Election Campaigns and Welfare State Change

Election Campaigns and Welfare State Change

Democratic Linkage and Leadership Under Pressure

STAFFAN KUMLIN
ACHIM GOERRES

OXFORD
UNIVERSITY PRESS

OXFORD
UNIVERSITY PRESS

Great Clarendon Street, Oxford, OX2 6DP,
United Kingdom

Oxford University Press is a department of the University of Oxford.
It furthers the University's objective of excellence in research, scholarship,
and education by publishing worldwide. Oxford is a registered trade mark of
Oxford University Press in the UK and in certain other countries

Impression: 1

Published in the United States of America by Oxford University Press
198 Madison Avenue, New York, NY 10016, United States of America

British Library Cataloguing in Publication Data
Data available

Library of Congress Control Number: 2022933689

ISBN 978–0–19–886921–4

DOI: 10.1093/oso/9780198869214.001.0001

Printed and bound by
CPI Group (UK) Ltd, Croydon, CR0 4YY

Till Liv och Elsa
Für Anna, Alexander und Andrea

Preface and Acknowledgements

At the end of a long project, it can be hard to remember exactly how it started. But we do recall our first meeting over lunch in a sunny Pisa square during the 2007 General Conference of the European Consortium of Political Research. We were survey researchers with a micro-level focus, but also shared a broader interest in the politics and policies of European welfare states. Further meetings and exchanges turned into concrete cooperation plans and we first discussed the possibility of this book in 2012. Almost ten years have passed and 'the book' accompanied us as we navigated through project applications, data collections, career shifts, moving between universities, parental leave, teaching obligations, the chairmanship of a department, family life, personal losses, and, in 2020–22, the Covid-19 pandemic with its challenging demands on university teachers and parents. With so much water having passed under the bridge, it is now difficult to know exactly whom to thank. We know that we are indebted to many institutions and individuals but apologize to those we somehow forgot.

We acknowledge financial support to Staffan Kumlin from the Research Council of Norway (project 217122), and the Swedish Research Council for Health, Working Life and Welfare (2009–1197). We are also grateful for seed money from the University of Duisburg-Essen.

We thank everyone contributing to the vibrant intellectual environments offered by our home institutions during these years. That is, the Departments of Political Science at the University of Duisburg-Essen, University of Oslo, University of Gothenburg, as well as the Institute for Social Research, Oslo.

We are grateful to the three anonymous OUP reviewers for insightful and helpful reports on the entire manuscript. Likewise, we have received useful comments on versions and portions of the book from many people in different settings: Ann-Helen Bay, Daniela Beyer, Christian Breunig, Marius R. Busemeyer, Henning Finseraas, Audun Fladmoe, Julian Garritzmann, Jane Gingrich, Christopher Green-Pedersen, Atle Haugsgjerd, Silja Häusermann, Niklas Jakobsson, Rune Karlsen, Christian Albrekt Larsen, Julie Lynch, Johan Martinsson, Maria Oskarson, Axel West Pedersen, Isabelle

Stadelmann-Steffen, Kari Steen-Johnsen, Stefan Svallfors, Pieter Vanhuysse, and Dag Wollebæk.

We must also acknowledge the importance of the many conferences where we presented our work: those organized by the Council for European Studies (2014 in Washington, DC and 2015 in Paris), the European Political Science Association (Edinburgh and Vienna), ECPR General Conference (Bordeaux), the Nordic Political Science Association (Gothenburg), Policy Network (Oxford), a 2016 workshop at Lund University (organized by Moira Nelson and Georg Wenzelburger), a 2016 workshop at the University of Konstanz (chaired by Marius R. Busemeyer), a 2015 talk at University of Bern (organized by Isabelle Stadelmann-Steffen) and at Goethe University Frankfurt in 2016, as well as numerous talks in our home departments. A collective round of thanks to the participants in these events!

Chapters 5 and 6 are based on previously published articles in the *Journal of Social Policy* and the *British Journal of Political Science* respectively (in parts reprinted with permission). We thank our co-author Rune Karlsen for agreeing to their inclusion here.

We thank our excellent research assistants over the years: Hanna Bugge, Manuel Diaz Garcia, Lukas Fiege, Hedda Haakestad, Josra Riecke, Hayfat Hamidou-Schmidt, Atle Haugsgjerd, Daniel Kihlström, and Louisa Cheng Seifert. This book and its data collections would not have been possible without you.

We wish to honour our friend and co-author Dennis C. Spies (1981–2021), Heisenberg Professor of Political Economy at the Heinrich Heine University of Düsseldorf, who unexpectedly passed away on 19 June 2021, aged 40, as we were finalizing the book. Our cooperation produced—among other things—an article using data from this book project (Goerres, A., Spies, D.C., and Kumlin, S. 2018, The Electoral Supporter Base of the Alternative for Germany. *Swiss Political Science Review*, 24: 246–69. https://doi.org/10.1111/spsr.12306).

Staffan would like to thank friends and family: Anders Linder with family, Fredrik Kornebäck, Martin Permer with family, Tobias Bach with family, and Frode Berglund. Special thanks to Achim Goerres for years of fun, pleasant company and friendship. Thanks also to my mother Barbro Kumlin for being there and for caring. And to Jeanette da Silva for so many things, including your unflagging ability to look on the bright side of life. I look forward to continue exploring the Oslo fjord, forests, and beyond with you! Finally, and most importantly, I thank my daughters Elsa Zeiner Kumlin and Liv Zeiner Kumlin. What a privilege to be your dad! You were small kids when this book took shape but soon you will be able to read and critique it. I look forward to the discussion!

Achim would like to dedicate this book to his best companion and wife Andrea. Firmly grounded in the professional world outside of academia, she always reminds me of the incredible academic freedom of pursuing a project of the heart across almost a decade; and of the privilege of working so intensely with the smartest people from other countries, such as Staffan Kumlin, who then become close friends.

Jointly, we dedicate this book to our children Liv, Alexander, Elsa, and Anna. This is after all a study of how 'your' democracies and welfare states deal with difficult challenges for the future. We suspect that the issues analysed in this book will stay relevant in the years to come.

Oslo and Duisburg, November 2021
Staffan Kumlin
Achim Goerres

Contents

List of Figures

List of Tables

PART I

RESEARCH PROBLEMS AND THEORETICAL FRAMEWORK

1

Introduction

Democracy and Welfare State Change

For several decades, mature welfare states in Europe have been on their way into a phase of austerity, marked by increasing demands and smaller, more insecure, revenues. A host of seemingly disparate reform pressures have gradually called into question the economic sustainability of social protection and services. The usual suspects include economic internationalization, which may trigger tax competition, capital flight, or redirect investment to emerging economies. Population ageing increases the proportion of people using pensions and health services, while fewer work and pay taxes. Public finances are further hurt by persistent unemployment (working-age adults who cannot find work) together with low employment (working-age adults not on the labour market). Periodic economic crises—such as 'the great recession' beginning in 2008—raise unemployment and benefit reliance in the short term, while scarring individuals and human capital in the long term. Meanwhile, changing family patterns, gender equality, and in particular female labour market participation alleviate these problems but also produce new trade-offs, for example between older social protection and better dual-earner policies. Finally, increasing levels of low-skilled immigration, not least in the wake of the 2015 refugee spike, raise the number of individuals with poor education and language skills generating further needs and potentially competition with other legitimate needs.

In this book, we investigate if and how political leaders publicly debate welfare state reform pressures and reforms at election time, and how citizens respond and draw political conclusions from such debate. At a more general level, we wonder what the answers to these questions reveal about the causes of welfare state change and about the nature of representative democracy in the early twenty-first century.

One rationale for raising these questions is that mature welfare states are changing. This was, until recently, far from obvious. Instead, welfare state researchers long tended to find policy stability despite the formidable challenges.

Election Campaigns and Welfare State Change. Staffan Kumlin and Achim Goerres, Oxford University Press.
© Staffan Kumlin and Achim Goerres (2022). DOI: 10.1093/oso/9780198869214.003.0001

Studies in this vein often relied on Paul Pierson's (1994, 1996, 2001) theory of a 'new politics of the welfare state' (shorthand: NPWS) (for overviews, see Levy 2010; Patashnik 2015). NPWS uses institutional theory to explain why political actors typically find it easier, cheaper, and more rational to stay close to long-trodden policy paths. It also emphasizes how parties and politicians think twice about welfare reform because of strong public support for already established policies. Policy change is occasionally possible, but mainly if coupled with 'blame avoidance' strategies that conceal what is going on and the political responsibility for it. A related idea is that multiple pressures in the new 'era of permanent austerity' generate ideological depolarization between left- and right-leaning parties. Most actors, regardless of ideology, must now simultaneously consider both the popularity and inertia of the welfare state *and* indisputable reform pressures. As a result, political parties advance increasingly similar and at best cautious reform agendas.

These ideas long seemed largely correct. No dramatic 'race-to-the-bottom' was (or is) in sight in most mature welfare states. Rather, policy changes were at first glacially slow and could be understood as institutionally path-dependent developments without radical breaks from past practices. In recent years, however, scholars documented how mature welfare states have begun to change more quickly and in more fundamental ways (see van Kersbergen and Vis 2014; Beramendi et al. 2015; Manow, Palier, and Schwander 2018). This process began in the late 1990s, gained momentum in the early 2000s, and was accelerated in several countries by the multiple crises experienced in Europe since 2009. Crucially, policy change appears multidimensional: it comes both as 'neoliberal' retrenchment (i.e. as benefit cuts and austerity policies), but also as less destructive, sometimes even expansive reforms in certain areas. This is captured by increasingly popular concepts such as 'recalibration', 'social investment', 'active labour market policy', and 'dual-earner policies', terms which we shall return to.

Anton Hemerijck, in *Changing Welfare States* (2013), juxtaposes these trends and the scholarly challenges they pose:

> the wide-ranging post-formative welfare reform momentum, with significant domestic variation, adds up to a broad, cumulative welfare-state (self-) transformation across the Member States of the European Union ... contrary to Paul Piersons's conjecture of change-resistant welfare states ... the majority of European welfare states have, interactively, made complementary reforms across macroeconomic policy, industrial relations, taxation, social security, labour market policy, employment protection legislation,

pensions, social services, welfare financing, and social and employment policy administration.

(Hemerijck 2013: 34–5)

Not only are these changes more fundamental and widespread than anticipated. Hemerijck (2013) also argues that they force us to reconsider how politicians and citizens respond to pressures operating on welfare states.

> we are in dire need of an alternative analytical perspective that allows a better and nuanced understanding of these more positive, multidimensional, and dynamic trajectories of social reform. ... As we observe more profound changes on the output side of the dependent variable of policy responses, we are confronted with a theoretical quest.... What we are looking for in the first place is a theoretical perspective that is more dynamic, and better able to gain leverage on social policy innovation and institutional transformation across time. Second, and most important, such a dynamic perspective should be able to conceptualize policy actors as more open and responsive to adaptive challenges.
>
> (Hemerijck 2013: 40–1)

Our book heeds this general call in specific ways. We investigate how political leaders and the public respond to reform pressures during a crucial period in a mass democracy: the election campaign. Do campaigns facilitate debate and attention to welfare state challenges? Do political parties present citizens with distinct choices as to how challenges might be met? Do political leaders prepare citizens for the idea that some solutions may be painful and unpopular? Do campaigns have adaptive consequences for how the public perceives the economic need for reform? Do citizens adjust their policy preferences as a result?

To address these questions, we have assembled a number of primary data sources:

- A data set covering 172 election campaigns in 18 European countries across three decades (EU15+ Norway, Iceland, Switzerland, 1977–2010). These data offer information about dominant campaign themes throwing light on the changing character of campaigns.
- Eighteen party leader speeches from the major left- and right-leaning parties in election years in Germany, Norway, and Sweden in the 2000s. These speeches, which comprise some 100,000 words of carefully formulated party messages under heavy media attention on the threshold to

an election year, reveal whether leaders publicly debate reform pressures and propose policy solutions that are distinct from those of other parties.
- A series of survey-embedded experiments gauging how political messages about reform pressures affect citizens' perceptions of welfare state sustainability in Germany, Norway, and Sweden.
- Panel surveys in Germany and Norway with waves collected between 2014 and 2016, allowing longitudinal analysis of how policy preferences along relevant dimensions are in turn affected by perceptions of welfare state sustainability.

Welfare state change and democracy: intertwined research problems

Our empirical results inform two broad and intertwined research problems. First, we want to understand the *role of election campaigns in processes of welfare state change*. What we are after, however, is not a straightforward estimation of 'campaign effects' on policy. For this we can rely on existing theory and research. Several studies clearly suggest that welfare reforms of different kinds become more likely as political systems pay greater collective attention to reform pressures and policy solutions. Taking a quantitative example, Jakobsson and Kumlin (2017) use time-series cross-section data and find that retrenchment in recent decades is more likely after election campaigns in which at least one welfare state related issue dominated the public sphere. Taking a more qualitative example, Schmidt (2002) followed six countries intensely. Focusing on a diverse set of reform types, she concludes that reform is more easily triggered in contexts with a pervasive, and often more public, reform discourse. Such discourse can advance new 'causal' ideas at odds with established institutional practices, interests, and ideologies favouring the status quo. In Schmidt's (2002: 169) formulation, 'discourse, understood as whatever policy actors say to each other and to the public more generally in their efforts to construct and legitimate their policy programs, is the missing element in the explanation of policy change in the welfare state'. She concludes that

> [c]ountries managed more or less successfully in their adjustment to the external economic pressures ... not only because of their greater or lesser economic vulnerabilities, their greater or lesser institutional capacities, and their better or worse policy responses but also because of their more or less convincing legitimating discourses.
>
> Schmidt (2002: 190)

Other scholars have developed the theory behind discourse effects on policy change. For example, Baumgartner, Jones, and Wilkerson (2011) emphasize how not only citizens, but also policymakers, operate under severe 'attention scarcity' such that policy changes occur earlier and to a greater extent in problem areas that actors devote more attention to throughout the political process (Baumgartner et al. 2011; see also Kingdon 2011 [1984]). Further, attention to problems is not only a scarce, but also highly dynamic resource. Attention can change more quickly compared to other important but inert factors such as values or institutions. Put differently, attention to problems is the key 'moving part' for understanding policy change (Baumgartner et al. 2011: 952).

While we contribute to research emphasizing discourse and attention in welfare reform, we also believe a crucial component is missing in this literature. Put simply, our contribution is to ask if campaign and discourse effects arise through democratic mechanisms. This leads to our second research problem, which concerns *the quality of representative democracy* in an era of challenges and resource scarcity. Can campaigns, and their constituent actors, respond to reform pressure while adhering to key democratic principles? What are these principles? What sort of observations would get us closer to answers? Democratic values are of course contested and not easily operationalized. Still, we hope to demonstrate the analytical leverage in identifying certain broad, but observable, principles most of us hope are not compromised even as pressures mount and welfare states begin to change.

We use the concepts of 'democratic linkage' and 'democratic leadership' as structuring devices. These are two 'visions' (Powell 2000) for what good political representation is and how it can be achieved. In this book, they function specifically as models for how political parties and citizens could and should communicate in campaign contexts.[1]

Now, most readers will probably agree that understanding the nature of representative democracy is interesting in its own right. What is more, however, these models inform our first research problem, that is, understanding processes of welfare state change. As we shall see, the models specify possible ways in which leaders and citizens may publicly adapt to, and communicate about, welfare state challenges and solutions. Hence, the models help us specify key democratic mechanisms through which campaign discourse may explain welfare state change.

---

[1] In other words, we will not examine all possible facets and implications of these models but rather concentrate intensely on a smaller number of key implications for the book's research problems.

Chapters 2 and 3 will revisit the notions of democratic linkage and leadership in detail. Chapter 1 will now give a first flavour of these chapters and indicate our contributions to current research. The remainder of Chapter 1 then samples highlights from the empirical chapters, discusses limitations inherent in our data, and finally foreshadows the concluding chapter.

Democratic linkage and the party decline debate

Democratic linkage is about the ability of electoral democracy to channel citizens' policy preferences into post-election policy. The linkage model envisages political parties presenting distinct and future-oriented policy platforms, addressing which societal problems now deserve attention while also proposing policy solutions. Citizens, for their part, use this information to develop informed perceptions of party differences and their own policy preferences. In turn, this allows them to vote for the party offering the best match. After the election, governing parties are honest and cohesive enough to let the policy mandates they asked for in the campaign translate into actual policy.

What explanation of welfare state change is implied by the democratic linkage model? A key implication is that campaigns in general, and political parties in particular, have increasingly put reform pressures on the agenda as these have become severe and consequential for policy. What is more, parties have told citizens which policy solutions will address growing challenges. Equally importantly, the problem/solution packages offered by parties are distinct from each other, allowing meaningful democratic choice in the face of outstanding challenges. Citizens, for their part, have the ability to use the information they receive to form their own views about reform pressures and—crucially under the 'linkage' model—adjust their prospective policy preferences.

Chapter 2 draws on a debate over whether political parties are losing their ability to provide democratic linkage. We note dramatically different views on the extent of party decline in this regard. The most pessimistic voices argue that dwindling party membership, more volatile and heterogeneous voters, and more complex conflict structures, make it harder for parties to link voter preferences with policies. By contrast, the most optimistic voices claim that even traditional mainstream mass parties reinvent themselves by developing their polices in the light of new societal challenges. Meanwhile, they also become better and more active in using modern election campaigns as a tool for communicating their problem–policy packages. This compensates for weakening traditional organizational and membership-based mass party linkage mechanisms.

A key contribution of this book is to analyse in detail the specifics of welfare state pressures and policy changes, that is, if/how such specifics are communicated to citizens, with which intensity, and with which effects. This sets our study apart from much research that still conceives of political conflict in very overarching terms; often this entails measures like general left–right self-placement among citizens, and broad measures of social spending to tap policy. This does not necessarily reveal which underlying pressures citizens are confronted with (if any), or which policies they are informed about (if any). Both of these components—salience of real-world problems and actual reform—is necessary to fully understand linkage in pressured welfare states where a complex landscape of problems and reform trajectories has opened up.

A further contribution is data related. In the words of Green-Pedersen and Jensen (2019: 805): 'we have almost no knowledge about what parties actually focus on when they address their would-be voters within the realm of the welfare state'. Admittedly, this is a drastic generalization, and we will discuss a number of exceptions along the way (see Busemeyer, Franzmann, and Garritzmann 2013; Green-Pedersen 2019; Green-Pedersen and Jensen 2019). On closer inspection, however, existing studies are not only few but often limited to measuring the issues parties discuss in their written party manifestoes. While such documents offer important windows into party competition generally, they are by definition less useful in revealing exactly what reform pressures and policy solutions citizens hear about in public campaign settings. Our data take us closer to such public campaign attention. Additionally, our experiments gauge how citizens' problem perceptions and policy preferences respond to information they are likely to encounter.

Democratic leadership and the study of changing welfare states

A good elected politician does more than diligently implement citizens' policy preferences. As Pitkin (1967) and other democratic theorists have argued, we want politicians who sometimes dare to defend unpopular but, as far as leaders can judge, sensible decisions while seeking to legitimize these. Influential scholars even suggest that such top-down democratic leadership is becoming more important in tandem with an alleged decline in democratic linkage.

Democratic leadership, then, requires daring—rather than blame-avoiding—politicians who, at least in principle and on occasion, have the courage to argue publicly that big challenges necessitate unpopular policies. Furthermore, democratic leadership also places demands on those who are led. Citizens are, at least in principle and on occasion, willing and able to listen. Leadership is compromised if citizens do not even in principle and on occasion have a capacity for accepting explanations made by democratic leaders. Leadership will not work if citizens can never readjust their perceptions of underlying challenges while at least accepting that they cannot have their prospective policy preferences satisfied.

Can accelerating welfare state change be explained by democratic leadership? The first half of Chapter 3 describes how older welfare state scholarship assigned a limited role to public sphere communication. From this vantage point, welfare state development was never, and is still not, due to broad open debate and ultimately policy changes in the face of popular preferences reshaped through such processes. This is true for a broad school of thought often labelled as 'institutional' theory. Pierson's (2001) 'new politics' framework is one example: it implies that political communication is seriously flawed. Politicians refrain from talking about uncomfortable pressures (unless there is a culprit to blame). Democratic linkage is compromised by ideological depolarization at the same time as democratic leadership will not work due to citizens' inability to let go of the status quo. This, in turn, is what forces policymakers to engage in blame avoidance rather than daring leadership.

Accelerating welfare state change, however, has challenged traditional welfare state scholarship. A growing body of work now suggests that leaders may develop new ideas about the welfare state and communicate to a greater and more consequential extent than older theories imply. A number of discourse-oriented concepts—examples to be discussed include 'credit claiming' (Weaver 1986; Bonoli and Natali 2012), 'strategic reframing' (Elmelund-Præstekær and Emmenegger 2013), and—particularly useful here—'ideational leadership' (Stiller 2010)—have gained currency in welfare state change research. This emerging literature goes beyond blame avoidance and suggests that parties may proactively put reform pressures on the public agenda, explain to citizens why *choosing* partly painful reform may be both economically smart *and* partly defensible with normative arguments. The latter arguments link reform pressures and solutions to ideas about fairness and 'deservingness' that the audience holds. The extent, nature, and consequences of such leadership, however, is currently less than clear. Past studies tend to concentrate on elite discourse itself rather than public communication. Alternatively, analysis is limited to dramatic cases or even anecdotal evidence about the contents and consequences of public discourse.

A parallel body of new findings concerns citizens. Their attitudes and behaviour now appear more ambivalent and malleable than previously appreciated. True, welfare state support appears relatively stable and strong. At the same time, electoral punishment for retrenchment is weak and contingent

(Armingeon and Giger 2008; Giger and Nelson 2010; Giger 2011). Case studies even suggest that politicizing pressures and championing retrenchment (sometimes in combination with more expansive policies) can be a road to electoral victory (Elmelund-Præstekær and Emmenegger 2013). Other studies report a readiness among citizens to react to some types of reform pressures (Naumann 2014, 2017; Jensen and Naumann 2016). Our empirics will allow progress in gauging the extent to which citizens are susceptible to information about reform pressures, as well as the types of normative arguments that may open the door to such influences.

A particular point made in recent work is that retrenchment is no longer the 'only game in town' (van Kersbergen, Vis, and Hemerijck 2014). Welfare reform is no longer merely a unidimensional struggle between the status quo and destructive cuts (Bonoli and Natali 2012; Häusermann 2012). Scholars have documented an ideational shift towards a "social investment" oriented welfare state (Morel, Palier, and Palme 2012; Hemerijck 2018). Concrete policy examples of this shift include expansive dual earner reforms in child care and parental leave as well as a host of activation policies meant to preserve and generate human capital on the labour market. Overall, what we will refer to as the *social investment/activation turn* builds on the promise that the welfare state is not just a problem to be downscaled, but is also part of the solutions that will alleviate reform pressures. Relatedly, the menu of policy responses is now longer and less exclusively destructive—and unpopular—than older theories imply.

This complex landscape of policy solutions generates key questions for this book. Has the social investment/activation turn—which is apparent in ideational and policy trends—also 'gone public'? It may have, in part because it allows politicians to debate pressures while having something more popular to propose than only retrenchment. Perhaps it has even permeated public debate to the extent that it *masks* more unpopular policy? If so, the social investment/activation paradigm may function as a vehicle for blame avoidance and an obstacle for true democratic leadership.

Empirical chapters at a glance

Let us take a brief look at the empirical chapters. These chapters are divided into two sections: one that examines messages and agendas that emanate from elite actors in campaigns, and one that studies citizens' reactions. Let us consider each in turn.

Campaign contents

Chapter 4 analyses 'systemic agendas'. Older research on the welfare state, we will note, has often promoted a somewhat reductionist view of elections, seeing these mainly as instruments for aggregation of exogenous preferences rather than for deliberation and preference change. Thus, as Chapter 4 will explain, much welfare state research has studied the policy preferences of specific actors, such as political parties and citizens. We know much less about policy agendas, that is, how prioritized and salient welfare issues are compared to other policy domains. In particular, this is true for the question of how much overall attention is being paid to welfare state issues in election campaigns. Do welfare issues ever dominate an election campaign? Have they become more or less dominant over time? Answers to these questions are crucial if we want to better understand the role played by election campaigns in welfare state reform (and better assess its democratic character).

Chapter 4 draws on recent work suggesting the meaningfulness of a 'systemic' approach to agenda-setting. We examine if welfare state issues become more—or perhaps less—likely to dominate entire election campaigns over time as most welfare states have delved deeper into the era of growing pressure for change. To the extent that there has been an attention increase, what about its *timing*? Have we witnessed a gradual increase in attention (as welfare states have experienced gradually mounting pressure)? Or have we rather seen a late and brief attention response to an 'era of permanent austerity' that really began in the early 1980s? The late-and-brief reaction, Chapter 3 will explain, is implied by theories of 'punctuated equilibrium' (Baumgartner et al. 2009) and 'attention cycles' (Downs 1972).

Chapter 4 also begins to analyse two sets of questions that cut through several chapters. One is about blame avoidance. Is welfare state debate a 'fair-weather sport' that was mainly exercised some time ago when pressures were less severe? Alternatively, perhaps we find such debate precisely during major economic crises because it can serve as a scapegoat for unpopular reforms? A second set of questions are about the social/investment activation turn. Have the well-documented elite- and policy-related shifts in this direction also shaped campaigns? Has social/investment activation even take over attention from less popular policies such as retrenchment?

By the end of Chapter 4 we hope to have convinced the reader that studying systemic agendas is worthwhile and can produce key insights. Yet, crucial questions cannot be answered using the systemic approach; these instead demand disaggregation and detailed analysis of 'meso-level' party messages.

This is the topic of Chapter 5. We use our primary data collection of party congress speeches in election years. Are reform pressures really put on the agenda by leading politicians? The simple fact that welfare issues are 'systemically salient' does not mean they do. Neither does systemic salience equal politicization of policy. So, do politicians really dare to connect pressures to reforms, and in particular to more unpopular ones? Finally, the empirics register whether politicians discuss pressures mainly in terms of economic sustainability (known in the discourse literature as 'cognitive' arguments), or whether they also appeal to various normative arguments.

A further set of questions concern actor-, context-, and country-related explanations of variation in party messages. For example, we test predictions about developments over time (particularly before and after the financial crisis of 2008). Other analyses look for party differences between left and right: what 'choice' are citizens presented with? Are there party differences in which pressures are stressed, in which policy solutions are emphasized, or rather in which normative concepts that are invoked to defend essentially the same policy responses?

Citizen reactions

Democratic linkage and leadership require more than leaders providing citizens with certain information. It also partly depends on citizens being, at least in principle, able and willing to listen. This is the starting point for the last three empirical chapters, which examine how citizens react to and draw political conclusions from information about reform pressures.

Chapter 6 develops a notion of 'reform pressure' framing and studies its effects on perceptions of the financial viability of the welfare state. Pressure framing refers to different ways of emphasizing and presenting information about pressures that challenge welfare state sustainability. The backbone of Chapter 6 is a comparative survey experiment fielded in our three countries, with respondents randomly provided with varying information veiled inside a survey question about reform pressures. This allows us to compare the impact of different reform pressures (including population ageing, low employment rates, EU and non-Western immigration, and international economic crisis). Moreover, the comparative component gives an insight into country variation, such as whether effects are different in economically exceptional Norway. Finally, the chapter draws on a number of studies showing the importance of how 'deserving' welfare recipients are (Tyler et al. 1997; Slothuus 2007; Petersen et al. 2010; van Oorschot et al. 2017). The concept of 'deservingness' helps us specify with greater precision a plausible normative component of successful leadership narratives.

The Chapter 6 experiment has a 'many-pressures, several countries' design that allows progress over the 'one-pressure, one-country' nature of extant research. But on the critical side, Chapter 7 notes, the treatments are somewhat removed from the messages citizens receive in the real world of democratic politics. There, citizens do not respond to subtleties veiled in survey questions, but to overt persuasion attempts by party politicians with an ideological stance and a policy agenda. Chapter 7 probes deeper into these last aspects of pressure framing, drawing on two experiments conducted in Germany and Norway respectively. These experiments introduce three types of realism. First, they increase message complexity. Real-world pressure frames are typically complex, nuanced, and vague. Do the generalizations from Chapter 6 hold for the 'messier' information provided by real-world party politicians? Second, real-world pressure frames quite often provide policy cues about how pressure is to be alleviated. Therefore, most treatments in this chapter combine pressure messages with various types of proposed policy (such as retrenchment or social investment). How important is the policy type for the acceptance of the underlying problem description? Finally, a third realistic feature is that the treatments clarify which party or parties says the welfare state is pressured. This allows us to examine which political parties are the most effective proponents of pressure messages. Relatedly, Chapter 7 develops and tests the idea that pressure messages with clear party- and policy cues might trigger resistance and counter-arguments among groups predisposed against sender and/or content. Resistance implies that effects are weaker or non-existent among those groups. Counter-arguments go further and imply polarization effects—rather than net negative persuasive effects—such that different groups may react in different directions to the same reform pressure message.

Finally, Chapter 8 uses our panel data to analyse if perceptions of reform pressures change policy preferences over time. Panel data are often called for in research on welfare attitudes but are hard to come by (but see Kumlin 2006; Margalit 2013). Such data can give a handle on the direction of causation: are welfare state preferences affected by information and perceptions about reform pressures or do people adjust perceptions to preferences already held? Panel data are also attractive as they provide insights into the longevity of opinion formation processes involving sustainability perceptions. Panel waves were collected roughly one year apart and thus indicate if sustainability worries matter over longer timespans than can be gauged in experimental research.

Most importantly, however, Chapter 8 addresses a key knowledge gap in research on the political consequences of welfare state sustainability perceptions. What we know from past research is that such perceptions can temper electoral punishment of governments for unpopular reforms (Giger and Nelson 2013). Less clear, however, is whether perceptions also transform underlying policy demands in a more fundamental sense.

Limitations (and opportunities) in space and time

The chapter descriptions show how our data cover certain countries, time periods, and political parties. For the most part, these limitations in space and time do not reflect strategic 'case selection', as much as the mundane but inescapable practicalities of organizationally complex and expensive research. Anyone who has attempted such projects knows that they are more feasible—and turn out better—with local knowledge and language skills. That said, our empirical material is likely to yield results that are systematically different from those that would arise for other countries, periods, and parties. As ever in comparative research, it is crucial to ponder the implications of the empirical windows offered by the arguably unique data sets that we collected.

To begin with, four out of five chapters draw on our primary data collected in Germany, Norway, and Sweden. This reflects the nature of our cooperation between a native German and a native Swede working in Norway. But what are the wider implications of studying these countries? To begin with, we would argue that they display a mix of differences and similarities that make them interesting cases in a comparative perspective. Importantly, they belong to the economically more affluent of Europe's welfare states. Relatedly, they were relatively unscathed by the financial- and Eurozone crises than other West and Southern European countries. So, at least before the Coronavirus pandemic starting in 2019, there had been few of the major crisis symptoms that the NPWS framework identifies as preconditions for welfare reform as well as significant political communication about it (by which is typically meant blame avoiding and defensive excuses). In contrast, then, these countries allow us to study if and how reform pressures and policy solutions enter campaigns, and affect citizens politically, also in more economically affluent and stable contexts. This feature of our cases becomes especially worthwhile given the state of the art in the field. Past research has convincingly shown that big economic crises often act as catalysts for sweeping policy changes, with blame-avoiding politicians publicly arguing that crisis makes retrenchment and other types of reform regrettable but inevitable (Kuipers 2006; Starke 2008). What remains less clear is how political communication processes work in the absence of such an immediate crisis (but still in the presence of long-term pressures and complex reforms). Do politicians still politicize pressures and reforms, and can citizens also process and react to such information in such settings?

The three countries are also different from each other in important ways. While all three have experienced significant welfare state reform including retrenchment as well as 'social investment/activation'-style reforms (Palier 2010; Morgan 2012) one must note Norway's position as something of Europe's big economic counterfactual. Fuelled by oil- and gas revenues it has experienced truly exceptional economic development in recent decades, with many employment-related and socio-economic indicators at the highest values worldwide. Norway also probably displays more policy stability overall, but with notable exceptions in pension, activation, and dual-earner reforms in the 2000s (Bay et al. 2019). Thus, in particular the inclusion of Norway allows studying political communication and its effects in a context of unusual fiscal affluence and stability, but where underlying long-term reform pressures and resulting reforms are reminiscent of those found elsewhere.

What about time periods? Here, the chapters on campaign contents study the period leading up to the financial crisis and the immediate aftermath. From here, Chapter 4 goes back in time to the late 1970s, whereas Chapter 5 concentrates intensely on the first decade of the 2000s. As is the case with country coverage, our particular empirical window constitutes a limitation, as we do not have data on the most recent years from well after the financial crisis. At the same time, the earlier period is also interesting exactly because it allows us to study the role of political communication well before the extraordinary series of crises experienced in Europe later on (Having said this, both Chapters 4 and 5 include a 2010 time point immediately after the financial crisis for comparison.). Also on the positive side, the period we study is (as Chapter 3 will discuss in-depth) of great theoretical interest for the field of welfare state scholarship. After all, it was in the late 1990s and early 2000s that European welfare states began to change in earnest along multiple dimensions. Moreover, Chapter 4 will show that this was also a period when the general systemic scale of campaign attention to welfare issues was at its highest (before declining again with the financial crisis). Overall then, this period constitutes an interesting 'pre-crisis laboratory' for studying the nature and role of election campaigns in welfare state change processes during a period of intensive reform.

Finally, we need to ponder our focus on the two largest parties in these political systems, that is, the social democratic and conservative/Christian-democrat parties respectively. More specifically, Chapter 5 studies how prime ministerial candidates from these parties politicize pressures and policy solutions. Relatedly, Chapter 7 examines how messages from these parties affect different groups of citizens. Again, there is no denying that our focus constitutes a limitation; it would in principle be interesting to study also, say, radical left, populist right, and green parties. But given that limitations are necessary due to budgetary and practical constraints, we would argue that social democratic and conservative/Christian-democrat parties are highly relevant. They are, after all, the two largest party families and the main contenders for the position of prime minister. Thus, they provide the ideological centres of gravity for the governments that are likely to form after the election. As such, they are arguably the single most important (if not the only) providers of democratic linkage for citizens. A similar observation concerns the concept of democratic leadership. As Chapter 7 will elaborate, these widely popular and trusted parties are likely to carry special weight in terms of persuading the public about the challenges and policy solutions in pressured welfare states. Overall, we follow Green-Pedersen (2019) who demonstrated that even declining 'mainstream' parties are likely to remain influential for the overall agenda in a political system, especially in welfare state issues where smaller emerging 'niche parties' (cf. Meguid 2005; Wagner 2012) are less prolific than in newer 'second-dimension' issues such as immigration and the environment.

Foreshadowing the concluding chapter

The final chapter will restate key results and analyse implications for the book's intertwined research problems. What have we learned about the quality of representative democracy and the nature of welfare state change? The discussion continues to be structured by the notions of democratic linkage and leadership.

In terms of democratic linkage, we will find a reason to start with some good news, noting an impressive capacity of these political systems to publicly refocus attention. The growing reform pressures operating on the welfare state have not only transformed policies but also reshaped campaign agendas. Pressures have neither been hidden away from public sight, nor have they surfaced only in times of severe crisis, as theories of blame avoidance imply. This is satisfying as we argue that systemic salience is an understudied precondition for most aspects of democratic linkage. Equally positive are findings suggesting that citizens can perform several of the key 'tasks' necessary for linkage. Especially in issues that are systemically salient, they can adjust their perceptions of welfare sustainability in light of pressure information and in turn update their prospective policy preferences.

Democratic linkage, of course, requires more than issue attention and informed citizens. It also assumes that citizens get to choose between distinct and clearly communicated party platforms. Our results in this regard testify to more fundamental shortcomings. Now, we hasten to avoid the vulgar accusation that 'there are no differences anymore' between parties. Quite clearly, research documents systematic party differences along multiple reform dimensions (Beramendi et al. 2015; Manow et al. 2018), even though these have probably declined over time (Stephens 2015; Jakobsson and Kumlin 2017). Our point, however, is to emphasize the difficulties parties seem to experience in communicating differences to voters in the increasingly complex landscape of multiple pressures and reform types. Based on our findings, we do not feel justified in concluding that election campaigns secure democratic legitimacy of welfare state change through a mandate given by a citizenry that could choose between distinct and coherent alternatives.

What about democratic leadership as a complementary legitimacy mechanism? After all, scholars have suggested that top-down legitimization becomes important as democratic linkage mechanisms allegedly weaken. Comparative welfare state scholarship has moved towards a similar position. Our empirical results, however, mostly indicate that blame avoidance—rather than courageous leadership—remains dominant in messages from the major parties studied in this book. The devil is in the detail, however, and several blame avoidance permutations largely fail to register; this applies to the 'agenda-controlling' strategy of hiding problems away and the use of crisis to argue that there is no choice. Relatedly, that we uncover significant attention to welfare state challenges in Germany, Norway, and Sweden—countries that are among Europe's affluent and less challenged welfare states—shows that it does not take a massive crisis, nor unusually severe pressures, to spark major campaign attention on these issues.

Instead, blame avoidance manifests itself in subtler ways. In particular, we shall find evidence of 'cherry-picking'. Systemic agendas of entire campaigns, as well as specific messages from prime ministerial candidates, are lopsided. In response to pressures, they typically propose expansion, social investment, 'enabling' activation, defend the status quo, or simply hint vaguely at 'improvements' that will happen despite pressures. You know you are witnessing a rare event when these politicians speak plainly about less popular types of reform such as retrenchment or punitive and demanding activation (these policies have shaped reform also in the countries under study). In important ways, then, politicians 'cherry-pick' politically marketable policy from a more complex and partly unpopular menu of reform. We even find that this imbalance has become more pronounced over time and gets worse as the leaders' speeches emphasize reform pressures to a greater extent. These tendencies, we conclude, do not reflect well on democratic leadership in an era of growing reform pressures.

The book closes by discussing two more specific 'mismatches' between how leaders debate welfare state change and how citizens reason about it. One mismatch concerns reasoning about reform pressures. A striking result in our experiments is that the strongest effects on welfare sustainability worries are triggered by suggestions that immigration puts pressure on the welfare state. By contrast, immigration is at best a secondary pressure on the agendas of mainstream parties. One can see this discrepancy as another symptom of suboptimal democratic leadership: despite the rise in attention to welfare issues and pressures, mainstream parties have not conveyed their sense of proportion to citizens. Once this 'mismatch' exists, moreover, it creates a strategic dilemma mostly working to the advantage of the populist right. Relatedly, we discuss if citizens' disproportionate responsiveness to pressure linked to 'undeserving' groups, and to immigration in particular, spells problems for the 'linkage' model's emphasis on 'informed' preferences.

The second elite–mass mismatch is related to how leaders and citizens treat policy solutions, in particular social investment/activation. In this regard, our results on campaign content capture a transition from neoliberalism and retrenchment in the 1980s to a more recent era when several aspects of social investment/activation became prominent. In fact, these new policy responses to pressures appear to have crowded out retrenchment issues, which were actually *more* salient back when welfare issues rarely dominated campaigns. Meanwhile, our experiments join past research in showing the importance of the policy cues people receive (Häusermann, Picot, and Geering 2012; Busemeyer et al. 2013; Häusermann, Kurer, and Traber 2019). It seems that acceptance of pressure messages becomes polarized and contentious when people are actually exposed to a balanced mix of retrenchment and social investment. In particular, this seems true as people become aware of possible 'trade-offs' where retrenchment in some areas pays for expansion in others. In closing, we juxtapose such results with our findings on how social investment and other 'popular' reform types dominate campaigns. We suspect that support for policy changes—and for responsible political actors—is exaggerated as citizens are not invited to ponder the totality of welfare state change.

***

But we are jumping ahead of ourselves. Chapter 2 will now situate our analysis in the broader scholarly debate on democratic linkage. Chapter 3 then revisits theories of welfare state stability and change, and how research on this topic has increasingly embraced the idea of democratic leadership.

2

Democratic Linkage and the Party Decline Debate

In an overview of research stimulated by Pierson's 'new politics' framework, Levy (2010: 561–4) makes a remark unusual for welfare state scholarship. There is something 'conspirational and unsavoury', he notes, about this theory: 'Pierson paints an unflattering picture of the politics of retrenchment, with governments manipulating and misleading the public in order to enact reforms that lack popular support'. This points us to one of the broader purposes of this book: evaluating political processes in pressured welfare states from a democratic perspective.

Welfare state scholarship has traditionally given surprisingly scant attention to the quality of democracy. Or in more nuanced words, it has been better at using democratic politics as an explanatory variable than at presenting a principled assessment of its performance. Or so Bo Rothstein (2009) argues in a critical review of research on the Swedish welfare state:

> The large body of specific findings on how representative democracy works in relation to welfare state outputs has not been assembled in overall analyses, with normative democratic ideals being confronted with empirical research. Some political scientists should have asked: is the ... welfare state a democratic project? If so, to what extent, and in which regards? Where democratic processes have faltered we should have been given a more general answer about how the actual decision process worked.
>
> (Rothstein 2009: 13, our translation)

This critique concerned a single country but we think it resonates broadly with the comparative welfare state literature. The democratic yardsticks that motivate research problems and conclusions are typically kept implicit at best. Meanwhile, the quality of democracy becomes more topical as welfare states probe deeper into the austerity era. What is increasingly at stake is democracy's

Election Campaigns and Welfare State Change. Staffan Kumlin and Achim Goerres, Oxford University Press.
© Staffan Kumlin and Achim Goerres (2022). DOI: 10.1093/oso/9780198869214.003.0002

ability to accommodate, and learn from, uncomfortable challenges, while staying true to its ideals. For sure, it is no easy feat to specify what it is that we want from a pressured but well-functioning democracy. Democracy, and its constituent values and mechanisms, are contested concepts that do not lend themselves to easy definition and operationalization. Still, we believe it is useful to identify certain core principles that most democrats would hope are not compromised as reform pressures mount and policies begin to change.

This chapter discusses 'democratic linkage'. It is a broad vision of how citizens and politicians should interact and communicate in a representative democracy. While deceptively simple in the abstract, it has complex implications for various aspects of the political process. In this book, of course, we are concerned with that subset of implications that relate to the role of election campaigns in processes of welfare state change.

Defining democratic linkage

Democratic linkage refers to processes through which political representatives act in accordance with the wants, needs, and demands of the public (see also Lawson 1980; Luttbeg 1981). Based on this or similar definitions, scholars have gone on to specify models of linkage; these are usually lists of requirements, activities, and patterns deemed central for successful linkage. One example is the widely applied notion of 'mandate-based representative democracy' (see Przeworski, Stokes, and Manin 1999; Naurin 2011). A closely related term is that of 'the responsible party model' (cf. Klingemann, Hofferbert, and Budge 1994). Under these models, linkage arises through democratic elections as political parties present distinct programmes about which societal problems deserve attention and the right policy solutions for them. Citizens become aware of party differences, and develop informed policy preferences of their own, allowing them to support the party offering the best match. After the election, the parties in government are honest and cohesive enough to base their policies on the policy *mandates* they asked for in the campaign.

There are many marginally different specifications of this process (for overviews, see Thomassen 1994; Mair 2006). An unusually inclusive account of linkage was provided by Russell Dalton, David Farrell, and Ian McAllister in *Political Parties and Democratic Linkage* (2011). They identify five aspects that must work for linkage to arise. While their model resembles those described above, it is crucial for us to note the inclusion of 'campaign linkage'. This refers to a set of activities[1] whereby parties collectively set the agenda for public discourse and inform citizens about their policy programmes and the underlying arguments. These last aspects matter also for citizens as they develop their perceptions of parties and their own informed policy preferences.

Party decline and weakening democratic linkage?

Models of democratic linkage see political parties as the main actors. It is parties that are to formulate coherent programmes of problem descriptions and policy solutions for citizens to choose between. Parties manage to communicate these programmes to citizens, in particular during election campaigns. And once in parliament, and especially government, parties strive to enact the policy mandates they asked for in the campaign.

Political scientists have for some time debated the possibility of a decline in the ability of parties to provide democratic linkage (Andeweg 2003; Saward 2008). The background is familiar enough: membership levels have dwindled and fewer citizens identify with a particular party. Voter turnout has decreased and voter volatility increased. Against this background, it is often said that the old notion of a *mass party* has lost its relevance: parties are no longer solidly anchored in the distinct interests and values of their many party members and in the distinct social groups and organizations these once came from. Parties are set adrift, as it were, transforming into volatile, centrist, and even opportunistic vote maximizers without a cause. Citizens can therefore no longer choose between cohesive, stable, and understandable programmes addressing how to solve society's problems. Once in government, parties have less clear mandates to implement. The overall result is weaker linkage between popular wants, needs and demands, and public policy.

In Peter Mair's (2006) discussion the decline in democratic linkage even generates a broad-based 'hollowing of democracy'. Not only citizens, but also political elites withdraw from the contacts and communication that democratic linkage requires. They come to focus less on their representative function and more on their official governing roles. This increasingly state-centred outlook among parties is paralleled by an increasing dependency on state funding. Thus, from Mair's (2006) viewpoint:

> beneath the beating of official breasts and the apparent distress at the hollowing out of mass politics, in practice there exists a clear tendency for political

---

[1] Candidate nomination is included as a further aspect in their discussion of 'campaign linkage'.

elites to match citizens' disengagement with a withdrawal of their own. Just as voters retreat to their own particularized spheres of interest, so too have political and party leaders withdrawn into the closed world of their governing institutions. Both sides are cutting loose.

(Mair 2006: 545)

How parties may still provide democratic linkage

Yet not all is lost. Empirical studies often provide more nuanced or even upbeat characterizations of democratic linkage. In *The Strain of Representation* (2012) Robert Rohrschneider and Stephen Whitefield examine political parties' ability to coherently package choices as well as achieve congruence between party and voter positions. Using expert and voter data they find that parties generally provide significant choices for citizens along major dimensions. More than this, party conflict is well-structured in that a large number of issues can be reduced to a few predictable ideological conflict dimensions. Likewise, voter-party congruence along key dimensions is rather healthy and does not seem to vary much across Western and Central/Eastern Europe. In Western Europe, however, two factors complicate the situation. First, a more clearly multidimensional policy space introduces the difficult task of formulating and communicating complex packages of positions across different dimensions of political competition. Second, the co-existence of strongly partisan and highly independent voters makes it difficult to appeal to both groups. Despite these difficulties, however, the empirics suggest that Western European parties manage to provide coherently packaged choices resulting in high levels of issue congruence.

The explanation may come as a surprise. The authors find that features of party organizations one associates with the old mass party are still in play. Parties that are larger, have more elaborate organizations, and frequent ties with civil society are better able to represent *both* partisans and independents. The invoked causal mechanisms are complex (and largely untested) but range from advantages in making members accept platforms, to party members persuading independents in social settings. Relatedly, larger and well-connected organizations generate networks and resources that 'can be used to organize campaigns, to communicate with voters, and to design strategies that appeal to both independents and partisans' (p. 119). Thus, the authors find support 'for the argument that attributes to mass organizations a critical role in providing a linkage between citizens and policies not only for partisans but also for the "new" types of voters—independents in the ideological center' (p. 135).

Dalton et al. (2011) provide further evidence of parties' continued relevance as providers of democratic linkage. Using data from the CSES[2] project, and assessing all their five key linkage aspects, they state:

> The empirical findings lead us to ask why analysts so often point to the decline of parties ... we agree that some features of partisan politics suggest a pattern of decline—such as decreasing party membership, and few citizens identifying with a political party. But these changes in citizens' connections have not been paralleled by a similar decline in parties' performance of their institutional roles in democracy. Rather political parties generally adapt to changing social and political circumstances to retain their preeminent role in the democratic process. In most nations, the decline in membership has been accompanied by new styles of campaigning, funding from public sources, and a more efficient campaign style.
>
> (Dalton et al. 2011: ix)

Interestingly, these authors focus less on internal party organization and more on adaptive abilities beyond any persistent potency of mass party organizational features. So where Rohrschneider and Whitefield (2012) emphasize the still considerable and consequential 'mass party' organizational features, Dalton et al. (2011) stress how parties are also *adapting* in largely new ways as mass party features are nonetheless slowly declining.

Two related adaptations are especially relevant here. The first has to do with campaigning. Dalton et al. (2011) present simple but powerful data suggesting that parties may have kept their hold on election campaigns in important ways. Developments in media access and presence suggest they still reign as the main characters of mass mediated election campaigns. A second adaptation has to do with *policy development*, that is, the capacity of individual parties, and the party system at large, to respond 'programmatically' to new societal challenges and resulting conflict dimensions. This happens because old parties have the capacity to adapt their programmes and communicate these adaptations to citizens. In more unusual cases, this can happen because new parties form when older ones cannot adapt. Overall, however, an important contention is that even old mass parties, of the type studied in this book, stay relevant through continuous policy development in the face of changing societal problems. More than this, they increasingly manage to communicate their stances through election campaigns in an era when mass party organizational features may have lost at least some relevance for achieving democratic linkage.

---

[2] Comparative Study of Electoral Systems.

These more upbeat accounts of democratic linkage resonate with two neigh-bouring accumulations of research. One is a sprawling literature on long-term changes in the general character of election campaigns (for overviews, see Far-rell and Schmitt-Beck 2002; Strömbäck and Esser 2014; Römmele and von Schneidmesser 2016). It addresses several complex topics that will not be dis-cussed here, such as campaign finance, media structures, and communicative strategies. The interesting thing to note, however, is the rationale for this lit-erature, that is, a widespread view among parties and pundits that campaigns have become very important as voters turn independent, late-deciding, and issue-oriented. This belief has in turn led scholars to pay much more attention to documenting their changing nature.

A second more focused literature has reported intensifying issue compe-tition among political parties in Western Europe. Several key findings are worth highlighting. For example, the number of issues that are actually politi-cized by parties (including large mainstream ones) has increased markedly over the last forty years or so. This expanding issue menu means that the relative attention paid to traditional economic left–right issues has declined. Conversely, several issues comprising the 'second' conflict dimension (exam-ples include crime and immigration) now receives more attention (cf. Kriesi et al. 2008; Kriesi et al. 2012). Of special interest to us, however, are findings suggesting a shift of emphasis among the broad class of economic left–right topics to which most welfare state issues belong. In *The Reshaping of West European Party Politics* (2019: 68), Christoffer Green-Pedersen concludes that 'the decline of other traditional left-right related issues like the economy and defense could lead one to expect that attention to the welfare state would also decline. However, the analysis here rather indicates that the conclusion cru-cially depends on which welfare state issues one is looking at'. Green-Pedersen's results suggested

> important changes in attention to the state-market related issues that tradi-tionally form the core of the left-right first dimension. Social policy issues remain an important and stable part of this, but health and education have grown and partly replaced economic issues in the sense of macroeconomics, the labour market, and business.
>
> (Green-Pedersen 2019: 70)

In summary, these recent arguments and findings suggest a persistent ability of political parties to provide linkage in at least some parts of the welfare state domain. Given these results it becomes possible that this domain is in fact marked by continued or even improved 'campaign linkage' in combination with visible policy development addressing the many challenges that now characterize this domain. More research is sorely needed, however. One case in point has to do with data. Chapter 1 noted how much of what we know about increasing issue competition comes from analyses of party manifestoes (Busemeyer et al. 2013; Green-Pedersen and Jensen 2019)). While such documents are crucial in studying issue competition generally, they are by definition less useful in revealing what reform pressures and policy solutions citizens get to hear about in public campaign settings.

The three upcoming sections will discuss aspects of linkage that we think demand our attention at this point. We first discuss the largely unexplored possibility that party systems as a whole put welfare state reform pressures on 'systemic campaign' agendas. Second, we ask if old mass parties communicate clear and meaningful choices about how to alleviate pressures along new (and old) policy dimensions. Third, we discuss how our analyses might shed light on the democratic linkage requirement that public preferences are 'informed' in an era of growing reform pressure.

Systemic welfare state campaign salience

The linkage process builds on several big assumptions. For example, citizens are assumed to be aware of party differences in terms of how they prioritize societal problems and their proposed policy solutions. Citizens are also thought to have well-considered attitudes of their own in these regards. As we shall discuss at the end of this chapter, concepts like 'well-considered' and 'aware' are difficult to define and measure. Regardless of how we define them, however, most would agree that citizens require information and open democratic debate to comply with these demanding assumptions. This may border on the obvious, but Chapter 4 will make a more specific argument. Research on welfare state change, we think, has not yet fully investigated the extent to which modern day election campaigns inform citizens about the increasing range of welfare state pressures and policy solutions. Especially absent is a consideration of the overall *scale* of public sphere attention. For a number of reasons discussed in Chapter 4, we largely lack answers to fundamental questions such as: are welfare issues widely debated in the public sphere during those crucial weeks and months leading up to Election Day? Has this changed as pressures have become more severe? Do welfare issues ever make it into that group of memorable struggles that will later define an election in the history books? If so, which issues?

These are questions about 'systemic agendas', that is, agendas transcending specific actors and applying instead to the overall character of a campaign. Systemic campaign salience is important to this book for several reasons. A general point is that most key aspects of democratic linkage depend on it. The extent to which citizens vote based on a particular issue dimension is sensitive to how much overall systemic attention is paid to that dimension (Stokes 1963; Iyengar and Kinder 1987). Relatedly, democratic representatives are more representative—in terms of attitudes and in policymaking—in salient areas (Esaiasson and Heidar 2000). Or take as a final example the communication of party positions to citizens. Several studies show that citizens are better at updating their views of parties in response to changes in policy positions when 'the wider informational environment' (Adams, Ezrow, and Somer-Topcu 2014: 976) allows such learning. Similarly, studies show how media campaign attention to a specific party increases the chances that citizens correctly perceive party positions (see also Banducci, Giebler, and Kritzinger 2017).

Two further points underscore the importance of systemic campaign salience. One is that systemic findings can change the democratic assessment of parties' and citizens' behaviour during campaigns. Imagine findings showing, say, that specific public statements made by leading politicians are generally very informative on pressures and policy responses, at the same time as citizens excel at drawing rational perceptual and attitudinal conclusions from such information. The meaning of these findings in terms of democratic linkage, however, will depend partly on whether this kind of information is generally present in campaigns or whether these issues remain systemically obscure.

Systemic salience, finally, may affect citizen responses to specific information about reform pressures and policy. Throughout the chapters on public responses we entertain the possibility that broad systemic salience functions as a 'trigger' for reactions to such messages. This applies to our analysis of which reform pressures, if any, citizens are prone to discover and worry about (Chapters 6 and 7). Likewise, it applies to our findings about the policy conclusions citizens draw once they have begun to worry about pressures (Chapters 8). Overall, we shall find that the systemic agenda context affects whether people recognize certain types of pressures and draw certain policy conclusions (while forgetting about others).

Do parties still provide coherent choice?

Democratic linkage is not only about attention and debate. It is also about eventually making a choice. In order to choose, however, there must be discernible differences between the alternatives. Numerous scholars have argued that linkage works better if differences across parties have a coherent 'programmatic' structure (Fuchs and Klingemann 1989; Thomassen 1994). It is desirable for parties to package their stances on a large number of issues into programmatic ideologies. Packaging makes it easier for parties to communicate to voters the mandates they are seeking. Rather than putting across a large number of disconnected issues, programmatic parties can signal general positions on a small number of ideological dimensions. Coherent programmes also make it easier for voters to grasp the policy packages on offer. After all, programmatic choice entails that a party's stance on one issue can be predicted by its stance on another issue and, more generally, by its overall programmatic character.

Scholars assessing democratic linkage have often assumed and found that parties compete along a single programmatic left–right dimension (where left means pro government social spending and redistribution whereas the right is anti those things for the benefit of the market, family, or civil society). For example, the upbeat conclusions reached by Dalton et al. (2011) build on findings suggesting that citizens can (still) correctly place parties along this continuum, that voters' positions along this one dimension predicts their party choice, and that leftist governments (still) spend more on the welfare state overall than other governments. There are also scholars working on parties and linkage who allow a more multidimensional policy space (e.g. Kriesi et al. 2008; Kriesi et al. 2012). However, they generally retain the idea that a single *economic* left–right dimension subsumes welfare state issues on redistribution, social spending, and benefit levels, but where this is complemented by one or several 'second' dimensions defined by migration, European integration, gender equality, and tolerance of diverse lifestyles.

Welfare state research has traditionally also upheld the idea of an all-important economic left–right programmatic dimension. The influential 'power resources' model (Korpi 1983, 2006) links general welfare state development to the political strength of the working class. Welfare state positions and policies among parties are seen as persistently structured by ideological left–right positions, in turn driven by class interests among the citizenry.

These assumptions are tested in research on how 'government partisanship' affects welfare state development (Korpi and Palme 2003; Allan and Scruggs 2004). This research analyses the effects of left- and right-leaning governments (with the latter sometimes divided between secular liberal/conservative parties and Christian democrats). For a long time, the hypothesis that government composition matters continued to receive support in explaining policy levels and change (van Kersbergen 1995; Huber and Stephens 2001; Korpi and

Palme 2003; Allan and Scruggs 2004; Castles 2007).[3] More recently, doubt has been cast on its continued success. Examining a larger number of dependent policy variables over longer time spans, recent research has found declining or, not least for new social policy, small left–right partisan effects in recent decades (Bonoli 2010; Nelson 2013; Stephens 2015; Jakobsson and Kumlin 2017).

But does a decline in left–right government effects on policy also equal a decline in democratic linkage? Not necessarily. In a magisterial review of research on parties and the welfare state, Häusermann et al. (2012) argue that parties might still link citizens with policy, but not in the manner that the 'power resources' model stipulates. Major left- and right-leaning parties do not have the same constituents as they once did. At the same time their traditional constituents, who are of some continued importance, have partly shifted their preferences in redistributive issues, or are more concerned with other dimensions. Still, the authors (Häusermann et al. 2012: 227) complain that 'studies that point to the absence of party differences or "unexpected" party behaviour (such as left-wing parties cutting back on welfare or different left-wing and right-wing parties pursuing very similar social policy agendas) interpret this as evidence for a loosening link between parties and their electorates, or even a "hollowing" of the representative function of parties'. As an antidote to this premature interpretation, Häusermann et al. (2012) suggest that scholars must pay attention to both the changing composition of voter groups and the actual policy preferences these hold.

We certainly agree that the composition and preferences of party voters provide crucial clues to understanding linkage. But to fully assess the role of parties we must also pay attention to a further element in the linkage process: which policy mandates, if any, do parties actually communicate to citizens? To what extent are welfare state issues systemically salient as well as present in concrete party messages? Do parties manage to communicate differences in their problem descriptions and policy solutions? These questions are analysed in Chapter 5, which assesses differences in party messages concerning welfare state pressures and policy solutions. Do any such differences conform to a traditional left–right programmatic structure?

The answer to the last question, as we have noted, is not self-evident. One major possibility is that messages and mandates are better understood as 'particularistic'. A distinct group of welfare state scholars has long

---

[3] Thus, (Schmidt 2010: 213) concluded in a fairly recent overview that 'the evidence of a wide variety of studies is that the "parties matter" hypothesis passes the empirical test reasonably well'.

demonstrated that policy positioning often serves to attract well-defined groups of strategic importance in a specific election (e.g. Baldwin 1990). In a similar vein, scholars have argued that the welfare state domain often provides *specific* rather than programmatic linkage. Such concrete and strategic issue competition may just as well obscure rather than clarify 'programmatic conflict' (Häusermann et al. 2012).

These possibilities may have become more prevalent. Some parties are alleged to have transformed from mass to 'catch-all' or even cartel organizations unbound by traditional class and ideology. Moreover, we noted in Chapter 1 that the policy landscape of pressured welfares states has grown more complex. The number of severe problems (i.e. reform pressures) to politicize has increased. The menu of policy instruments to alleviate pressure has also expanded. In Chapter 3 we shall develop this last point when discussing 'the social investment/activation turn'. For now, suffice it to say that we are observing an expanding universe of available particularistic narratives, the possible result of which is that programmatic party differences are poorly communicated. We will now discuss two different versions of the particularistic democratic linkage that may be on offer in the absence of programmatic left–right linkage. The results in Chapter 5 will be compared also to these two models.

'Issue ownership' and problem-oriented party messages

The first model explains why politicians may well debate specific societal problems (i.e. reform pressures) at the same time as they remain largely silent on specific policy solutions. This model has been around a long time (Robertson 1976; Budge and Farlie 1983; Carmines and Stimson 1990) under names such as 'saliency' theory or 'issue competition' but is now mostly referred to as the 'issue ownership' model (e.g. Petrocik 1996; van der Brug 2004; Aardal and van Wijnen 2005; Green and Hobolt 2008; Martinsson 2009; Lefevere, Tresch, and Walgrave 2015; Stubager 2018). The model envisages party competition as a struggle to make citizens attend to the particular problem areas where they themselves are regarded as the most competent problem-solver (i.e. issues that they 'own'). In these areas, parties present themselves as competent and committed, without telling voters in detail how problems will be solved. Thus, parties develop particularistic problem 'specialties' that are not necessarily well captured by left–right programmatic stances.[4]

---

[4] While issue ownership has traditionally been regarded as a stable party trait, reflecting a history of performance and image-building, recent research finds that parties can develop their image in the

Issue ownership-based party competition might seem unsatisfying when held against a gold standard stipulating that democratic choice should be about policy, or even programmatic ideology. At the same time, it does provide a modicum of choice as citizens get to vote for different narratives concerning which problems we must prioritize. What is more, this competition type may have a secret democratic advantage that does not show at first sight. More specifically, it could have an in-built capacity to secure party differences in an era of programmatic left–right depolarization. Under issue ownership competition parties have strong incentives to 'speak past each other' and engaging in 'selective emphasis' highlighting only issues that they 'own' while avoiding the issues that benefit opponents.

This last assumption, however, seems to be increasingly challenged. Summarizing a large comparative longitudinal study, Green-Pedersen and Walgrave (2014: 222) report that most parties try to capitalize on a very limited number of salient real-world problems with 'a lot of issue-overlap, a finding that challenges the issue ownership thesis. Thus, issue priority differences between parties and between governments in the same country are surprisingly small'. More than this, 'the pervasive finding that parties' issue priorities are not very different and that, when they enter government, parties do not pursue systematically diverging agendas challenges the core idea of party government and mandate politics' (Green-Pedersen and Walgrave 2014: 226).

We take away from this discussion a realization that the in-built capacity of issue ownership-style competition to generate party differences in priorities cannot be taken for granted. Our analysis in Chapter 5 contributes by studying the extent to which major left–right parties politicize different or similar sets of reform pressures, and the extent to which they remain silent on policy altogether.

The 'multiple streams' framework and policy solution-based agenda-setting

A second possible model of particularistic messages implies that politicization of reform pressures comes with clearer policy solutions than predicted by the 'issue ownership' model. In a seminal study, John Kingdon (2011

light of changing real-world circumstances (Butt 2007). Voters, for their part, are seen as problem-rather than policy-oriented: they worry deeply about societal developments and they form an idea about which parties are the most competent and engaged in addressing them. At the same time, under this model citizens are not necessarily very clear on what should be done in terms of concrete policy to solve salient problems.

[1984]) conceived of 'agenda-setting' as the result of interactions between three independent 'streams' of events. There is the 'problem stream', in which objective indicators of real-world problems are defined (or more commonly, not defined) as worthy of scarce attention. Second, there is the 'policy stream', in which experts and eventually politicians form new ideas for policy solutions. And third, there is the 'political stream', in which political actors judge which problems and solutions should be attended to—for example in election campaigns—given the nature of public opinion and its implications for re-election and coalition-building.

These three streams of events are seen as largely independent of each other. Every now and then, however, the streams are 'coupled' in ways that allow problems and solutions to climb the agenda of a political system and, eventually, produce policy change. A 'policy window' opens up through which key actors connect a particular problem with a particular policy solution. These solutions may well have been under development for some time in distinct expert circles independent of those who have been concerned with the problems that the solutions are now meant to solve. Kingdon (2011 [1984]) also emphasizes that policy solutions take shape slowly, often for unrelated reasons, and initially as responses to other problems. A key upshot for this study is that objective real-world problems such as welfare state reform pressures may not be enough for agenda change. Instead, such problems may only enter public agendas once they can be coupled with new policy ideas that might reasonably alleviate underlying problems *and* conceivably be marketed to the public and to coalition partners.

The 'multiple streams' framework originated in the USA with its individualist, candidate-oriented, and presidential system in mind. The theory envisages problem–policy coupling done by 'policy entrepreneurs' such as individual experts, candidates, or corporate actors (Zahariadis 2004). Quite reasonably, however, several scholars have argued that in parliamentary European political systems it is political parties that assume the leading role in this regard. Political parties weave together expert concerns about growing real-world problems and couple these with new available policy solutions, forming coherent marketable narratives (Herweg, Huss, and Zohlnhöfer 2015; Knaggård 2015). At the same time, the process becomes time consuming when complex collective entities such as parties act as policy entrepreneurs. Problem descriptions as well as policy ideas must first develop among expert communities, and then be imported into party platforms in ways consistent with party history and ideology, perhaps making concessions to rival factions.

This is where our study connects with the multiple streams tradition. Chapter 5 investigates if and how parties couple welfare state reform pressures with policy solutions. Which combinations of welfare state problems and solutions (if any) do parties put across to voters? Which policy solutions (if any) enable the politicization of reform pressures? In a sense, we will be looking for traces in campaign communications of the policy development in response to a changing environment that is seen as one explanation of allegedly well-functioning democratic linkage (Dalton et al. 2011). Does this linkage follow a left–right structure or is it better understood as particularistic and non-programmatic? And perhaps most important: is democratic choice safeguarded in the process, or do large mainstream parties promote similar sets of marketable problem–policy combinations?

In sum, we have two distinct notions of the particularistic 'mandates' parties might promote. Each has its own implications for democratic linkage. 'Issue ownership' implies that citizens get to choose between clearly different narratives about the societal problems that deserve attention. The drawback of this form of competition and voter choice is that citizens may not be informed about concrete policy. In the welfare state domain, parties may simply signal how concerned they are with some reform pressures, without revealing concrete reforms to alleviate pressure. At the same time, traditional accounts of 'issue ownership' models may have overestimated the inclination of parties to 'speak past each other' as opposed to capitalizing on the same problems. In the worst case, citizens get to choose between parties that are very similar in terms of which welfare pressures they prioritize, while remaining largely silent on policy solutions.

The multiple streams framework, by contrast, implies that parties will not politicize reform pressure until they have formulated a concrete, credible, and marketable policy solution. From a democratic linkage perspective, the clear advantage is that this brand of competition seems to ensure concrete policy information. A corresponding problem, however, stems from considerations made in the 'political stream'. These may narrow the scope of the actual policy solutions that are deemed possible to market to the public. In effect, citizens may come under the impression that the welfare state is more pressured than before at the same time as the amount of choice offered by parties has also shrunk. In the worst case, this public impression is accompanied by a wide variety of actual ongoing welfare reform out of which only a biased selection is ever marketed to the public. This is a possibility that we shall sustain into Chapter 3. There we will discuss the possibility that the social investment/activation turn functions as a blame avoidance device, or smokescreen if you like, for a larger and in its totality less popular set of policy changes.

Can citizens perceive pressures and update preferences?

Models of democratic linkage assume, often in passing, that the public preferences parties link with policy are 'informed'. What does this mean and how do we shed light on the problem?[5] As one of us has discussed,[6] there are two broad conceptualizations of informed public opinion. First, an 'objectivist/expert-driven' definition sees public opinion as informed if it complies with, and is logically responsive to, 'objective' facts and consensual expert views on how a situation should be perceived. This objectivist notion is for example found in economic voting research. Here, scholars assume the existence of a 'real' economy and investigate if it is correctly perceived and responded to by the public (cf. Anderson 2007; Achen and Bartels 2016).[7] In the most elaborated accounts, scholars examine a causal process where a small set of objective macroeconomic indicators affect consensual interpretations by elite experts, which in turn shape citizen's perceptions, and ultimately voting behaviour (MacKuen, Erikson, and Stimson 1992).

We use the objectivist notion, but it must be said that it is limited in several ways. We can therefore not claim to capture but a few interesting aspects of informed public opinion in the area of reform pressures and policy solutions. One limitation is that the objectivist notion is hard to apply to substantive policy preferences. Instead, it is more relevant when studying underlying perceptions of societal problems (i.e. welfare reform pressures) and the preference formation processes that these perceptions trigger. A second limitation arises from difficulties in identifying objective facts. Some would even argue that the bulk of political conflict in modern democracies is precisely about different, but legitimate, views on how reality should be portrayed. Not even macroeconomic performance—for all the availability of hard data—is necessarily only about an 'objective' state of affairs (see Mutz 1998). Thus, objectivist yardsticks for assessing the public are mainly relevant in situations where we accept the

---

[5] To ask this question is to potentially invoke a gargantuan political science literature that started with early classics (Converse 1964) and is still ongoing (see Achen and Bartels 2016) In this section, however, we shall stay clear of such a broad exposition. The more modest, but still important, purpose is to note some more pointed contributions that our empirics make in this regard.

[6] This section builds on Kumlin (2014).

[7] The indicators used to measure the objective state of affairs vary (ironically enough), but Lewis-Beck and Paldam (2000) emphasize 'the big three': unemployment, GDP growth, and inflation.

existence of major objective facts and find it problematic if citizens are ignorant or unable to draw conclusions from them.

Partly due to these issues, scholars also tend to rely on a 'subjective/deliberative' notion of informed public opinion. Here, there is no assumption of objective facts. Perceptions and substantive preferences are inherently subjective; they are open to argumentation and interpretation in democratic debate. Informed public opinion is secured through exposure to a procedurally satisfactory information flow and refers to whatever perceptions and preferences people hold afterwards. This subjective/deliberative notion is found both among democratic theorists[8] (e.g. Dahl 1989), 'deliberative polling' studies (cf. Luskin, Fishkin, and Jowell 2002; Delli Carpini, Cook, and Jacobs 2004), as well as survey research 'simulating' what the public *would* prefer if everyone were highly and equally informed (Bartels 1996; Althaus 1998).[9]

A number of our empirical results are useful in a discussion concerning objectivist yardsticks of informed preferences. Importantly, they require that we can accept the objective existence of serious reform pressures that call for a policy response. Here, we follow, among others, Vis and van Kersbergen (2013: 841) who have argued that welfare states must be seen as seriously constrained by how:

> existing 'objective' problem pressure influences the range of ideas that political actors consider. Pressures are 'objective' to the extent that they threaten the existential conditions of material survival of a system. ... The 'objective' pressure tends to facilitate the adoption of certain ideas and the neglect or abandonment of others. These ideas, in turn, affect the type of reform that political actors pursue. Different ideas may thus lead to different reform proposals, but not all ideas are feasible.
>
> (Vis and van Kersbergen 2013: 841)

Leaning against this assumption of objectively existing pressure the chapters on 'public responses' make several relevant observations. The first one has to do with how exposure to pressure information affects perceptions of welfare

---

[8] The subjective/deliberative model is consistent with Robert Dahl's discussion of democracy as a procedure for forming and implementing an 'enlightened understanding'. Dahl does not put substantive restrictions on what people are 'supposed' to think with full information, or what the 'correct' enlightened views may be. Rather, what is important is that the informational context gives citizens the possibility to find *their own* enlightened understanding in dialogue with an open, fair, and balanced information flow (Dahl 1989).

[9] While the subjective/deliberative view seems less restrictive and more sympathetic in that it does not require objective truth, it does introduce the meta difficulty of objectively defining a democratically satisfactory opinion formation process.

state sustainability. Do citizens at all react to such information under the 'non-crisis' conditions offered by our three country cases? Put differently, can citizens process information about sweeping transformations such as, say, population ageing and incorporate these into updated perceptions of welfare state sustainability? Even if they can, there may be biases and obstacles in such processes. For example, Chapter 6 examines if citizens process arguably milder pressure related to 'undeserving' groups (i.e. immigration/immigrants), while ignoring very severe pressure related to 'deserving' groups (i.e. population ageing/the elderly). Moreover, both Chapters 6 and 7 assess whether pre-existing welfare support and partisan leanings function as 'perceptual screens' that stop, or even create backlash against, the processing of even the most severe reform pressures. Finally, Chapter 8 studies if perceptions of sustainability can ever produce adjustments in policy preferences, along with the reciprocal possibility that sustainability perceptions are instead explained by existing preferences (Chapter 8). All these biases and tendencies may seem unsurprising and 'normal' features of opinion formation in mass democracies. But taken to extremes they may be hard to square with the notion of informed public opinion, at least if we are willing to treat pressures as major objective facts that threaten the 'existential conditions' of the welfare state.

In conclusion, our results provide input for assessing an important sense in which public opinion is informed in an era of objective reform pressure. Moreover, the answers also inform our view of whether linkage processes can help explain welfare state change. How likely is it that this change happens partly because information about reform pressures transforms perceptions of sustainability which in turn reshape the public demand that parties and governments are linking with policy? If so, does that transformation in demand correspond to the broad contours of actual policy change? Negative findings would cast doubt on the notion that continued democratic linkage in the welfare domain has been secured through policy development, communicated to citizens through improved campaigning processes that offset other aspects of party decline.

3

Democratic Leadership and the Changing Study of Changing Welfare States

Representative democracy entails more than 'democratic linkage': it also requires leadership by those elected. Few want representatives who only execute the mandate already given by the public. Most of us, upon reflection, also expect leaders to consider what the people *would* want if they knew and understood what leaders know and understand. We expect politicians to sometimes stand for potentially unpopular policies that they think make sense in the long run (cf. Jacobs 2011). Crucially, we also expect them to make such arguments in public, even when the stakes are high during an election campaign.

In *The Concept of Representation* (1967: 209), Hanna Pitkin adopted a widely influential conception of political representation that captures these sentiments. To be a good representative is defined as 'acting in the interests of the represented, in a manner responsive to them'. One implication is that politicians are indeed entitled to propose and enact policies that are out of touch with current public opinion, provided they do so in a *responsive* manner. Crucially, 'responsiveness' means that while policies do not have to correspond to current public opinion, representatives must always *motivate* unpopular decisions to citizens in terms of their own enlightened interests. This notion of responsive democratic leadership directs our attention to the public sphere in general and to election campaigns in particular (see Esaiasson and Wlezien 2017 for recent analyses of responsiveness).

Democratic leadership also places demands on citizens. When exposed to responsive leadership, citizens cannot be slaves under the status quo. They can, at least in principle, process arguments about reasons for unpopular policy and adjust their perceptions and preferences accordingly. And at least sometimes, and to some extent, they are able to process information and draw conclusions that run against their short-term interests. Otherwise, responsive leadership would always be in vain. Overall, then, democratic leadership entails citizens that are, at least in principle and on occasion, able to adapt in view of new societal challenges.

Election Campaigns and Welfare State Change. Staffan Kumlin and Achim Goerres, Oxford University Press.
© Staffan Kumlin and Achim Goerres (2022). DOI: 10.1093/oso/9780198869214.003.0003

Leadership was always an ingredient in representation, but some argue that it is becoming more important. Because of the alleged decline in linkage and prospective policy mandates discussed in Chapter 2, representatives must now increasingly govern *for* the people rather than *by* the people (Manin 1997; Scharpf 1999). To stay democratically legitimate, it is now more crucial than ever that representatives convince citizens at least 'after the fact'. Said differently, they need to legitimize policies top down, instead of representing bottom up. In this spirit, Peter Mair (2006) has argued that 'responsible government' is outflanking 'representative' government. Or in van Biezen's (2014: 13) succinct summary: 'the key problem of the mainstream parties in modern democracies has become that of legitimising their governance in the face of their weakened representative capacity'.

Also welfare state researchers are warming to the idea that accelerating policy change now happens partly because of democratic leadership and adaptive citizens. In the process, scholars have started to go beyond institutional explanations of stability as well as pure 'blame avoidance' explanations of change. This chapter discusses this shift in the literature and outlines our contributions to it. The first part of the chapter covers selected parts of institutionalism. This conglomerate of theories, which grew in popularity in the 1980s and 1990s, was at first focused on explaining policy stability and divergence between countries. Later work adapted institutional theory to account for uniform policy change. But overall, scholars in this rich tradition still assign a limited role to electoral democracy in general and public sphere communication in particular. To illustrate this, we first discuss the literature on 'gradual institutional change' (Streeck and Thelen 2005), which implies only a minor role for electoral contestation as an explanation for a sweeping 'liberalization' of advanced political economies. We then discuss research stimulated by Pierson's NPWS (new politics of the welfare state) framework and the neighbouring study of blame avoidance. This research regards the public sphere as more important but still views it in negative terms—as a site for normatively flawed processes serving as obstacles for both welfare state change and for the democratic leadership that could legitimize it.

The remainder of the chapter moves to discussing newer approaches that assign greater importance to political communication. It would be wrong to advertise this research as some sort of unitary 'movement', however. It is as of now a set of loosely connected research literatures. They are united, however, in emphasizing that information spread in the public sphere by political leaders may be a potent and democratically positive factor in an era of accelerating welfare state change. Specifically, this discussion starts with work on political leaders who, after all, do not only engage in democratically dubious blame avoidance. They are increasingly regarded as capable of absorbing new policy ideas that break with the institutional environment. Relatedly, we discuss research using concepts such as 'credit claiming', 'strategic reframing', and—above all—'ideational leadership' to understand how actors publicly politicize new (and old) policy solutions to reform pressures. While we see our study as a part of this development, we also argue that the democratic optimism exuded by this important research may be premature. Ongoing work is useful but often limited either in terms of methods or in its scope.

The chapter then discusses actually ongoing policy changes in European welfare states, focusing especially on the 'social investment/activation turn'. Is this a new policy paradigm? How is it different from both the earlier expansive 'golden age', and from the 'neoliberal austerity' era beginning in the 1980s? We highlight research on how new 'social investment'-related social policies have become popular, and how they open up a more multidimensional landscape of party and voter preferences, with implications—and rarely debated democratic perils—for campaign communication. Unresolved questions here concern the extent to which social investment clouds less popular policy in public communication, and the extent to which this new paradigm offers coherent democratic choice for citizens.

Finally, we will consider public opinion research on how citizens perceive and respond to information about reform pressures and policy changes. A surprising finding is that citizens rarely punish incumbents for welfare state retrenchment and dissatisfaction. The correct interpretation of this tendency is unclear, however. Does weak electoral punishment signal suppressed anger over malperformance that cannot find an outlet in voting? Or does it reflect successful democratic leadership resulting in public realism and acceptance of the fact that reform pressures constrain welfare states? We contribute to knowledge about this second possibility by asking two sets of questions. First, are citizens' perceptions of welfare state sustainability sensitive to information about reform pressures; if so, which pressures among which people and contexts (Chapters 6 and 7)? Second, can citizens draw meaningful policy conclusions based on such perceptions (Chapter 8)? We explain our contribution to past research as well as how these questions inform our understanding of welfare state change and democracy.

Gradual institutional change: secretive liberalization under the public radar?

Political science took an 'institutional turn' in the 1980s and 1990s (Rothstein 1996; Immergut 1998; Peters 1999; Schmidt 2010). Western welfare states displayed mostly institutional and policy stability, or even path-dependent institutionally structured divergence. Hence, it was natural for scholars to formulate institutional theories that could account for the stable and structured situation in front of them. As welfare states have begun to change along multiple lines, scholars have not only turned to more political and discourse-oriented explanations. They have also developed institutional theory itself to better explain change. Nonetheless, even this adapted version of institutional theory tends to assign a marginal role to the factors studied in this book.

An example is *Beyond Continuity: Institutional Change in Advanced Political Economies* (2005), edited by Wolfgang Streeck and Kathleen Thelen. These authors sought to steer a path between two ideas implied by institutional theory: on the one hand, long periods of stability and, on the other, the occasional 'window of opportunity' or 'punctuated equilibrium', allowing outbursts of purposeful and salient institutional transformation. Instead, these scholars argue, institutions themselves—as they interact with changing real-world conditions—give rise to *gradual* but eventually important institutional transformations. This change seems insignificant when experienced step-by-step but adds up to considerable 'gradual but transformative' change over longer periods.

The precise mechanisms of gradual change are complex and we will not discuss them in detail. Just briefly consider 'policy drift' as an example. Policy drift happens when policies remain formally inert 'in spite of external change resulting in slippage of institutional practice on the ground' (Streeck and Thelen 2005: 31). For example, growing 'new social risks' may be poorly handled by existing welfare state policies. This poor performance may in turn produce increased de facto reliance on alternative markets and other private alternatives among groups not protected by long-standing benefits and services (see Hacker 2005). This 'liberalization' may be helped along by complementary mechanisms of gradual institutional change. For example, previously peripheral private alternatives may become more important. Similarly, seemingly insignificant private alternatives may be introduced, after which they gradually outcompete and undermine the old institutional order they were supposed to buttress.

The 'gradual change' framework contrasts with our approach in two ways. First, purposeful democratic politics explains welfare state change only to a limited extent. Change is rather seen as a gradual, opaque, and politically uncontrolled affair. It is hardly perceptible, let alone debated, at any given point in time. It does not happen because reform pressures and policy solutions burst onto the scene in election campaigns during which governments establish democratic linkage and exercise leadership. At best, electoral democratic politics takes a reactive role in gradually adjusting the welfare state to exogenous changes prompted by the interaction between institutional practices and real-world conditions. True, Streeck and Thelen's discussion allows for occasional and reactive 'political contestation' of these already ongoing gradual change processes. Thus, while the core of the argument is that 'significant change can emanate from inherent ambiguities and "gaps" that exist by design or emerge over time between formal institutions and their actual implementation or enforcement' they also acknowledge in passing that 'these gaps may become key sites of political contestation over the form, functions, and salience of specific institutions whose outcome may be an important engine of institutional change' (Streeck and Thelen 2005: 19). However, as Hemerijck (2013: 97) objects: 'The more purposeful interventions, aimed at a more comprehensive problem-solving remain, I believe, undertheorized [...] they do not allow for the institutional ambiguities they underscore to help (re)shape the cognitive understandings and normative orientations of relevant policymakers'.

Of course, in this book we ask questions about the prevalence and impact of the political contestation of changing real world conditions (reform pressures) in election campaigns. Do campaigns function as intense periods of debate reshaping perceptions and attitudes? Chapter 4 even asks if these periods can in fact be characterized as 'punctuated equilibria', that is, as rather sudden and massive changes in systemic agendas. Meanwhile, the chapters on public responses help to establish if such systemic salience assists perceptual and attitudinal change processes among the public. Well-founded answers to these questions clarify the extent to which welfare state change is a secretive process that goes mostly unnoticed in election campaigns and among the citizenry at large, as might be implied by the gradual change framework.

A second notable feature is that the gradual institutional change framework mainly explains 'liberalization'. Thus, it focuses on state retreatment from policy ambitions assumed in earlier decades. Streeck and Thelen (2005: 2), like many others writers in the early 2000s, saw liberalization as the 'prevailing trend in the advanced economies during the last two decades of the twentieth century and beyond'. Having the benefit of writing more than a decade later, we can recognize the limits of this assessment. As will be discussed later in this chapter, welfare state change has for some time involved both retrenchment in a liberalizing direction *and* a menu of less destructive or even expansive reform trajectories. More than simply limiting the scope of the theory, however, focusing on liberalization has implications for how we understand the very process of change. As we shall see, social investment/activation reforms in particular are generally assumed to be more popular than retrenchment and cost containment policies. This may open the door to the public sphere and election campaigns as a more potent and positive factor in welfare state change. Work on agenda-setting—as we noted in Chapter 2—suggests that societal problems (in our case reform pressures) are more likely to shape policy agendas once there is a set of fresh policy solutions that is palatable to the public (e.g. Kingdon 2011 [1984]). Other research (e.g. Häusermann 2012) shows how such new social policies also open up for majority coalitions supporting multifaceted reform packages containing both popular and less popular types of policy change. These matters will be discussed later in this chapter. For now, suffice it to say that this book pays close attention to how the emerging social investment/activation paradigm shapes 'systemic agendas', party messages, and their impact on citizens. In going beyond 'liberalization', we question the notion of welfare state change as a one-dimensional, largely destructive, and democratically secretive process.

A new politics of the welfare state?

A rather different institutionalist theoretical lens is provided by Pierson (1994, 1996, 2001) in his work on a framework known as 'the new politics of the welfare state' (NPWS) (Green-Pedersen and Haverland 2002; Levy 2010; Hemerijck 2013).[1] The NPWS framework builds on a recognition of multiple growing reform pressures that collectively define an era

---

[1] Although much recent scholarship argues that NPWS theory cannot on its own explain nearly all welfare state change it continues to be a prominent theory in the research field, as evidenced by a recent anniversary special issue (Patashnik 2015).

of 'permanent austerity' beginning sometime in the early 1980s (Pierson 2001; Hay and Wincott 2012). However, the framework makes assumptions about institutions, citizens, policymakers, and the nature of reform, to explain why welfare state change is nonetheless modest, and incremental, with radical reform being restricted to certain areas and situations. Here we shall focus specifically on NPWS assumptions about public opinion and political communication.[2]

One key assumption is that the welfare state has built strong support for itself such that changing the status quo is unpopular. This is partly due to the rise of large and self-interested constituencies that now defend their own benefits and services. However, the welfare state has also generated broader normative support for itself, not least due to institutional mechanisms; these extend support for the status quo beyond specific policies where an individual has a direct stake. Furthermore, citizens are 'risk-averse': their fear of welfare state deterioration is stronger than their desire for improvements (Vis 2011). Relatedly, any societal gains from retrenchment are diffuse, long-term, and uncertain, while losses are visibly concentrated to identifiable, self-interested, and easily mobilized groups, often protected by interest organizations.

All this produces an aversion among office-seeking decision makers against politicizing reform pressures and advocating retrenchment. As Pierson (2001) put it:

> [t]here are strong grounds for scepticism about the prospect for any radical revision of the welfare state [...] The broad scale of public support, the intensity of preferences among programme recipients, the extent to which a variety of actors (including employers) have adapted to the existing contours of the social market economy, and the institutional arrangements which favour the defenders of the status quo make a frontal assault on the welfare state politically suicidal in most countries.
>
> (Pierson 2001: 416)

Throughout this book we put a number of key implications of this storyline to a test. For example, in Chapters 4 and 5 we examine the extent to which

---

[2] Other assumptions explain why institutions are hard to change. This is in part due to the manifold 'veto points' in affluent democracies, such as coalition governments, bicameralism, federalism, referenda, etc. These features inhibit radical change, typically by requiring more than simple majorities. Institutional stickiness also arises from mechanisms producing 'path dependence' through 'positive feedback'. Such mechanisms constrain policymaking by making it (seem) easier, cheaper, and generally more rational to stay close to long-trodden policy paths.

election campaigns are ever shaped by proposed retrenchment, and if this has become more or less unusual as reform pressures have mounted.

The NPWS framework also has implications for our analysis of citizen responses to campaign information. The ideas of status-quo supporting and risk-averse citizens guarding their stakes would imply a predisposition against the message that the welfare state is not economically sustainable. NPWS thus suggests limited room for what Chapter 6 will call 'reform pressure framing', particularly among status-quo supporting and self-interested citizens, but also among those who display more generalized support for existing social protection.

A further implication of NPWS is increasing similarities between political parties, especially those that are contenders for government office. The action space of these parties is limited by, on the one hand, a universally perceived reform pressure and, on the other hand, the need to remain in office. Pierson (2001: 417) therefore predicts increasingly centrist tendencies in the 'era of austerity': 'we should expect strong pressures to move towards more centrist—and therefore more incremental—responses. Those seeking to generate significant cost reductions while modernizing particular aspects of social provision will generally hold the balance of political power'. Also, this aspect of NPWS is part of our examination of whether the leaders of the large parties communicate distinct choices to citizens in terms of prioritized reform pressures and policy solutions. Are there such differences in campaign messages and, if so, do these have a coherent programmatic left-right structure? Or are these best described as particularistic messages that emphasize specific reform pressures and policy solutions?

The 'Nixon goes to China' logic

In an oft-cited article, Fiona Ross (2000a) added a party-political dimension to NPWS. She discussed a 'Nixon goes to China' logic, whereby leftist governments may end up retrenching and restructuring the welfare state just as much, or even more than, because of issue ownership and perceived trustworthiness in most welfare state areas. Left-leaning parties can more credibly adopt the centrist and pragmatic reform stance identified as crucial by NPWS theory. The left can thus exercise more effective leadership by talking more about pressures and unpopular reform, while still managing to exude welfare state support at a more general and normative level. This narrative is difficult for right-leaning governments as they can often be accused of actually *wanting* retrenchment for deeper ideological 'neoliberal' reasons. As Ross (2000a) explains:

> There is an old adage associated with Nixon's 1972 visit to China: [...] the latitude for successful policy leadership is largely reserved for those who seem least likely to act. [...] According to this logic, rightist parties should be more vulnerable in their retrenchment efforts than parties of the left—and especially so on explosive issues like welfare reform. The principal psychological mechanism conditioning voters' response to issue-associations appears to be trust [...]. Very simply, voters do not trust rightist parties to reform the welfare state whereas they assume that leftist parties will engage in genuine reform rather than indiscriminate and harsh retrenchment.
>
> (Ross 2000a: 162–4)

The key party difference here, then, is a legacy of issue ownership and trustworthiness. This helps leftist parties to communicate the message that the welfare state is under pressure and must be reformed. This advantage is also what gives them the confidence to put welfare state reform pressures and potentially unpopular policy solutions on the campaign agenda.

This theory, too, will be put to the test. Chapter 5 will examine if social democratic parties politicize uncomfortable reform pressures and policy solutions to a greater extent than their liberal-conservative competitors in our three countries. Chapter 7 gives a handle on whether such messages from social democrats are really more widely accepted and consequential among citizens, such that social democrats have a greater capacity to exercise political leadership.

While the 'Nixon goes to China' hypothesis seems reasonable, there is an alternative view. It has been argued that messages about reform pressures and policy solutions may in fact be more persuasive if they fit the party's ideological pedigree and issue ownership record. Under this alternative view, voters get confused, irritated, and feel betrayed when parties' welfare state messages seem to deviate from expectations. If true, the 'Nixon goes to China' phenomenon should not be very effective or common. Rather, citizens would then be prone to punish parties that deviate from, or underperform relative to, their own ideology and issue ownership profile. For example, social democratic parties would suffer *more* than other parties from politicizing welfare state reform pressures and champion retrenchment. Interestingly, this latter idea has been supported in several empirical studies: although electoral punishment for retrenchment is weak overall, it seems stronger for social democratic parties (Schumacher, Vis, and van Kersbergen 2013; Vis 2016).

'The blame game'

The NPWS framework does allow for more significant welfare state change under some circumstances. However, the institutional mechanisms and electoral incentives discussed above require that any remotely unpopular reforms, and the responsibility for them, are muddled using *blame avoidance strategies*. The explicit focus on blame avoidance means that NPWS is an institutional theory with direct implications for the public sphere and election campaigns compared to gradual institutional change, which mostly downplays electoral contestation and communication.

Blame avoidance as a concept was introduced into political science by Weaver (1986). He clarified that there is a diverse menu of possible blame avoidance strategies. Unfortunately, there is no established general definition, typology, with agreed-upon operationalizations. Part of the problem, we suspect, is that the concept is inherently vague because of its negative character; after all, the universe of options for *avoiding* a problem is potentially infinite. Since *any* action or non-action that serves to somehow avoid or reduce blame might conceivably be 'blame avoidance', it is not surprising that conceptual or operational consensus has not materialized.

Still, the welfare state literature revolves around a finite number of tendencies. A basic but useful three-fold distinction is offered by Hood (2007, 2011). The first type of blame avoidance refers to *institutional* strategies through which actors may strategically equip several political levels with overlapping responsibilities. A second type of strategies is *policy-related*, where actors may strategically rely on low-key non-decisions, opaque policies, or delay policy effects. Third, *presentational* blame avoidance strategies are more immediately about the topic of this book, that is, public communication between elites and citizens, which the rest of the discussion focuses on.

Even the presentational strategies defy easy definition. The possibilities in the literature range from *not* talking about a problem with an associated painful policy, to actively convincing citizens that the solution does not incur pain after all, that it is fair, or that it is painful but that most people will get some compensation (Vis 2016). Confusingly, the term 'blame avoidance' has been used for conveying to citizens that most parties agree on unpopular reforms anyway (Pierson 1996).

While we use blame avoidance as a convenient shorthand, it is important to be precise given this multitude of meanings. Empirically, we measure a small number of presentational aspects of blame avoidance that lend themselves to more precise definition and measurement. They are united by a conceptual restriction that we think makes sense, but which is not always explicit in past research. More precisely, all the measured strategies view presentational blame avoidance as relevant when actors accept—and so to speak 'work around'—the fact that a policy is potentially unpopular and is not the party's first preference. We reserve attempts to redefine problems and policies in positive terms for a different conceptual framework to be discussed later in this chapter.

A first strategy is *playing the crisis card*. This means arguing that a reform pressure is so severe and uncontrollable that 'we have no choice but to act now'. The most common version is probably the idea that an immediate economic crisis, with high unemployment-related budgetary strains, necessitates policies that neither citizens nor decision makers prefer. The idea of a crisis as the catalyst for retrenchment through this type of rhetoric is inherently part of the NPWS framework (Pierson 1996). It is also well-documented empirically in that several studies suggest that governments have exploited economic and fiscal crises in this way (Kuipers 2006; Starke 2008; Hay and Wincott 2012).

The final group of presentational blame avoidance strategies concern, not so much what is said, but what is *not* said. We will speak here of 'agenda control'. Politicians may try to keep a problematic set of reform pressures, and associated unpopular solutions, off the public sphere agenda. If reform pressures are very severe, they may even refrain from politicizing certain policy areas altogether. Thus, politicians who think population ageing is a severe reform pressure that will have to be solved by retrenchment and cost-cutting may campaign on other issues than pensions and elder care, or at least be silent on the reform pressure in question. If several major actors have this idea at the same time, the systemic salience may also be affected such that the whole public sphere pays less attention to reform pressures and associated policy areas as problems become more severe.

A distinct agenda-controlling technique is 'cherry-picking' of the actual policies marketed as solutions. This is a more subtle strategy compared to taking issues off the agenda altogether. Leaders do not necessarily shy away from the underlying and possibly uncomfortable societal problems. They may even launch clear policy solutions to address the problem. At the same time, however, they take care not to display the full range of policies citizens can expect after the election. It is useful here to recall that welfare reform has become more multidimensional over time. Thus, cherry-picking opportunities have increased. A particularly acute point discussed later in this chapter concerns the social investment/activation turn (cf. Morel et al. 2012).

The empirical chapters will examine possible manifestations of these blame avoidance strategies. Chapter 4 will examine if growing reform pressures increase or decrease the systemic salience of welfare state issues. Chapter 5 will, among other things, tell us if specific political leaders engage in presentational 'cherry-picking'. The empirical answers have implications for democratic linkage and leadership. Starting with linkage, one can make the point that agenda control strategies imply that citizens may not get the information they would need. Chapter 2 holds that citizens need to develop an informed understanding of problems and solutions in pressured welfare states. Alternatively, cherry-picking of policy solutions may inform citizens that there are problems while conveying an overly rosy picture of how these problems will be solved. Finally, linkage may also be compromised as politicians play the crisis card. This narrative does not entail, as linkage-based democracy would have it, solving reform pressure by making a *choice*. Rather, politicians make the defeatist argument that 'you have no choice, regardless of what you might think or what the opponents might say'.

Democratic leadership, too, has an uneasy relationship with presentational blame avoidance. Democratic leaders are expected to motivate unpopular decisions in terms of citizens' own enlightened long-term interests. This involves being prepared to make such arguments in public when the stakes are high during an election campaign. By contrast, blame avoidance would, on several accounts, seem to be the inverse of democratic leadership. These strategies imply everything from hiding reform pressures away from public sight to focusing only on less controversial policies. Alternatively, politicians need an immediate crisis before they dare politicize uncomfortable reform pressures and policy solutions. The crisis card allows them to opt out of democratic leadership as defined above. Instead, they tell citizens that there is really no choice at all.

The growing emphasis on discourse and leadership in welfare state research

In recent years, scholars have uncovered more—and more multidimensional—welfare state change. A growing body of work suggests that political leaders and citizens are less constrained by their institutional environment than previously assumed. Leaders can formulate and implement new policy ideas that address reform pressures. They also communicate these ideas to citizens who may be able to listen and adapt to a greater extent than previously appreciated. Thus, neither 'gradual institutional change', nor NPWS-inspired blame avoidance explanations, may provide the full story behind welfare state change. We must also consider discourse and democratic leadership explanations.

The remainder of this chapter discusses three components of this partial shift in the literature. The first concerns how elite actors may be able to formulate and communicate new policy *ideas*. A second section deals with a key substantive ideational shift: the social investment/activation turn; this shift has made welfare state change increasingly multidimensional, with implications for democratic leadership. The third section discusses citizens' attitudes and behaviour, which may be more malleable than previously thought.

Transformative ideational change

Ideas can be defined in many ways. However, the literature on transformative ideational change typically concerns actors' *causal* beliefs about how society and public policy relate. For example, the metaphor of a reform pressure describes a causal idea: that factor X exerts pressure on policy Y. Similarly, propositions about how policy change alleviates pressure adds another causal idea: that a pressure, say population ageing, would case if policy were reformed.

The crucial proposition in this literature is that the development of, and discourse around, new causal ideas impact on policymaking and political behaviour. Relatedly, ideas are not determined by interests and institutions. They are something more than reflections of such material and structural variables. Humans have the capacity, intellectually, to break out of the most stifling structural environment, convince others that they are right in their analysis, and build a coalition for change. Importantly, ideas and corresponding policy choices develop as actors communicate with each other in an evolving *discourse*. Overall, as Robert Cox and Daniel Béland explain in *Ideas and Politics in Social Science* (2011),

> the unique claim of ideational scholars is that these choices are shaped by the ideas people hold and debate with others. These ideas, in turn, are based on interpretations people have of the world and of those around them. There is a material reality but it lends itself to many interpretations that open endless options for human agency.
>
> (Cox and Béland 2011)

Several comparative (Cox 2001; Schmidt 2002) and single-country (Ross 2000b; Wincott 2011) studies of welfare state change draw conclusions broadly consistent with this storyline (see also Taylor-Gooby 2005). What contributions do we make to this research? As already said in Chapter 1, a fundamental contribution is to ask if discourse, as it manifests itself in election campaigns, fulfils the requirements identified by the 'democratic linkage' and the 'leadership' models.

There are several other contributions beyond the application of these democratic lenses. One arises as many studies are elite-centred. As a result, less is known about the contents and consequences of more public discourse, also involving communication between leaders and citizens. Theoretically, ideational scholars often discuss an interesting variation where 'ideas can take the form of high-profile public frames, discourses, and ideologies at the foreground of the political arena or constitute lower-profile assumptions and paradigms that often remain at the background' (Cox and Béland 2011: 6). Empirically however, high-profile public discourses are tapped by somewhat sweeping characterizations of the public sphere during historical phases, references to univariate distributions of public opinion and election results, but rarely by detailed data of the type we have assembled. The otherwise impressive studies by Cox (2001) and Schmidt (2002) are cases in point here. Relatedly, 'very little quantitative research into ideas has been attempted' (Cox and Béland 2011: 17; but see Kemmerling 2015: 20).[3] One of our contributions to this important literature, then, is systematic quantitative analysis of the contents of campaign discourse and public responses in the welfare state domain.

Some further contributions are inspired by advancements made in Sabina Stiller's (2010) *Ideational Leadership in German Welfare State Reform*. Stiller argues that a convincing ideational explanation needs specificity in terms of who the ideational agents are, what they say about the effects they might trigger on others and ultimately on policy change. 'It is difficult to imagine', she writes:

> that ideas have an impact by themselves, detached from what policy-makers do, let alone to show such a connection empirically. Ideas [...] cannot enter the policy-making arena on their own and, for that reason, need an agent to gather them, put them on a political agenda and further communicate them to a certain audience.
>
> (Stiller 2010: 32)

---

[3] Kemmerling (2015) shows how citizens' causal ideas about how labour markets work can be logically explained by individual and contextual variables. Meanwhile, he finds that such ideas also structure policy preferences, and that these patterns in turn explain labour market reforms. But beyond such exceptions we still have limited empirical knowledge of the public scope and causal effects of ideational discourse.

Stiller's solution is to link ideational strategies, not just to a vague discourse, but to identifiable leaders—usually ministers or other key individuals with pivotal positions. Our contribution is to specifically focus on how prime ministerial candidates from the principal government alternatives put reform pressures and policy solutions on campaign agendas (Chapter 5). Relatedly, we study how messages from leaders affect citizens (Chapters 6 and 7). Leaders of these large and comparatively trusted parties should carry special weight in leading the public on matters of difficult challenges and controversial policy.

Finally, Stiller argues that scholars need to specify the type of arguments one can expect from true ideational leaders. In her model, leaders advance a causal narrative that begins with what Heclo (1974) called 'policy failures'. In Stiller's (2010: 35) formulation, 'they link the existing situation in a policy area to themes like failure, inefficiency, crisis, welfare loss, and the like'. In our terminology, they put a reform pressure firmly on the agenda explaining how it makes the search for reform alternatives necessary. Besides problem-solving, this allows politicians to boast about their daring leadership while accusing opponents of sweeping problems under the rug. This last aspect is worth emphasizing: unlike typical blame-avoiding actors, ideational leaders are pro-active agenda-setters for serious problems that challenge the status quo and may require partly unpopular but ultimately sensible reform.

A related feature in Stiller's model is open legitimization of policy solutions using both 'cognitive' and 'normative' arguments. Cognitive arguments explain why new policies work. In terms of the reform pressures studied in this book, this might involve an argument about how a new policy alleviates unsustainability brought on by, say, population ageing, low employment rates, and the like. Normative arguments, by contrast, link policy failure and solutions to normative ideas about values, fairness, and deservingness that an audience already holds. Why does reform beat the status quo in, say, helping the truly deserving or in establishing procedural justice in service delivery? Such arguments differ from the archetypal blame avoidance attitude that somebody else or an economic crisis immediately *forces* us to do what is *all bad*. Rather than avoiding blame, leaders openly declare which popular and unpopular policies will be required to address serious but manageable problems. In doing so, they use a mix of cognitive arguments about what works and normative arguments about what is right in explaining why we could and should *choose* reform.

Stiller's model is suitable for our purposes. It combines welfare state pressures and policy solutions in one framework, while encouraging us to be specific about which actors are ideational leaders and what they say. More than this, the model links the focus on ideas in welfare state change with the broader notion of democratic leadership. Invoking Pitkin (1967), we argue that political representation is something more than just the linking of policy with existing demands. Representation is also about being 'responsive' in a broader sense, whereby representatives are allowed to deviate from a mandate they have been given. Crucially, they are only allowed such leeway if they motivate their actions publicly in terms of the 'interests of the represented'. The model of ideational leadership offers a specification of this democratic ideal while remaining grounded in concepts and observations from the welfare state literature.

Overall, we argue that ideational explanations of welfare state change become more convincing if broad-based ideational public discourse is both present and consequential. Specifically, Chapters 4 and 5 examine if campaigns function as public fora for the advancement of ideas about reform pressures and policy solutions. Are party leaders also ideational leaders who, in public, bring attention to reform pressures and argue that we should choose policy change because it alleviates pressure while having some normative advantages? Do they only stick to the most popular policy options or do they lead the way also on unpopular and painful policies? Finally, we also draw citizens into the picture. Chapters 6 and 7 ask if people can process and react to messages containing the *idea* that the welfare state is financially pressured. If so, which pressures are influential? For example, are pressure messages more influential if combined with a normative cue about 'deservingness'? Chapter 7, finally, studies if citizens can move from the idea of pressure to increased support for a particular policy response.

The social investment/activation turn: a smoke-screen for unpopular welfare state change?

How has the ideational landscape changed and what are the implications for this book? To begin with, scholars argue that we have seen more policy change in mature welfare states than institutional theories anticipated (e.g. Hemerijck 2013; van Kersbergen and Vis 2014; Beramendi et al. 2015). Part of this is true for those reform types that institutional frameworks were meant to explain, that is, retrenchment and 'liberalization'. There has been an increasing focus on cost control (Palier 2010; Taylor-Gooby 2001) coupled with certain cutbacks of entitlements and services (Korpi and Palme 2003; Scruggs 2008; Palier 2010; Stephens 2010; Häusermann 2010; Hay and Wincott 2012). However, retrenchment is not the only reform trajectory (van Kersbergen et al. 2014). The notion that welfare states are 'recalibrated' has gained currency (see Ferrera 2008). This involves a re-balancing of policy such that 'new' risks and needs receive more attention, typically at the expense of protection against 'old' ones related to health, unemployment, and old age (Bonoli 2005).

More recently, in what might be the most general attempt to theorize such changes, scholars discern a shift from traditional welfare state goals, such as income security and equality, to a social investment oriented welfare state geared towards the creation and preservation of human capital (Ronchi 2018). It is even debated whether social investment constitutes a new 'policy paradigm' (cf. Hall 1993; Morel et al. 2012). Hemerijck (2013) makes the following proposal:

> Most comparative welfare state researchers divide the post-war era into *two* periods: a 30-year Golden Age of welfare state innovation and expansion, from the end of World War II to the mid-1970s, and one of fiscal austerity and retrenchment from the mid-1970s, to the early years of the twenty-first century.... I put forward an alternative periodization by subdividing the post-war period to the early twenty-first century into *three* distinct phases of welfare state configuration. These are: (1) the era of welfare state expansion and class compromise starting at the end of World War II; (2) the period of welfare retrenchment and neoliberalism, which took shape in the wake of the oil shocks of mid to late 1970s; and (3) the more recent epoch since the mid 1990s in which social investment became popular.
>
> (Hemerijck 2013: 118)

The third phase, which we refer to as the 'social investment/activation turn', has expanded the menu of responses to reform pressures. It has also moved policymaking towards less obviously destructive and 'neoliberal' responses to pressure, compared to the 'blame avoidance'-enabled retrenchment analysed by NPWS, and the piecemeal 'liberalization' predicted by the 'gradual change' framework. The social investment/activation turn instead promises that the welfare state is not only a problem to be downscaled in the face of pressures. It can also be part of the solution. If correctly re-designed, the welfare state is an economically productive factor that protects and generates human capital.[4] In turn, this helps social inclusion by improving employment and unemployment.[5] In Morel et al.'s (2012) explanation:

> The social investment perspective is intended to sustain [...] the knowledge-based economy. In this new economy knowledge is considered as the driver of productivity and economic growth. The knowledge-based economy thus rests on a skilled and flexible labour force, which can easily adapt to the constantly changing needs of the economy but also be the motor of these changes. The social investment perspective also aims at modernizing the postwar welfare state so as to better address the new social risks and needs structure of contemporary societies, such as single parenthood, the need to reconcile work and family life, lack of continuous careers, more precarious forms of contracts and possessing low or obsolete skills.
>
> (Morel et al. 2012: 1)

The social investment/activation turn has diverse roots and is hard to define in traditional left–right terms. Some roots are academic and include Giddens' *The Third Way* (1998) and Esping-Andersen et al.'s *Why We Need a New Welfare State* (2002). Other roots are party-political, emerging not least from debates about the future of European Social Democracy.[6] Meanwhile, international organizations with a liberal bent such as the OECD have been attracted by the idea of economically productive social policy. The EU has also been an important driver through the European Employment Strategy and the Lisbon Agenda.

Despite its success as an elite idea, scholars conclude that social investment/activation is not yet a full-fledged 'policy paradigm' (cf. Hall 1993).

---

[4] In a popular play on words, it is a welfare state concerned with *preparing* citizens for postindustrial society, helping them to adapt to the ever-changing needs of a knowledge-based society, rather than only *repairing* their situation with passive benefits once risks are realized.

[5] That said, the notion of income security at a high level is retained as a part of the social investment philosophy, not least as such security is thought to breed acceptance and reduce fear of the increasingly quick transformations of the post-industrial economy. Furthermore, while the social investment perspective agrees with the 'golden age' philosophy that the welfare state is a productive factor in the economy, it also critiques a traditional focus on passive benefit reception by male breadwinners, as well as its idea of economic growth stimulus mainly through Keynesian countercyclical demand management and 'automatic crisis stabilization'. And while it shares with the neoliberal paradigm a general belief that the existing welfare state is not sustainable in the face of multiple reform pressures, it also critiques neoliberalism with its increasing poverty and inequality coupled with a documented inability to actually deliver on growth, employment, and fiscal sustainability.

[6] Gerhard Schröder's concept of 'Die Neue Mitte' or Tony Blair's 'New Labour' were prominent examples. Other examples of politicians pursuing these ideas are Wim Kok in the Netherlands and Romano Prodi in the Italy of the 1990s.

It is best described as an 'emerging' paradigm reflected in ideational development and in key concrete reform trends. For example, there have been expansive reforms in 'dual-earner' policies such as child care and parental leave in several countries (Morgan 2012; Ellingsæther 2014). Subsidized childcare and generous parental leave schemes for men and women stimulate female employment while reconciling careers and reproduction. These policies also indirectly address population ageing and are seen as an educational investment in children.

Another integral trend is the 'activation turn' in welfare state change. This refers to a complex set of policies (Bonoli 2010), where some aim at investments in 'life-long' education among those not working. Such policies are also known as 'enabling' active labour market policies (for a discussion see Fossati 2018). Other activation schemes aim at better exploiting already existing human capital by improving work incentives and tightening benefit conditionality. These reforms are sometimes labelled 'demanding' activation (Fossati 2018), or 'workfare', meant to make job search and reemployment more rational.

Crucially for our purposes, social investment/activation reforms are typically assumed to be popular among the public (Busemeyer and Garritzmann 2017). Cases in point include dual earner policies, enabling activation, and most types of education spending. In particular, such policies go down well among the growing and electorally mobile 'new middle classes' (Gingrich and Häusermann 2015). At any rate, they are assumed to be more electorally viable than pure retrenchment and austerity policies. Relatedly, investment-type policymaking is marked by small and unstable left–right party differences that fluctuate greatly with context and policy details (Gingrich and Ansell 2015).

The relative popularity of social investment/activation is important here because, as Chapter 2 discussed, reform pressures may not climb campaign agendas until *coupled* with new policies that are palatable to the public and to plausible coalition partners. The social investment/activation turn might have helped put reform pressures on campaign agendas by allowing leaders to debate growing challenges while still offering something more uplifting than either retrenchment or simply clinging to the apparently unsustainable status quo.

A further point concerns the *dimensionality* of the policy space. Silja Häusermann (2010, 2012) has argued that "new" social policy has opened up a multidimensional reform landscape. An old social policy dimension concerns defending the status quo versus retrenchment. In contrast, a new social policy dimension is about the status quo versus an expansion of mainly the emerging social investment paradigm discussed above (see also Beramendi et al. 2015).[7]

Some key points about this second dimension are useful for our purposes. First, not only does the expansion of new social policy—especially social investment—suit the median voter better than retrenchment in old social policy. The two dimensions are also distinct in that party families and voter groups align themselves differently. Reform-minded actors exploit this multi-dimensionality to 'package' complex welfare state change deals involving both retrenchment and new social policy. As Häusermann (2012) explains:

> large parts of the literature have analysed these reform trends separately, and tried to identify the distinctive driving forces for each [...] this is a mistake [...] old and new social policies are raised and politicized in one and the same policy reform space. Hence, if we want to understand the politics of the post-industrial welfare state, we need to look at them simultaneously.
>
> (Häusermann 2012: 115–16)

Thus, increasing multidimensionality may itself help explain the increasing rate of reform. Political parties include aspects of old and new social policies in reform packages finding unexpected majorities for some combination of the two reform types, even though some components would be a hard sell on their own. As Häusermann (2012: 116) argues, 'these package deals have become a pattern in post-industrial welfare reform' (see also Knotz and Lindvall 2015).

We examine several implications of the social investment/activation turn for campaigns and democratic leadership. One possibility is that the popularity and increased multidimensionality makes it easier for parties to put uncomfortable pressures and even unpopular policy on election campaign agendas. They might publicly use the notion that reform is not entirely 'bad', 'destructive', 'or neoliberal', and is even partly about popular expansion. They pre-empt negative reactions to retrenchment by presenting it as a necessary part of a more encompassing modernization strategy.

But there is a more sinister possibility. Do citizens really get to hear about *both* major dimensions of welfare state change? Given that social investment is more popular it may enable blame avoiding 'cherry-picking' rather than

---

[7] Additionally, 'new social policy' is also about 'repairing', by redistributing to those exposed to 'new social risks' in the labour market and in the family realm. This sub dimension of the new paradigm, however, might be not as relevant for campaigning, given Kingdon's arguments, because these parts of new social policy might be more redistributive and contentious, compared to social investment, thus being less fit for campaign marketing.

balanced ideational leadership. Perhaps the social investment paradigm has enabled parties to politicize reform pressures while *only* talking about popular reforms that are assumed to win votes?

These public sphere implications of the social investment/activation turn have rarely been examined. Therefore, Chapters 4 and 5 investigate if the public has been invited to salient debate about the emerging social investment paradigm, and whether it has eclipsed unpopular and contentious welfare state change, thus ultimately hindering courageous democratic leadership.

Citizens and democratic leadership

To assess democratic leadership as a motor behind welfare state change, we must examine how citizens react to it. Do people ever accept messages saying the welfare state is under pressure? Do they ever adjust their policy preferences in the face of perceived pressure? Research on idea-based discourse and ideational leadership implies that such adaptation processes are part of what now allows mature welfare states to change. Institutional theories are of course more sceptical. The gradual institutional change framework sees the reform process as comprising many tiny steps towards 'liberalization', each largely under the radar of electoral democracy. NPWS, for its part, implies stable support for the status quo. A resulting fear of electoral punishment creates reform hesitation among political parties unless 'blame avoidance' can be achieved. Publicly arguing that pressures require reform is a risky business, partly because citizens are predisposed against the message.

Empirical research on public opinion increasingly questions these storylines while partly embracing the idea of leadership effects. To start with, several studies find that reforming governments are rarely punished at the polls (despite stable normative policy support). Cuts in replacement rates and dissatisfaction with public services exercise small and conditional effects on government survival and popularity (Kumlin 2007; Giger 2011; Alesina, Carloni, and Lecce 2012; Arndt 2014).

But how should we interpret this apparent lack of electoral punishment? Does it reflect suppressed outrage or successful democratic leadership? Supporting the former interpretation, a recent overview concludes that while welfare retrenchment and dissatisfaction only rarely spark electoral punishment, these variables are consistently associated with generalized political distrust in democratic institutions and actors (Kumlin and Haugsgjerd 2017). This suggests that electoral frustrations are real but for whatever reason rarely expressed in the voting booth. This could in turn be due to well-documented institutional accountability deficiencies in most Western political systems (Powell 2000). Additionally, blame avoidance strategies of different types may obstruct electoral accountability (Wenzelburger 2014).

Other studies, however, report signs of successful leadership and a considered public acceptance in the face of reform pressures. For example, perceptions of economic welfare state sustainability are typically more negative than, and only partly correlated with, normative welfare state support (e.g. Roosma, Gelissen, and van Oorschot 2013). Sustainability perceptions also have behavioural consequences. In an important study, Natalie Giger and Moira Nelson (2013: 1091) found that citizens who support the welfare state on a normative level, but who worry about troublesome welfare state effects on the economy, are less likely to punish reforming incumbents, compared to welfare state supporters who see no economic problems. Giger and Nelson (2013: 1091) concluded: 'the perceived economic strain of social spending tempers generalized support for redistribution and makes many voters relatively more tolerant of a retrenchment agenda'. They also suggested for future research that '[...] fiscal austerity and severe economic conditions together with the demographic challenges might make people more responsive to claims of endangered economic sustainability of the current system of social welfare'.

Chapters 6–8 examine various facets of this suggestion. Chapter 6 discusses extant experimental evidence that citizens respond to information about reform pressures. This is a valuable emerging literature but almost all research concentrates on one reform pressure/policy area in one country. Often this has meant a narrow focus on pressure related to immigrants/immigration. Therefore, we do not know if the uncovered results imply a universal (in)ability to process reform pressure, or whether effects vary with topic and context. Chapter 6 presents an experiment that compares the effects of argumentative emphasis on different reform pressures, in three different countries, using perceptions of economic welfare state sustainability as dependent variable. Are some reform pressures more consequential than others?

Chapter 6 draws on 'deservingness' theory to answer this question. A host of studies have shown that welfare attitudes depend on information about how deserving recipients are (e.g. Tyler et al. 1997; Slothuus 2007; Petersen et al. 2010; van Oorschot et al. 2017a). These studies are important as they help us specify a plausible 'normative' component of ideational leadership narratives. Having said this, deservingness studies generally leave economic sustainability issues aside. In the language of the 'ideational' literature, they concentrate on normative arguments of deservingness while mostly ignoring cognitive arguments about economic pressure. So beyond notable exceptions (e.g. Kangas, Niemelä, and Varjonen 2014) we do not know if an emphasis on economic unsustainability matters over and above deservingness, or—crucially—whether these classes of arguments operate in combination. Are citizens more susceptible to economic pressure if provided with the right deservingness cue? The experiment reported in Chapter 6 addresses this by comparing the effects of messages about different pressures, some of which are linked to 'deserving' or 'undeserving' groups.

Chapter 7 advances these issues further in two experiments on variation in party-political statements rather than in subtle question wording. These real-world statements, which come from leader speeches and election manifestoes, increase the complexity of messages and involve nuances, uncertainty, and vagueness. Can respondents process these complex but realistic messages? Moreover, the information comes from a party-political messenger who typically advances a policy solution. Some involve expansive social investment whereas others foreshadow retrenchment and liberalization. Chapter 7 draws on political psychology to theorize how these features make reactions contingent on political values and partisanship. We ask if some messages even trigger 'counter-arguing'—that is, effects in an unintended direction—among those predisposed against them, producing 'polarization' between subgroups rather than net persuasion. This would tell us something important about the prospects and contingencies of effective democratic leadership in welfare state change. Finally, these experiments allow comparison of political parties. We test the 'Nixon goes to China' hypothesis that Social Democrats are more effective communicators of the message that the welfare state is pressured and must be reformed.

Chapter 8, finally, adds an element to our knowledge of how sustainability perceptions can have political consequences. As mentioned, Giger and Nelson (2013) found that negative perceptions of economic welfare state consequences moderate electoral punishment for retrenchment. Chapter 8 takes this analysis a step further and uses our panel data to detect if negative sustainability perceptions also impact welfare state support itself. A broadly affirmative answer would mean sustainability perceptions do more than 'only' temper a key electoral expression of policy demand. More fundamentally, sustainability perceptions would then appear to reshape policy demands themselves. This would indicate a more transformative impact of reform pressure information. Such results would also be interesting given the book's distinction between democratic linkage and leadership. Democratic leadership minimally requires that leaders motivate unpopular decisions and that citizens (sometimes) accept the explanations for why their preferences cannot be fulfilled. This acceptance may be expressed in various ways, for instance in manifest worries about the sustainability of preferred policies and in a reluctance to hold policymakers to account for unpopular policies. Democratic linkage, by contrast, revolves around informed prospective policy preferences. Thus, if pressure information also restructures prospective policy preferences, it becomes possible to explain welfare state change in terms of reshaped democratic input that is subsequently linked by parties to new public policy. Conversely, if preference adjustment is nowhere to be found, then we must turn to democratic leadership and public acceptance to explain how welfare state change can still be democratically legitimate.

PART II
CAMPAIGN CONTENTS

4

Up and Down with the Welfare State

Systemic Agenda Shifts in Europe

Are welfare state issues widely debated and contested during those crucial weeks and months leading up to Election Day? Are they ever among the issues that will later define an election in the history books? These are questions about 'systemic agendas', that is, campaign agendas that transcend specific actors and concern most players in the political system. Of course, later chapters will look closely at party leaders' messages and citizens' reactions to those messages. The rationale for this chapter, however, is that answers to those more specific questions can only be fully understood with knowledge about the *scale* of debate at a systemic level. Therefore, this chapter examines systemic agendas during a 33-year period between 1977 and 2010 when pressures intensified and eventually resulted in the multidimensional reform trajectories described in Chapter 3.

We will address three questions. First, did the systemic salience of welfare issues *change over time*. This is relevant for the book in several ways. Chapter 2 emphasized a need to assess the overall scale of democratic discourse, alongside other more commonly recognized preconditions for 'democratic linkage'. Moreover, Chapter 3 discussed 'blame avoidance' strategies as possible enablers of reform; for example, problems that could imply unpopular and painful policy changes may be kept off the agenda altogether. If so, big-time welfare state debate may resemble a 'fair-weather sport' that was mainly exercised when resources were plentiful but has become rare as pressures have grown. However, Chapter 3 also demonstrated how increasingly popular concepts such as 'ideational leadership' and 'credit claiming' imply continuing or even increasing salience as challenges grow.

Second, we examine the *timing and the shape* of agenda changes. Has there been slow and gradual change in response to gradually growing pressures? Alternatively, maybe agenda change is better described as a 'late-and-brief' but large response to long-standing challenges? The latter possibility is not very consistent with the notion of gradual welfare state change (cf. Streeck

Election Campaigns and Welfare State Change. Staffan Kumlin and Achim Goerres, Oxford University Press.
© Staffan Kumlin and Achim Goerres (2022). DOI: 10.1093/oso/9780198869214.003.0004

and Thelen 2005) discussed in Chapter 3. It would fit better with work on 'punctuated equilibria' in agenda-setting, which we will discuss later in this chapter.

A third set of questions concerns the *content* of agenda change. Here, Chapter 3 discussed the 'the social investment–activation turn' in European welfare state politics that began in the mid-1990s. Did this well-documented sea change in elite-level ideas and policy also leave a systemic imprint on election campaigns? The analysis in this regard is informed by the 'multiple streams' framework (Kingdon 2011 [1984]), which suggests that neither intensifying real-world pressures—nor simply the passing of time—are enough to trigger agenda change. Politicians also need a new, big, and politically feasible set of ideas to dare to put reform pressures and policy solutions on the agenda. The emerging investment–activation paradigm might have played this role, allowing policymakers to politicize pressures in ways that resonate with voters. Perhaps social investment/activation even allowed a 'cherry-picking' blame avoidance strategy such that citizens are not exposed to unpopular aspects of welfare state change. Such cherry-picking stands in contrast to genuine democratic leadership, under which leaders are brave and open about painful but necessary adjustment.

Despite so much high-quality research on welfare state development we have at best patchy answers to these questions. One explanation is, as we shall see, theoretical. Scholars have focused more on the policies that elites and citizens prefer and less on policy *agendas*, that is, the extent to which preferences are prioritized and given attention. A second reason is data availability: there are few longitudinal comparative data sets on welfare state salience in election campaigns. The studies that exist typically use data on the contents of party manifestos (Busemeyer et al. 2013; Green-Pedersen 2019; Green-Pedersen and Jensen 2019). Such studies are valuable and will serve as important points of comparison. Still, party manifestoes do not necessarily measure systemic campaign agendas. They tap a longer list of pre-election issue priorities of specific parties but do not necessarily reveal what smaller number of issues will actually dominate the public sphere on a systemic level come the campaign. We have therefore collected our own data on systemic agendas spanning 18 European countries and the period 1977–2010 (Kumlin, Kihlström, and Oskarson 2021).

The chapter next proceeds by highlighting recent developments suggesting the meaningfulness of a systemic comparative approach to agenda-setting. Subsequent sections develop specific hypotheses rooted in the theoretical discussion from Chapters 2 and 3. The empirical part of the chapter then starts with data presentation.

Towards a contextual and comparative study of agenda-setting

The premise of *agenda-setting* is that power is not only exercised by obvious and tangible means such as military force, voting strength, or economic clout. Rather, influencing more subtle aspects of the informational context is also important, particularly in open and stable democracies. Crucially, this 'softer' brand of power is not mainly about persuasion aimed at shifting policy preferences, but rather about affecting which problems and issues are prioritized and worthy of attention. Or, according to an often-used play of words: it is not only important to affect what others think, but also what they *think about* (see Cohen 1963).

There has been a tremendous amount of research on agenda-setting since the concept was launched (for overviews, see McCombs and Shaw 1972; Funkhouser 1973; Dearing and Rogers 1996; Soroka 2002). A by now stylized fact is that perceived issue importance among citizens is affected by the size of mass media attention. In turn, agenda priorities can shift the evaluative ingredients of voting decisions (e.g. Iyengar and Kinder 1987; van der Brug 2004). Effects running in the opposite direction—that is, from citizens' agenda priorities to the media—do exist but they are weaker (Dearing and Rogers 1996).

Agendas and agenda-setting also have broader effects in a political system. Parties and politicians devote more energy to realizing preferences that are high on the agenda. Relatedly, agendas moderate the quality of representation with better opinion congruence between voters and elected politicians in high-attention policy areas (e.g. Esaiasson and Heidar 2000). Finally, agendas may affect public policy through mechanisms operating on policymakers (e.g. Klingemann et al., 1994; Baumgartner, Green-Pedersen, and Jones 2008; Mortensen 2010). Findings such as these, then, make it interesting to examine the extent, timing, and content of agenda change in the welfare state domain.

It is still fair to say that comparative welfare state research has been more preoccupied with policy *preferences* than policy agendas. More energy has been devoted to studying which types of policies enjoy support across groups of citizens, political parties, organized interests, welfare regimes, time, and how such preferences affect policies (see Korpi 2006; Scruggs and Allan 2006; Brooks and Manza 2007; Carnes and Mares 2007; Svallfors 2010). Much less scrutinized are questions about where welfare issues rank in terms of priority, that is, the extent to which they are perceived as important and attended to at various stages of the policy process.

Bringing agenda-setting into comparative welfare state research has proven to be difficult: researchers examining agenda-setting have usually not operated at the same aggregated, comparative-historical level as welfare state research (Blumler and Gurevitch 1975; De Vreese 2003; Strömbäck and Aalberg 2008). Instead, agenda-setting studies often analyse how actors influence and interact with each other. This has led to disaggregated theoretical models at the meso- and micro levels, and to research designs in which a single process, issue, country, election, etc. is studied one at the time. For example, scholars have often conceived of party conflict in terms of 'issue competition' (e.g. Robertson 1976; Carmines and Stimson 1990) and envisioned agenda-setting as a three-way power struggle between citizens, the mass media, and political actors (e.g. Asp 1983). In a complex reality, all these actors influence each other's agendas (Soroka 2002). However, the weight of the evidence depicts agenda-setting as an elite-driven process in which purposeful parties and the mass media battle each other's agendas, with citizens as mostly passive but receptive bystanders (cf. Van Aelst and Walgrave 2011).

Disaggregated approaches have clearly been very valuable. But they may obscure broader cross-national and historical processes and differences. Agenda-setting scholars know less about whether agendas may also be fruitfully thought of as an overall 'contextual/systemic' characteristic of a political system, group of countries, era, or even a continent. Is there a meaningful and measurable 'overall essence' of the agenda that transcends many actors and groups in a place and point in time? How, why, and when do such overall agendas vary across countries and change over time?

Some scholars have recently taken certain steps towards a broader historical and comparative study of agenda-setting. Scattered observations suggest the possibility of more gradual, even linear agenda shifts, over extended periods and many actors (Baumgartner et al. 2008; Baumgartner et al. 2009; Baumgartner et al. 2011). For example, Green-Pedersen and Wilkerson (2008) show that in both Denmark and the USA overall attention to health care in parliamentary hearings, bills, questions, and debates increased gradually over five decades starting in the 1950s. This was interpreted as a result of similarly incremental changes in external reform pressures, such as rising demand for health care and rising costs. Continuing the US example and considering roughly the same period, issues of taxation, spending, and social security became more common as presidential campaign topics. Defence and issues of race declined. These overall systemic shifts were eventually larger than cross-sectional differences in salience between actors at any given point in time (Baumgartner et al. 2011; Sigelman 2004).

Traditionally, 'issue ownership' assumptions, as discussed in Chapter 2, have suggested that actors 'talk past each other' emphasizing their own favourite issues. However, scholars now increasingly acknowledge the possibility of an overall agenda essence, captured in terms such as 'issue convergence' or 'issue overlap' (Damore 2005). Green-Pedersen and Mortensen (2010) even explicitly separate between agendas of constituent actors and the overall agenda of the *party system*. The latter is the agenda that emerges in settings where actors interact and thus give up some control over the relative attention given to issues. As the authors explain: 'An agenda is thus a structural phenomenon in the sense that it constrains the relevant actors at any given time. They must address the issues that are prominent. ... At the same time, they compete to influence the composition of the agenda' (Green-Pedersen and Mortensen 2010: 260).

We sustain these developments by examining systemic agendas in election campaigns. We argue that it is fruitful to apply the notion of a systemic agenda to campaigns as these are shaped by a multitude of actors, including parties and candidates, the mass media, interest groups, and citizens. Precisely because campaigns involve many actors during a crucial but limited period, it becomes interesting to ask not only micro questions about 'the struggle for the agenda' but consider which issues manage to rise above the cacophony of competing agendas.

Agenda change in the face of growing reform pressures?

Let us now formulate hypotheses that will structure the analysis. Our starting point is a broad agreement among welfare state scholars that the expansionist 'golden' age in the early post-war decades has been gradually succeeded by an 'era of permanent austerity'. Its starting point is hard to pin-point, but the early 1980s is a frequently used watershed point, when a number of reform pressures began to intensify over time. Against this background of generally and gradually increasing pressures, we formulate the simple hypothesis that welfare state issues have gradually climbed up the election campaigns agenda since the early 1980s. This 'positive response' hypothesis posits that political systems react rather rationally to objective real-world indicators of pressure on the welfare state. And since the austerity era is a story of gradually accumulating pressures and challenges, the salience of these policy areas would increase in a similarly gradual fashion.

This broad hypothesis has received some support from party manifesto data. As mentioned in Chapter 2, Green-Pedersen (2019) finds that while the relative attention to economic left–right issues has declined, this is not the case for key welfare state related issues. Crucially however, the response seems dependent on specific issue characteristics. Green-Pedersen and Jensen (2019) argue that social protection and services related to the life course, for example health care and pensions, display greater increase. In such issues, most citizens have a long-term vested interest at the same time as the old are almost universally regarded as very deserving. This would explain why attention to welfare issue areas related to life course issues would increase, whereas attention to more contentious and more clearly horizontally redistributive social protection related to labour market risks is likely to remain, at best, stable in the light of growing pressure. We will test the 'positive response' hypothesis with an eye towards such possible contingencies. Again, recall that past results draw on party manifestos: we still know little about how welfare issue salience has developed at a more public and systemic level.

The 'positive response' hypothesis can be questioned using blame avoidance theory. Chapter 3 discussed several such strategies. One is 'agenda control' where uncomfortable reform pressures are simply kept off the agenda by office-seeking parties. Another strategy was referred to as 'playing the crisis card'. This means putting reform pressures on the agenda while arguing that they are so severe and uncontrollable that 'we have no choice but to act now'. The most well-documented version is the storyline that an immediate economic crisis necessitates policies that neither citizens nor decision makers prefer. Thus, we can formulate a 'crisis contingency' hypothesis stating that welfare state issues have become more salient, but mainly in times of economic downturns.

Both hypotheses so far assume that objective real-world problems are important driving forces behind agenda attention. But this is not necessarily consistent with existing evidence. Real-world indicators of the severity of societal problems have at best a tenuous relationship with the attention they receive at various stages in the policy process; there are even examples of agenda attention and problem severity being negatively correlated (for overviews, see Dearing and Rogers 1996; Soroka 2002). For these reasons, we now consult two prominent theories from agenda-setting research: 'punctuated equilibrium' theory and 'multiple streams' theory, to arrive at more fine-tuned hypotheses about how agenda shifts may have played out over time.

Punctuated equilibria: the possibility of a late-and-brief response

So, the standard view holds that mature welfare states gradually have entered a more problematic 'era of permanent austerity' since the early 1980s. On the other hand, as discussed in Chapter 3, it is only from the mid-1990s and mainly in the 2000s, that welfare state change accelerated along multiple dimensions. This points to significant inertia in policymaking and, potentially, in agenda-setting. How can we understand such inertia?

A useful theoretical idea is that of 'punctuated equilibrium' (for overviews and evidence, see Baumgartner et al. 2008; Baumgartner et al. 2009). Here, agendas are seen as slow-moving animals showing little change from one year to another. They are held firmly in place by strong institutional and psychological forces affecting both political parties and citizens (i.e. the party system, the media landscape, patterns of public spending, norms, or simply poor imagination). Interestingly, such inertia can occasionally give birth to massive transformations by delaying more or less inevitable change, thus exaggerating agenda shift once it finally happens. A late but large effect arises exactly because agendas could not change freely in the first place, while external change pressures persist. When the agenda eventually does change, involved actors will feel the need to make up for past negligence. Attention to a previously ignored issue briefly becomes much larger than it would in a structurally unconstrained environment. Thus, the theory of punctuated equilibrium implies that agendas respond in late outbursts of attention to long-neglected problems.

The evidence for punctuated equilibrium mainly comes from studies of policymaking (i.e. in committees, bills, etc.). We know less about whether the theory also applies to earlier phases in democratic processes such as election campaigns. For sure, scholars have long been mindful of the possibility of sudden and short-lived outbursts of attention in public settings. In the much-cited article 'Up and Down with Ecology', Anthony Downs (1972) argued that:

> a systematic 'issue-attention cycle' seems strongly to influence public attitudes and behavior concerning most key domestic problems. Each of these problems suddenly leaps into prominence, remains there for a short time, and then—though still largely unresolved—gradually fades from the center of public attention.
>
> (Downs 1972: 38–9)

As for the initial increase, Downs argued that it takes a series of dramatic events to ignite the spark causing an explosion in attention. The subsequent and equally sudden decline is explained by a combination of resignation ('this problem is difficult and expensive'), moderation ('there may be positive aspects of this problem'), combined with competition from fresh issues that are currently at an earlier stage in the attention cycle. All in all, then, we hypothesize that welfare state issues became markedly, but temporarily, more salient during a well-defined period occurring well after the early 1980s. We call this the 'late-and-brief' response hypothesis.

'Multiple streams': new policy ideas as catalysts for agenda change

Chapters 2 and 3 discussed John Kingdon's (2011 [1984]) seminal framework for agenda-setting studies. One of its many upshots is that objective real-world problems mainly shape agendas once they can be coupled with new policy ideas that might reasonably alleviate underlying problems *and* be marketed to the public and prospective coalition partners. Importantly, new policy ideas cannot be taken for granted. Kingdon emphasizes that they take shape slowly, for unrelated reasons, and as responses to other problems. Furthermore, policy ideas might develop first among expert communities, perhaps at another political level. They must then be imported into party platforms in ways consistent with party history and ideology, making concessions to rival factions (Herweg et al. 2015).

This book considers the possibility that the social investment/activation turn has functioned as a catalyst for agenda change in election campaigns, allowing actors to couple welfare state reform pressures with new and palatable solutions. Social investment, as we have emphasized, is one of the more general attempts to conceive of welfare state change. Scholars have identified a shift, beginning in the mid-1990s, from traditional goals of social protection, such as income security and equality, to a welfare state geared towards the creation, preservation, and efficient use of human capital. It has even been debated whether social investment constitutes a new 'policy paradigm' (cf. Hall 1993; Morel et al. 2012). Similarly, Hemerijck (2013) proposes that social investment constitutes a 'third phase' of welfare state transformation, one that has succeeded both the golden age of expansion, and most recently a neoliberal era of retrenchment and cost containment.

Two key points about the social investment–activation turn were made in Chapter 3. First, many social investment policies tend to be relatively popular. Specifically, dual earner policies, education spending, and strengthening of employment incentives all tend to go down relatively well among the growing and electorally mobile 'new' middle classes (Gingrich and Häusermann 2015). A second point has to do with the *dimensionality* of the policy space. Häusermann (2010, 2012) has argued that new social policy has opened up a multidimensional reform landscape. Whereas an old social policy dimension concerns defending the status quo versus retrenchment, a new social policy dimension is about the status quo versus expanding the emerging social investment paradigm. Reform-minded actors can exploit this to 'package' complex reform strategies (Häusermann 2012: 115–16). If so, it might also help to put welfare state reform on campaign agendas, or at least reduce any past resistance in this respect. Politicians might make public use of the notion that welfare reform is not all that 'bad', 'destructive', or 'neoliberal', or else embed unpopular reform as necessary parts of a more encompassing modernization strategy.

Three further hypotheses can now be formulated. First, we test the 'social investment' hypothesis that from the mid-1990s, social investment-related themes became an increasingly present component and driver of welfare state salience in campaigns. Preliminary support for this hypothesis comes from studies of party manifestoes showing that in several countries education issues have become more salient Green-Pedersen (2019), but also contested Busemeyer et al. (2013) during the decades studied here.

Conversely, we can formulate the flipside prediction that retrenchment and cost containment show a stable or possibly a negative trend, even in the face of increasing overall welfare state salience, precisely because social investment/activation allows politicians to debate pressures and reform while having something more popular to propose. We call this the 'declining salience of retrenchment' hypothesis. A third corollary is that an increasing emphasis on social investment alleviates the need for blame avoidance that existed in the neoliberal retrenchment phase of the 1980s and early 1990s. We examine this by testing whether welfare state salience becomes less associated over time with economic crisis and macroeconomic concerns, and gradually begins to occur more often in good times than before; we refer to this as the 'weakening crisis–welfare nexus' hypothesis.

The data

Our data set draws on election reports published in the two political science journals *West European Politics* (WEP) and *Electoral Studies* (EL). Since 1977 and 1981, respectively, these reports have been written by a large number of country experts observing specific elections closely, and later summarizing and interpreting events for an academic audience in a limited number of pages. At their heart, they provide a qualitative documentation of historical events. Interestingly however, studies indicate that key aspects of the contents can be systematically coded and quantified across space and time. Therefore, we have coded a number of variables related to the overall thematic content and character of systemic election campaign agendas. The units of analysis are national parliamentary elections in 18 West European countries (EU15, Iceland, Norway, and Switzerland). The overall time period is 1977–2010.

The idea to code and quantify the information found in these election reports is not new. However, past studies have typically been limited to a specific phenomenon, time period, and/or a rather limited number of elections. For example, Kumlin and Esaiasson (2012) measure the incidence of a specific phenomenon—election scandals—and find that these have become more common over time. In an innovative study of government electoral support, Armingeon and Giger (2008) measure the campaign saliency of large cuts in welfare generosity. Their coding, however, was restricted to the rather unusual elections preceded by significant cuts in welfare generosity and made no distinction between policy areas (see also Giger 2012). Encouraged by these efforts we have taken a broader approach in terms of coverage and substance. All in all, the data set contains 172 national election campaigns.

Operationalizing election themes

We employed the concept of an election theme to capture what the campaign 'was about' in an overall sense. Coding instructions defined an overall theme as a topic that, according to the expert, was particularly significant and salient in the public sphere during the election campaign. Election campaign themes, moreover, can concern past, present, or future policies, performance, or outcomes. But they can also concern basic political institutions and processes, political actors such as parties and politicians, coalition formation, the governing ability of governments, as well as political features of the public (such as growing mistrust and non-participation).[1]

---

[1] Corruption can feature as an election theme if it does not only concern immediate scandals involving identifiable politicians. Information about concrete election scandals is provided by Kumlin and Esaiasson (2012).

We adapted a coding scheme previously used to categorize European MPs' survey answers to a 'most important issue' question (1996 European Representation Study; see Schmitt and Thomassen 1999). The resulting adapted scheme identifies 12 broad policy domains, within which a number of more concrete codes are provided. Conceptually, the coding builds on Green-Pedersen and Mortensen's (2010) discussion of agendas, which separates between, on the one hand, actor-specific priorities and, on the other, the systemic or contextual distribution of attention that emerges in a setting where actors interact. All involved actors are assumed to partly contribute to this systemic agenda at the same time as no one entirely controls it. We apply this notion to systemic agendas in election campaigns in order to measure which issues and concerns have temporarily risen to such prominence on the overall agenda that they become key characteristics of entire campaigns.

The coding of election themes involved several steps. Reports were first checked for passages where substantive issues and conflicts of the types mentioned above were discussed. Second, it was determined which of usually several issues qualified as overall campaign themes, according to our definition. In doing this, we used the existing coding scheme as our point of departure, but also added some new categories where needed.

Two rules were used to identify themes. First, we looked for instances where the expert author explicitly states that a topic has been important for the election or public campaign in some overall sense, has created visible conflict or agreement across several parties, or aroused significant overall attention in the media or among the electorate. Thus, simply the fact that an issue is said to be present in the manifesto or on the agenda of a single party, interest organization, or voter group is not, on its own, enough to qualify a topic as an election theme. Second, we looked for instances where an expert does not simply mention or list a topic, but devotes considerable space to explaining its contents and political role (i.e. by devoting a paragraph or several sentences to it, or by returning to it in several places).

Operationalizing sub-issues

We gradually discovered that experts often mention further issues in conjunction with an overarching campaign theme. These are so to speak 'nested within' a broader theme. To capture this, we invented the concept of a sub-issue, defined as an election campaign topic that is a concrete manifestation of, a constituent part of, or is otherwise linked to, an overarching theme. The same coding scheme was used for election campaign themes and sub-issues. Furthermore, two rules were used to identify sub-issues. First, a topic was coded as a sub-issue if the expert explicitly states, or otherwise signals, that a topic is to be regarded as a sub-issue thus defined (i.e. by using expressions such as 'for example', 'in particular', etc.). Second, a topic is coded as a sub-issue if it is mentioned in passing inside a system of sentences (for instance a paragraph) describing a broader theme.

The coding of overarching campaign themes was both the most substantively important as well as the analytically demanding aspect of this project. Therefore, extensive reliability tests were performed focusing on these variables. To begin with, an intracoder reliability test of the coding of the 12 policy domains was conducted by the main coder 6–12 months after the first coding. This involved recoding a randomly sampled subset of 15 per cent of elections. The results indicated good reliability, with 91 per cent of the total number of coded themes coded to the same policy domain in a consistent way across elections (WEP = 88 per cent; EL = 94 per cent).

Intercoder reliability tests were performed in a similar fashion, recoding another randomly chosen 15 per cent of the material. Intercoder consistency was also satisfactory, albeit predictably lower than intracoder consistency. Here, the overall domain consistency of coded themes was 82 per cent (WEP = 84 per cent; EL = 79 per cent). This test focused on whether a theme from a domain was coded or not, that is, not on counting how many themes from a specific domain were coded in a report. When allowing several themes from the same domain, reliability dropped from 82 per cent to a still reasonable 75 per cent. Nonetheless, since most theme variation is dichotomous anyway, we will generally analyse dummies rather than count variables, that is, measuring whether a particular policy domain is present or not (rather than counting how many such themes there are). Still, it is perfectly possible to construct and use count variables from the theme variables (given that one can accept 75 per cent intercoder reliability).

Empirical results

Figure 4.1 gives a first feel for the data by showing the proportion of elections in which a particular broad domain was represented by at least one discussed theme in one journal.[2] Four broad areas appear to have dominated West

---

[2] The coding scheme contained a thirteenth policy domain (social community and planning). We do not report it further here as it only concerned six elections (3.5 per cent).

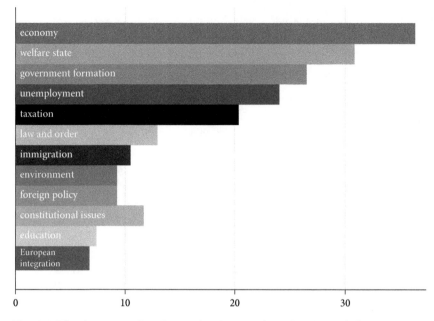

Fig. 4.1 Election campaign themes in 18 countries, 1977–2010 (%).

Note: Based on elections with at least one expert report (N=165).

European election campaigns: the macro economy, welfare state issues, the unemployment/labour market, and issues related to government and coalition formation. These show up as broad themes in between one-fourth and one-third of elections. A fifth domain—taxation—forms a middle group on its own at around 20 per cent, whereas all other domains are parked at lower levels around 10 per cent or less. This is true for immigration, law and order, foreign policy and relations, European integration, education, constitutional issues, as well as environmental/agrarian policy.

A detailed longitudinal view of the welfare state domain is given in Figure 4.2, showing trends using unweighted 'moving averages'.[3] The solid lines represent the welfare domain dummy used in Figure 4.1, although now broken down by journal. While the journals differ somewhat in the general attention given to welfare state issues, they display similar trends, such that the proportion of elections associated with any welfare theme grows to a peak in the early 2000s and then drops. During this peak, moreover, attention to welfare issues

---

[3] Like all longitudinal graphs in this chapter, it was produced using Stata's 'graph lowess' procedure, where we set the window of the moving averages to 20 per cent of the data. This corresponds to 6–7 years. We have experimented with larger and smaller windows, but substantive conclusions remain the same.

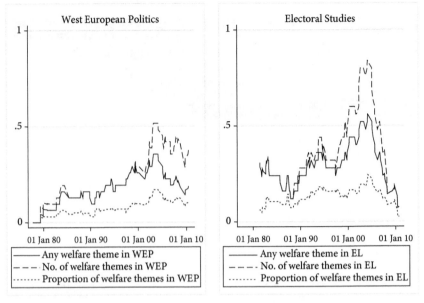

Fig. 4.2 The welfare state domain as election campaign theme (moving averages).

intensifies somewhat in the sense that the average *number* of simultaneously salient welfare themes increases. The solid and the dashed curves are similar up until the late 1990s. Thus, up to a certain point there were few elections with more than one welfare state theme and thus little information was gained by registering more than one such theme. From the late 1990s, however, the curves diverge, and the average number of welfare themes rises more sharply than that of the simple dummy. Put differently, some election campaigns came to be dominated by several welfare state themes simultaneously.

Overall, the patterns of change are relatively consistent with the notion of a 'late-and-brief' agenda response to reform pressures. True, from early on there seems to have been a gradual but weak increase (at least looking at WEP). But it is some 15–20 years into the era of permanent austerity in the 2000s that we see a more intense reaction in the form of the simultaneous presence of several welfare areas, clearly registered in both journals.

The dotted lines standardize for the overall number of themes from any domain reported in the journal in question. This is relevant as past research suggests campaigns and party agendas have become more issue-oriented as political parties have come to compete over a greater number of issues over time (Green-Pedersen 2007). This is also true for our data with weak to moderate correlations between the total number of themes and linear time (EL = 0.11; WEP = 0.22).[4]

From now on, we will generally rely on summary measures that combine the two journals. Furthermore, we generally dichotomize measures. This is to keep the reporting of the results simple, but it is also the case that the distinction between count and dichotomy is minimal as soon as we begin to unpack the components of the broad welfare state domain. Relatedly, even for the broad domain we have seen that only a small and period-specific portion of the variation extends beyond 0 and 1 anyway.[5]

The solid line in Figure 4.3 shows moving averages for a dummy taking on the value 1 if at least one journal reports a campaign theme related to the welfare state. It is only missing if reports are lacking for both journals. This has the advantage of exploiting as many elections as possible and the full-time range offered by the data set. Again, we see the up-and-down pattern with a slow rise to a peak in in the early 2000s and a subsequent decline. The dashed line shows

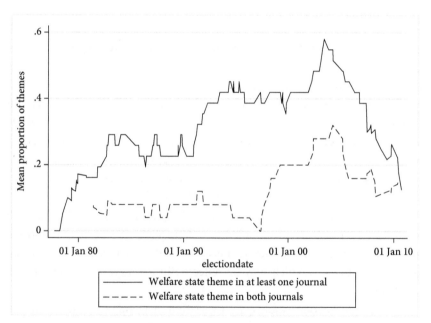

Fig. 4.3 Welfare state campaign themes in one and both journals.

---

[4] Further analyses show that while WEP indeed shows a mild linear increase over time EL rather displays more cyclical volatility. Moreover, it is only in EL that we also see the late up-and-down pattern for the total number of themes registered.

[5] Also recall that reliability tests showed slightly worse reliability beyond simple dichotomization. Figure 4.3 illustrates two possible summary dichotomies for the two journals.

moving averages for a dummy that only takes on the value 1 if both journals report a welfare state theme. This variable is defined as missing as soon as at least one report is lacking and therefore only exploits 124 elections for which we have two reports. Here there is less variation: only 11 per cent of elections are coded as welfare state elections thus defined (compared to 31 per cent for the less restrictive dummy). Nonetheless, this variable also shows a late rise and fall of welfare state campaign themes over time. This time, however, the increase is registered later and more quickly, mainly from the last half of the 1990s to the early 2000s. The comparison underscores the observation that this period seems to have been one of particularly widespread and intense election debate over the welfare state, such that in up to one-third of elections both experts bring up at least one theme pertaining to this policy domain. Interesting as this observation is, however, we will from now on mainly analyse dummies of the kind represented by the solid line. We do this as this simplification of what is going on in the two journals offers more welfare state content to analyse over a longer time span.[6]

Differences and similarities between welfare regimes

It is useful to consider variations across countries to get a feel for these data. Specifically, the comparative welfare state literature may well be taken to imply that agenda levels and trends vary across welfare regimes. An initial assumption here, one well in line with the theory of 'punctuated equilibrium', is that agendas typically reflect the broad institutional environment. For example, we would expect more attention to be paid to welfare state issues in the largest and most costly welfare regime types, especially social democratic welfare states located in the Nordic region, but also in the high-spending conservative states located in continental Europe. Liberal welfare states (here: the UK and Ireland) and, in particular, Southern European states are generally seen as less generous and costly, which may be reflected in a comparatively lower level of saliency.

One might also conceivably expect variation in agenda *shifts* across institutional environments. For example, greater social expenditure, more generous benefits, and heavier taxation may underscore the perceived urgency of external and internal pressures. At the same time, resistance to change may also be

---

[6] Further analyses of the 'any journal' dummy show that coding elections as missing only when we lack both journals correlates strongly with a more restrictive approach using missing as soon as at least one journal is missing.

stronger in exactly such environments, thus producing more contestation of reform pressures (for a similar argument, see Swank 2002: 56). The prediction would therefore be that trends towards greater campaign salience are more pronounced in larger welfare states (i.e. especially in social democratic, but also conservative ones), than in smaller welfare states (i.e. liberal and Southern welfare states).

Two further remarks can be made before we look at the data. First, these predictions follow in a straightforward way from mainstream institutional theory in the sense that existing institutions guide actors' attention in an evolving and uncertain environment. Second, the relationship with the theory of punctuated equilibrium, is more complex. On the one hand, this theory expects the institutional environment to structure attention during long periods of agenda stability. On the other hand, the theory implies that institutional structures are better at explaining initial and 'static' variation than subsequent rapid change once it happens. The delayed but large shifts highlighted by this theory represent a movement away from priorities long encouraged by an institutional environment. Under this view, then, agenda shifts show no or even a negative correspondence with institutions.

Figure 4.4 divides the data into early and late periods. We refrain from using moving averages as the number of elections is small, especially among the two representatives of the liberal regime (Ireland and UK). Looking first at our preferred measure (salience in any of the reports), two observations can be made. One is that regime predictions about levels of attention are only partly borne out. They are most clearly confirmed in the sense that southern countries consistently score the lowest. Likewise, in the early period, the welfare state provided dominant election themes more often in social democratic welfare states and, in both periods, conservative welfare states are found somewhere in between. The empirical surprise, though, is that campaigns in liberal countries attend in a major way to welfare state issues roughly as often as in Scandinavia. Looking at the more restrictive measure of whether both reports register salience even shows somewhat more salience in liberal countries, with social democratic and conservative welfare states on an equal footing in the early period.

Turning to changes over time, the regime framework loses whatever ability it had to explain levels. Increases over time are found for all regime groups and indicators, with the biggest increases (in absolute terms) in liberal and social democratic welfare states. Minor exceptions to this generalization include that by 2010 there had still not been an election in the southern countries where both journals registered major welfare state salience. Similarly, such attention

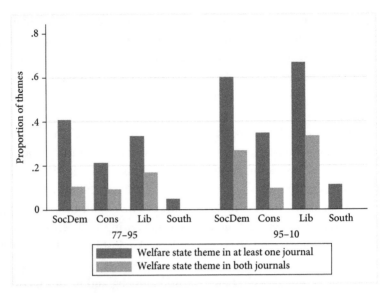

Fig. 4.4 The welfare state domain as an election campaign theme across welfare regimes.

is still as unusual in conservative countries as it used to be. The big story here, however, is that all four groups of countries have indeed seen an increase in systemic campaign attention to welfare state issues.

Covariation of welfare state issues with other policy domains

The data also offer an insight into the extent to which welfare state issues are systemically salient at the same time as other policy domains. Figure 4.5 shows the development of five domain categories that are not part of the broad welfare state domain but are nonetheless theoretically interesting. For each topic, we see the development of systemic salience over time among all elections, as well as among the subset of elections where one welfare state issue or another dominated the campaign at the systemic level. Thus, comparing the two lines tells us whether the topic in question is over- or underrepresented in welfare state dominated campaigns, and if this has changed over time.[7]

The top row reveals an interesting development for unemployment and the economy. While none of these domains show clear overall trends, they became less synchronous with welfare state issues than they used to be.

---

[7] In this analysis the parameters of the moving average were increased from 20 to 30 per cent, as the analysis of welfare state elections relies on a smaller number of observations.

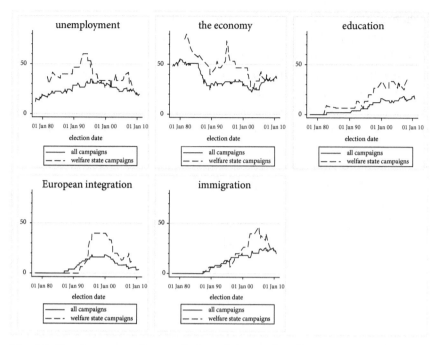

Fig. 4.5 Simultaneous salience of selected themes (in all campaigns and in campaigns where welfare state themes were salient).

Macroeconomic topics used to be very common in elections dominated by welfare state issues. But beginning just before or around the turn of the millennium the lines move closer. In terms of our hypothesis, this fits the 'crisis contingency' hypothesis in that welfare salience and macroeconomic concerns tended to go together in the early period. However, there is also support for the 'weakening crisis–welfare nexus' hypothesis in that the synchronicity has become less pronounced.

The education graph conveys two messages. One is that education, from near invisibility in the late 1970s, has become more common as a major election campaign theme. This finding fits past research based on party manifestoes showing that education issues became more salient among political parties (Busemeyer et al. 2013; Green-Pedersen 2019) in roughly the same countries and time period as those studied here. In terms of our hypotheses, these results already provide some support for the 'social investment' hypothesis suggesting issues related to human capital have grown more salient. What is more, however, the rise of education is more pronounced in elections dominated by (other) welfare state issues. This fits with the idea that issues related to human capital and the welfare state respectively have become more inter-twined over time, that is, it is consistent with the notion of social investment as a catalyst for welfare state salience.

The bottom part of the graph in Figure 4.5 shows the development for Euro-pean integration and immigration. These two domains are less immediately relevant for our hypotheses, but nonetheless they are interesting for the book overall. Both of these topics can be construed as reform pressures that raise costs or otherwise impose constraints on national welfare states over time. And indeed, the results suggest that both domains have increasingly become part of the thematic context in which welfare state issues are salient. This was especially so during the period around the turn of the millennium, during which both immigration and European integration tended to be more salient in elections dominated by welfare state issues.

A more particularistic welfare state debate?

So far, we have treated multiple welfare state topics and areas as members of a broad policy domain. We will now dig more deeply into the precise ingredi-ents of agenda shifts. We first ask if welfare state campaign themes have become more *general and abstract* or more *particularistic*. After all, the notion of a gen-eral age of 'permanent austerity' (cf. Pierson 2001) implies that several reform pressures increasingly challenge the entire welfare state by applying general sustainability pressure on public finances. True, some pressures are cognitively linked to certain policy areas—for example, one may link population ageing to pensions or (more controversially) non-western immigration to social assis-tance. But even such reform pressures can potentially affect many policy areas because spending and funding adjustments brought on by a given pressure may be paid for in many different ways. This increasing cross-over of pressure raises the question of whether the welfare state is increasingly politicized and debated as a broad policy domain. Evidence that this is the case would be rel-evant for the notion of democratic linkage discussed in Chapter 2. There we distinguished between 'particularistic' and ideological 'programmatic' linkage and noted that it was an open question which one (if any) has become more important.

A couple of ideas can be developed here. First, if the causal mechanism is a broad challenge to overall social expenditure, one would expect politiciza-tion trends in *several* welfare state areas rather than in just a single one. The next section on the salience of specific policy areas will deal with this question. Second, we would expect a potential for rhetorical connections across specific areas, as evidenced in various ways, for example by being *simultaneously* on the agenda. We have already seen some evidence for this in that some campaigns came to be dominated by several welfare state themes around the turn of the millennium. A related idea is dealt with in this section. Is the increasingly pressured welfare state domain also increasingly conceptualized and made visible in more *abstract and encompassing* terms and not just only in terms of specific policy areas? Put differently, is the welfare state increasingly present in terms of encompassing abstractions such as public services, social transfers, social protection, and the like?

Figure 4.6 differentiates three sub-categories within the welfare state domain. The dotted line registers elections for which social outcomes (i.e. 'inequality' or 'poverty') or underlying normative values (i.e. 'justice', fairness', 'solidarity', 'security') are identified by experts as dominant themes. The thick line, in contrast, represents themes concerned with straightforward policy areas or programmes (i.e. 'health care', 'pensions', 'child care', etc.). The dashed line, finally, captures themes where the expert uses some sort of abstraction to capture a larger sector of the welfare state (i.e 'public services', 'social

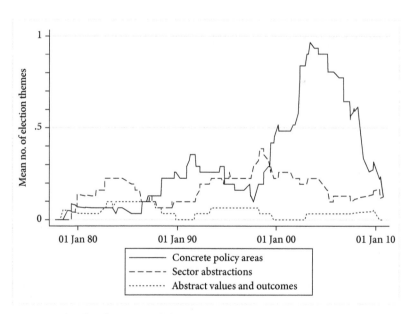

Fig. 4.6 The development of abstract campaign themes and concrete policy areas (moving averages).

insurances') or even more encompassing and abstract themes pertaining to the entire welfare state.

It is mainly concrete policy areas that drive the previously uncovered trends. Here, one recognizes once again an overall increase over time, in particular the late-and-brief reaction in the 2000s with a subsequent decline. Broader area abstractions, in contrast, have been less common and display no clear trend. Finally, themes constituted by general values or outcomes have been very unusual throughout. Overall, these results suggest that it is concrete areas rather than encompassing themes that for a period had a significant presence on the election campaign stages in Western Europe.

Which policy areas grew more salient?

So which concrete areas? Overall, there are six concrete policy areas present as election campaign themes in more than one election. These are shown in Figure 4.7. In addition to major campaign themes (dark grey), the figure also shows how areas surface in the material as sub-issues, that is, as smaller topics on the fringe of bigger campaign themes. The figure excludes two additional policy areas (student aid and active labour market policy) that only registered as sub-issues once and twice respectively.

The upper half of Figure 4.7 shows the development for areas showing a clear increase over time: health care, pensions, and elder care. Health care is the most frequent area, surfacing in around 15 per cent of campaigns over the whole period. Moreover, health care increases from around 10 per cent in the early period to over 20 per cent in the late period, an increase reflected in broader campaign themes as well as in sub-issues. Pension issues have also become more common over time, although at a lower level and where the increase is not as pronounced. For elder care, in contrast, one notices a clear shift in that this policy area was basically invisible in the early period, but clearly present later as a theme as well as a sub-issue to other themes. Overall, these results support the argument made by Green-Pedersen and Jensen (2019) that agenda responses to reform pressures are more likely in issues related to the life course, where more people have a long-term vested interest and because the older members of the population are regarded as very 'deserving'.

The bottom half of Figure 4.7 contains policy areas that show no increase over time. Also, most salience here is of the weaker sub-issue type rather than systemic dominance. This is true for unemployment and sickness benefits,

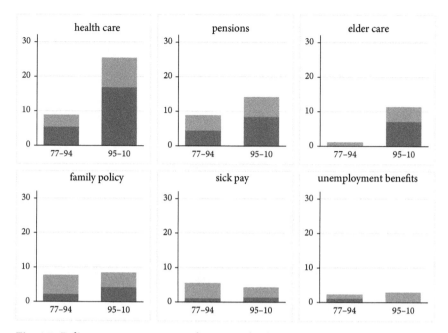

Fig. 4.7 Policy areas as campaign themes and sub-issues.

Note: Percent of elections with at least one theme/sub-issue in one journal (N=165 elections in 18 countries). Dark grey=campaign theme; light grey=sub-issue.

where the former in particular hardly registers on our scale of salience, with a small percentage of campaigns containing major themes. Family policy, finally, was more prevalent at just below 10 per cent already in the early period.[8]

The three growing areas—health care, pensions, and elder care—largely follow the general trends for the welfare state domain shown previously (Figure 4.8). Again, this entails a modest increase over time, an especially pronounced spike in the 2000s with a decrease in recent years. Specifically, while health and elder care adhere closely to this pattern, the curve for pensions shows a more gradual increase over a longer time span, albeit with the same dip towards the end.

Overall, we conclude that the rise (and more recent fall) of welfare issues applies to concrete policy areas rather than to encompassing sectors and abstractions. However, this by no means applies to all conceivable welfare state policy areas. Instead, we found that the concrete areas that receive more attention in tandem over time tend to be used more by the elderly (i.e. health

---

[8] Note however that this policy area is in a sense broader than the others as it unites several parts of our coding scheme (not only general 'family policy', but also 'child care', 'child allowance', and 'sick pay care for children').

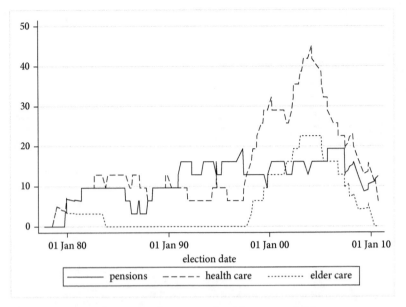

Fig. 4.8 The development of pensions, health care, and elder care (moving averages).

Note: For each area, the graphs show average proportion of elections where there is at least one election campaign theme or sub-issue.

care, elder care, pensions). Hence, a particular aspect of permanent austerity—the demographic challenge—seems to have left a particularly large systemic imprint on European election campaigns during the examined period.

Retrenchment and social investment

Chapter 3 evoked Kingdon's (2011 [1984]) 'multiple streams' framework and posited that big agenda shifts in the face of real-world problems are more likely once combined with new and politically palatable policy ideas. Specifically, we look at the social investment/activation paradigm, surfacing in elite-level ideas during the mid-1990s, with an emphasis on human capital, education, dual earner polices, and active labour market policy. This emerging paradigm might be more likely to act as a catalyst for major shifts in election campaign agendas compared to the earlier neoliberal paradigm of the 1970s and 1980s suggesting reform pressures should be met with retrenchment, austerity, and liberalization.

What do our data say about these lines of differentiation as tools for understanding the agenda shifts uncovered so far? One characteristic of the social

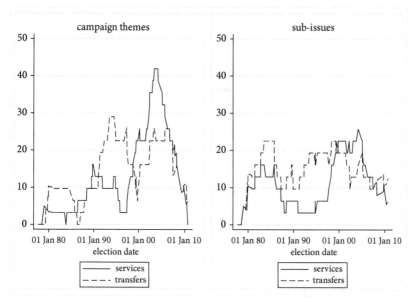

Fig. 4.9 The development of campaign themes and sub-issues related to public services and cash transfer systems (moving averages).

investment/activation turn is that it shifts the focus from passive social transfers to a wide range of public services meant to activate the inactive so that their human capital is better utilized (Hemerijck 2013). Against this background Figure 4.9 shows how the presence of transfer systems of various kinds as well as public services have developed over time. Both have generally become more common over the long term and both experience a downturn during the late 2000s. Relatively speaking, however, a comparison between the two reveals that transfers used to be somewhat more common both as broad campaign themes and as sub-issues. Over time, this gap has closed and during the familiar peak in welfare state attention around the turn of the millennium it is actually public services that more often occupied the top spots on the public agendas of European election campaigns.

Let us now look at education, a broad policy domain that has been put centre stage and increasingly linked with other welfare state policy goals through the social investment/activation turn (see Nikolai 2012). As Figure 4.1 indicated, education was not part of the broad welfare state domain analysed so far. There is some disagreement about how well this policy domain fits under the broad 'welfare state' umbrella. We are largely agnostic about this debate and simply note that education is relevant in an analysis of social investment

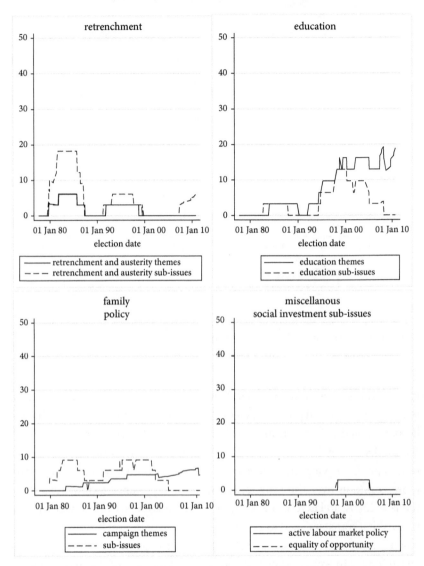

Fig. 4.10 The development of retrenchment/austerity and social investment related themes and sub-issues (moving averages).

Comment: The graphs show the average proportion of elections where there is at least one campaign theme/sub-issue.

(Nikolai 2012). Figure 4.10 shows the development for social investment-related topics over time and contrast these against the development for codes that can be said to represent the neoliberal retrenchment paradigm.[9]

---

[9] One such code is 'cutbacks and austerity' in the welfare state domain, which we combine with two macroeconomic codes of relevance here ('budget deficit' and 'austerity programme').

The retrenchment paradigm has usually not been a prominent part of sys-temic agendas, except for the early 1980s. Even then, however, it was often present in the form of sub-issues, rather than as a major campaign theme. Moreover, the retrenchment paradigm has receded and largely disappeared by the end of the 1990s, only to make a small comeback as a sub-issue in elec-tions held between the 2008 financial crisis and the end of our data window in 2010. Education travelled in the other direction. It was a rather unusual item on systemic campaign agendas until the mid-1990s after which it experienced a linear-looking increase as a campaign theme and a curvilinear up-and-down pattern as a sub-issue.

Beyond education, Chapter 3 emphasized some further policy areas associ-ated with the social investment/activation turn. The lower part of Figure 4.9, first, takes a closer look at family policy. Predominantly, we saw stability when we divided the data into two major periods (Figure 4.6). Thus, it is not surpris-ing that more fine-tuned moving averages also mostly display stability. But a further observation can be made, however, that whatever salience there is tac-itly shifts from minor sub-issues to major campaign themes from around the millennium and onwards. Relatedly, the presence of family policy as a major campaign theme grows over time such that after 2005 between 5 and 10 per cent of all elections have a systemic family policy campaign theme. The sec-ond graph displays a couple of categories intimately related to the idea of social investment: active labour market policy and equality of opportunity.[10] Both, however, are almost absent from the data except for two election campaigns. Interestingly however, these were again held around the familiar welfare state peak around the turn of the millennium.

Conclusions

This chapter has taken a comparative-historical approach to welfare state agenda-setting by asking questions about broad variation in systemic agendas across countries, welfare regimes, and in some cases parts of an entire conti-nent. In general, the results show that systemic agendas constitute a dynamic contrast to the well-documented preference stability in mature welfare states. There seems to be wide and systematic variation between political systems and periods, ranging from near-invisibility to near-domination of election cam-paigns. The political landscape of Europe's welfare states, it seems, is not only

---

[10] Equality of opportunity is often associated with social investment, while pitted against the more traditional welfare state goal of 'equality of condition' (see Morel et al. 2012, Chapter 1).

marked by relatively stable preferences but also by marked systemic agenda dynamics.

What have we learned about such dynamics? To begin with, that salience of welfare issues increased during a period of increasingly problematic challenges. This does not support the most drastic versions of 'blame avoidance' theory such as 'agenda control', where political parties and other actors conspire, as it were, to keep uncomfortable challenges off the agenda altogether. Instead, actors appear to have collectively responded to reform pressures by increasing public sphere campaign attention towards the welfare state domain. However, the revealed systemic agenda shifts were not linear. Europe's welfare states did *not* react to increasing reform pressure over these decades by gradually paying more attention to the welfare state. Rather, it is some 15–20 years into the 'era of permanent austerity' that we saw an especially intense, but brief, attention spike. This pattern is consistent with the 'late and brief response' hypothesis inspired by the theory of 'punctuated equilibrium'. Conversely, it is less consistent with the theories predicting a 'gradual' and not so publicly perceptible welfare state change discussed in Chapter 3 (cf. Streeck and Thelen 2005).

The overall rise in salience provides, in and of itself, some good democratic news. Chapter 2 emphasized systemic salience as an understudied but important precondition for democratic linkage. We hasten to add, however, that the salience increase concerned mainly concrete policy areas rather than abstract concepts. This provides a first clue about exactly which type of linkage citizens have been increasingly exposed to. The more ideological 'programmatic' linkage discussed in Chapter 2 would reasonably have been visible especially in themes dominated by broad concepts such as values or outcomes, or in themes that concern larger chunks of the welfare state. But such general topics have remained unusual at the systemic level examined here. Instead, what we see is a periodic rise in the salience of certain concrete policy areas. This is more consistent with the notion of particularistic, issue-specific linkage.

The salience increase, finally, did not concern all conceivable welfare state areas. Rather, the results fit Hemerijck's (2013) suggestion that the classic historical periodization of the post-war era into *two* periods no longer suffices. The classic dichotomy, of course, starts with a 'golden' age of welfare expansion, followed by an era of neoliberal austerity and retrenchment from the mid-1970s or early 1980s. However, our results also support the notion of a third and more recent epoch in which the focus on retrenchment and austerity, especially in conjunction with macroeconomic concerns, wanes. Said differently, we found support for both 'the declining salience of retrenchment' hypothesis as well as the 'weakening crisis–welfare nexus' hypothesis. In fact, since the mid-1990s, specific aspects of social investment appear to have helped to crowd out the neoliberal paradigm, thus supporting a 'social investment' hypothesis. In particular, we saw evidence that social investment helped to drive welfare state salience around the turn of millennium. This increasingly happened in 'good times' when macroeconomic issues were *not* salient.

5

What Politicians (Don't) Tell You about Welfare State Change

Do political leaders publicly put welfare state reform pressures on the agenda? Do they explicitly couple pressures with concrete policy solutions and normative ideological cues? Partial answers to these questions surfaced in Chapter 4, where we analysed aggregate patterns in 'systemic agendas' across decades and countries. Among other things, we learned that the salience of (some) welfare issues increased over time and peaked just after the turn of the millennium. Yet, several facets of our research questions cannot be fully answered using the systemic approach. Taking one example, simply the fact that welfare state issues are systemically salient does not necessarily mean that *pressures* are at the centre of debate. Neither does systemic salience equal a presence of policy solutions. These examples illustrate that we also need a detailed analysis of specific party messages.

In this chapter, we analyse 18 election-year party congress speeches by prime ministerial candidates from the two largest parties in Germany, Norway, and Sweden. We zoom in on the first decade of the 2000s; this allows us to dig more deeply into a period that Chapter 4 found to be especially intense and that past research has singled out as marked by accelerating welfare reform (Chapter 3). Moreover, election-year congress speeches are interesting for our purposes as they provide parties and leaders with the opportunity to address publicly, in a coherent and uninterrupted manner, the issues they want to put on the agenda for the upcoming campaign and frame them in their preferred way. Party congress speeches are therefore strategic enterprises and party specialists, consultants, personal advisors, and leaders themselves can be expected to use the occasion to maximize electoral appeal. Importantly, party congresses, and especially those of major parties, have become significant public events in West European politics. Excerpts from and commentary about leaders' speeches are likely to feature on national TV, in online and radio news, and in the print media.[1]

---

[1] See Farrell, Kolodny, and Medvic (2001) for a general discussion about the professionalization of parties in Western Europe.

Election Campaigns and Welfare State Change. Staffan Kumlin and Achim Goerres, Oxford University Press.
© Staffan Kumlin and Achim Goerres (2022). DOI: 10.1093/oso/9780198869214.003.0005

The data thus allow us to examine several issues of importance to this book. Some of these are about 'democratic linkage', in particular the nature of the choices put before the citizenry. What type of party differences, if any, concerning welfare state pressures and policy solutions do major parties display when speaking uninterrupted, at length, and under heavy media attention on the threshold to an election year? Chapter 2 discussed several conceivable possibilities in this regard. Traditionally, party and welfare state scholars alike have argued that parties compete along a single coherent economic left–right dimension (where left means pro government social spending and redistribution). However, several influential scholars in both traditions— examples include Peter Mair and Paul Pierson—have converged on the idea of ideological depolarization as pressures have intensified and as the representative function of parties allegedly deteriorated. Ross (2000a) has even suggested a 'Nixon goes to China' logic (see Chapter 3), under which social-democratic parties now have greater leeway in politicizing uncomfortable pressures and unpopular policies such as retrenchment, because of a greater perceived trustworthiness in the welfare state domain.

Meanwhile, ideological linkage may increasingly be complemented by particularistic party messages and differences. Parties may focus on specific combinations of pressures and policies that do not entirely resemble traditional left–right conflict. Such unexpected and particularistic narratives may be especially likely in the currently expanding universe of pressures and policy. In this regard, we have emphasized the 'social investment/activation' paradigm under which the left-right impregnated 'retrenchment versus status quo' struggle is only one component of increasingly multidimensional conflicts over welfare state change. Specifically, Chapter 2 discussed two different versions of particularistic messages. 'Issue ownership' implies that parties or candidates expose citizens to narratives about which problems (i.e. reform pressures) deserve attention. But they are not well informed about concrete policy. In the worst case, citizens will face parties that are similar in terms of the pressures they prioritize, while they remain silent on policy. The 'multiple streams' framework, by contrast, implies that the politicization of reform pressure requires a new, credible, and popular policy idea. From a democratic linkage viewpoint, the advantage is that this logic ensures policy information. A potential problem, however, is that strategic considerations could narrow the number of actual ongoing policy changes that are deemed marketable to the public.

This chapter also answers questions about 'democratic leadership'. Do prime ministerial candidates publicly engage in the proactive and unbiased agenda-setting of pressures and solutions imagined in work on ideational change and leadership (Cox 2001; Schmidt 2002; Stiller 2010; Cox and Béland 2011)? According to this research, leaders openly legitimize the totality of reform policies using cognitive as well as normative arguments. 'Cognitive' arguments explain the logic behind proposed solutions, such as why they alleviate resource scarcity and unsustainability brought on by reform pressures. 'Normative' arguments link solutions to values such as fairness and deservingness.

Alternatively, politicians may resort to the 'blame avoidance' variants that we recognize from Chapter 4. For example, they may keep a problematic set of pressures and unpopular solutions off the agenda altogether. Another strategy—'playing the crisis card'—involves parties putting pressures on the agenda while arguing that they are so severe that 'we have no choice but to act now'. To the extent that this strategy shapes rhetoric, we would expect talk about pressures and more unpopular reform to be generally unusual in these affluent welfare states but become more common after the 2008 financial crisis and then concern immediate macroeconomic pressures. Finally, we will assess if prime ministerial candidates engage in 'cherry-picking'. This subtler blame avoidance strategy involves emphasizing possibly uncomfortable problems while hiding the full range of policy citizens can nonetheless expect. Crucially, the increasingly multidimensional welfare reform landscape has increased cherry-picking opportunities.

Research strategy and contributions to past research

We seek to improve on past research in three ways. First, past studies often examined country contexts where it was clear that dramatic reform, usually retrenchment, had actually happened (Stiller 2010; Elmelund-Præstekær and Emmenegger 2013; Ervik and Lindén 2015). Scholars then worked their way backwards and analysed the various reform arguments used both behind the scenes and in public. Our approach, instead, begins by identifying relevant material that generally captures communication between leaders and citizens. We then examine how much 'reform pressure' talk there is in general, what it is about, and how it is linked to policy solutions and normative arguments. This strategy should give a fuller, more realistic and broad picture of public politicization of reform pressures and policy solutions. In addition, it allows us to consider a longer menu of policy options. This is important because the expanding universe of welfare reform has dramatically increased opportunities for 'cherry-picking'. This may go unnoticed with an exclusive focus on dramatic retrenchment cases. As we have emphasized, the general turn towards activation and 'social investment' is particularly interesting in this regard as several ingredients of this shift—examples include dual-earner policies and education and employment incentives—are typically assumed or found to be popular, not least among growing and electorally mobile 'new middle classes' (Gingrich and Häusermann 2015). This gives us reason to ask if the emerging social investment/activation paradigm has allowed leaders to put pressures on the agenda while drawing attention away from the not insignificant retrenchment that, frequently, citizens now have reason to expect after elections. More generally, gauging the public presence of the social investment/activation turn contributes to a broader debate about just how paradigmatic these ideational shifts have been (see Morel et al. 2012; Vaalavuo 2013; Raffass 2017). Is the social investment/activation turn an elite- and policy-level phenomenon, or have citizens been invited to a debate about it?

A second contribution begins with the fact that much research has investigated how economic crises trigger welfare reform and public legitimization (e.g. Kuipers 2006). In contrast, our design also incorporates other, more long-term, and diffuse pressures. In addition, we study three countries that are in the more affluent half of Europe's welfare states. This allows us to probe the contextual and substantive limits of 'ideational leadership'. That said, we follow these countries over time, before and after the financial crisis of 2008, to see whether it takes a massive economic crisis for significant public debate over reform pressures and policy solutions to arise.

Third, our material provides encompassing and systematic information at a 'soundbite' level about what politicians actually say to voters. As Chapter 3 noted, much past research has been impressionistic in its treatment of the public side of welfare reform, often relying on broad historical analyses of reform-intense phases (e.g. Cox 2001; Schmidt 2002; Bonoli and Natali 2012). Scholars have drawn on initiated but general summaries of the ideas, positions, arguments, and policies espoused by political actors, sometimes combined with anecdotal examples of public statements. It seems essential at this point to analyse more systematically what leaders actually say to voters in campaign settings.

Design, data, and methods

The speeches were made by social-democratic and conservative/ Christian-democrat prime ministerial candidates, usually the party leaders, during the 18 party congresses preceding national elections in Germany, Sweden, and Norway between 2000 and 2010. They vary in length from 3,500 to 8,400 words, with a mean of approximately 5,500. In total, the analysis includes almost 100,000 words of carefully crafted party-political messages.

The first coding step was to identify statements about welfare state institutions and policy. Here, we followed a classic definition of the welfare state (Flora and Heidenheimer 1981) as comprising all of those institutions, policies, and resources that are intended by publicly authorized allocation to reduce socio-economic inequality and increase the social security of individuals and households. Passages that dealt with the welfare state were delineated in thematic units, meaning parts of the speech that belonged to one overarching specific argument. So, the beginning and end of a coded passage was defined by the overall argument in which the welfare state was mentioned.

Over time we created three code families, each of which comprised a theoretically driven 'starting set' of codes. We then gradually added codes in an iterative and partly inductive process, ending up with a total of 44 codes across the families. Specifically, the first code family is 'reform pressures and opportunities'. These were defined as the social, economic and political developments or patterns that affect preconditions of, create challenges for, open windows for action to bring about, or force outright changes in the welfare state policy domain. The second family is 'policy responses' defined as concrete policy solutions in welfare state politics. The third code family is 'normative values and outcomes'. These were defined as desired values and outcomes that are linked to the welfare state domain or a change thereof.[2]

The coding was performed by a Scandinavian team and a German team, each consisting of primary researcher(s) with assistants who were (near-)native in the languages they coded. These teams communicated throughout the iterative development of the coding scheme. Both teams first coded two documents per country, before conferring with each other, after which the coding scheme was revised and harmonized. They then coded six speeches using the revised scheme, conferred again, and finally coded all the speeches. In each step, the code list was developed further, creating new codes, improving code definitions, and restructuring the code hierarchy. In total, there were 12 iterations, each one yielding a slightly different codebook with the number of changes decreasing substantially with each iteration.[3]

---

[2] Details of the coding development and examples are available upon request from the authors.
[3] For an overview of challenges in comparative content analysis, see Peter and Lauf (2002).

Due to the demanding coding exercises with a complex codebook and three different languages (German, Norwegian, and Swedish) with English as the target language, we finalized each coding with a group decision across national teams (for a discussion of reliability in high-number coding exercises see Krippendorff 2004: 417). Here, the one person on the team who is proficient in all four languages served as an inter-language anchor in comparing coding decisions and interpretations. Thus, each coding decision was discussed by this person and at least one other native speaker/researcher, and a consensual decision was made. Any disagreement about code application was explicitly discussed and solved. In total, six coders were involved in the exercise, being guided by the codebook with detailed coding instructions.[4]

Empirical analysis

The analysis proceeds in three steps. First, we look at the univariate patterns in the code family of reform pressures and opportunities ('rpos'). Relatedly, we explore changes over time as well as bivariate relationships with party family, country context, and incumbency. In a second step, we analyse relationships between rpos and the second code family, that is, policy responses. In a third and final step, we examine questions related to the third code family, that is, normative outcomes and values ('novs').

Patterns of reform pressures and opportunities

Table 5.1 displays the 14 thematic codes in the rpo family. It reveals the absolute number of words coded and the relative proportion given the overall number of words. A first observation is that reform pressures are clearly salient in these 18 speeches. Recall here that these are general speeches about all sorts of issues while our coding only pertains to passages where the welfare state was the focus of attention. Nonetheless, 15.8 per cent of all words are part of a discussion that could be attributed to at least one rpo topic. Put differently, about one-sixth of the speeches were associated with at least one mentioned welfare state reform pressure. The mean number of rpos per speech was 4.7. This high salience of reform pressures does not sit well with blame avoidance understood as agenda control, that is, not talking about uncomfortable problems at all.

---

[4] For a methodological discussion about inter-rater reliability approaches in qualitative content analysis, see Armstrong et al. (1997); Pope, Ziebland, and Mays (2000).

Note that our definition of rpos is in principle neutral regarding the assessment of the development or pattern referred to. Before the data collection, we expected some reform pressures to be spun into something positive, creating 'opportunities' for further developing the welfare states rather than for creating negative challenges. Yet, almost all rpos turned out to be negatively framed. Thus, politicians very rarely frame structural preconditions of welfare state change as opportunities. For example, the issue of ageing societies is rarely connected to better life expectancy and a longer, healthy lifespan, positive facts that could arguably be linked to welfare state changes. Likewise, migration could be portrayed as an opportunity in several ways, but is generally not in these speeches. An exception in the form of a purely positive opportunity is the rare linkage between the wealth of natural resources in Norway (gas, oil) and the welfare state. But overall, what we have in Table 5.1 are problematic 'pressures' rather than positive 'opportunities'.

From the list of rpos in Table 5.1, we can discern four dominant meta themes: (1) labour market (low employment 4.4 per cent, unemployment 4.3 per cent); (2) the economy (lacking health 2.5 per cent, economic internationalization 0.6 per cent); (3) population change (international migration 1.0 per cent, population ageing 0.7 per cent) with the work–family nexus at the intersection between labour market and population change (1.7 per cent), and (4) inequalities (economic inequality 1.3 per cent, interregional inequality 0.7 per cent). These four themes—labour market, economy, population change, and inequalities—make up the bulk of reform pressures addressed. Among these, pressure related to the labour market takes centre stage as the dominant reform pressure. This finding adds an important nuance to the book when it comes to which reform pressures are salient. Whereas Chapter 4 found that 'life course' pressures and polices have driven systemic agendas in Europe over the long haul, we now see that labour market pressures also figured prominently in messages from the major parties in these three countries at the beginning of the 2000s.

Moreover, the results show that macroeconomic pressures are clearly present but not all-important. Pressure talk in these speeches also concerns a number of more diffuse and long-term pressures that do not allow for the immediate crisis rhetoric emphasized in some variants of blame avoidance theory. Examples include pressures such as ageing, immigration, low employment (as opposed to unemployment), and work–life squeeze. Relatedly, recall that these three countries are generally among the more affluent and sustainable among Europe's welfare states and that they weathered the financial crisis well. Apparently, then, party messages about pressures do not need a

Table 5.1 Fourteen thematic codes related to reform pressures and opportunities

Thematic code reform pressure/opportunity	Code definition	Number of words	Relative % of all words
Low employment	Too many people are not at the disposal of the labour market.	4389	4.4
Unemployment	Too many people available to the labour market but who still cannot/will not get a job.	4277	4.3
Lacking health of the economy	Lacking health, or a full crisis of the overall economy.	2510	2.5
Work–family nexus	Changes in how people cohabit and plan their families OR tensions that arise for those with children from combining paid work in the labour market and unpaid work in the family.	1695	1.7
Economic inequality	Income and/or wealth inequality between individuals.	1302	1.3
International migration	Inflow of migrants into the country from another country or outflow into another country.	1008	1.0
Population ageing	The increase of the relative proportion of the elderly populace.	738	0.7
Interregional inequality	Inequality of life chances, economic opportunities or any other sort between regions of the same country.	684	0.7
Economic internationalization	Increase in trade of goods and services across borders.	628	0.6
Inefficient bureaucracy	Efficiency problems in the implementation of welfare state policies.	416	0.4
Public debt	Size of public debt.	268	0.3
National resources	Wealth in natural resources.	184	0.2
Intra-national migration	Migration within parts of the same country.	165	0.2
Environment	Link between ecological issues and the welfare state.	103	0.1
Total % of words that had *at least* one rpo code			15.8

Table 5.2 Reform pressures and opportunities themes across three
time periods between 2000 and 2010

rpo themes	overall	2000–02	2003–06	2007–2010
Labour market	10.1	8.9	10.7	10.7
Economy	3.2	0.8	1.0	7.9
Population change	3.7	5.6	2.8	2.6
Inequalities	1.7	3.3	0.0	1.9

Notes: rpo theme measures is a sum of the salience of constituent rpos.
The rpo code 'work–family nexus' is used twice to calculate population change and
labour market.

massive economic crisis to arise, nor are they always about the immediate
macroeconomic situation.

The overall salience of reform pressure talk increases somewhat towards the
end of the period. If we first merge all the categories and divide the first decade
of the 2000s into early, middle, and late periods, the average proportion of
speeches dedicated to at least one rpo was 14.1 per cent in period 1 (2000–02),
12.9 per cent in period 2 (2003–06), and 19.5 per cent in period 3 (2007–10).
The moderate increase towards the end could be explained by crisis-oriented
blame avoidance assumptions. These would predict that the crisis after 2008
eased the politicization of pressure and possibly contentious welfare reform. At
the same time, the change was hardly massive nor significant (ANOVA analysis
of group differences in means, $p = 0.38$). Reform pressures were clearly also
salient before the crisis.

Table 5.2 follows more closely the four meta themes over time. The most
important observation here is that the slight overall increase is driven by talk
of macroeconomic pressure, with the economy category increasing after the
onset of a crisis (a significant change at $p = 0.01$). By contrast, there is no
general trend beyond the macroeconomy as pressure. Labour market related
pressures were consistently present between 2000 and 2010, with no significant variation. Demographic pressures and inequalities, both relatively slow
processes, varied little with no significant trend. Overall, the effect of the financial crisis in these countries appears to have been that the *composition* of the
pressure debate, rather than its volume, changed. Apparently, reform pressures
were also present in party messages in non-crisis periods in three of Europe's
more affluent and relatively speaking more sustainable welfare states.

We also explored how the salience of rpo topics co-varies with characteristics of the speeches or the speakers themselves (not shown in Table 5.2).
This was achieved by looking at the relative salience of any of the 14 rpo

codes across the 18 speeches. In general, we found few and minor differences between the two party families examined here. Leaders of the conservative parties used slightly fewer words on rpos (14.0 versus 17.0 per cent; not significant, t-test, $p = 0.46$) than those of the main left parties.[5] Further analyses revealed that this slight difference is consistently found across all three countries, and for most subcategories of pressures (especially the common ones).[6] Overall, these negligible party differences do not fit a traditional left-right conception under which the right focuses much more on the welfare state's underlying economic problems. Neither do the small differences fit the 'Nixon goes to China' hypothesis (according to which the left finds it much easier to politicize pressures).

Incumbent prime ministers speak slightly more about reform pressures (17.3 per cent) compared with the opposition candidates (13.2 per cent) ($p = 0.32$). Incumbents also address more pressures per speech on average (4.1) than the opposition parties (3.4) ($p = 0.38$). Arguably, this observation does not support the blame avoidance perspective as one would expect the opposition to talk more about problems they can less plausibly be blamed for. This finding seems to suggest a more proactive rhetoric on the part of governments than 'blame avoidance' suggests.[7]

How do leaders couple pressures with policy responses?

We now move on to our second code family—policy responses. We start by looking at univariate patterns and then ask how pressures and policy responses are linked. We define a policy response as the speaker's own statements about his/her party's actions in government or in parliament (rather than remarks about those of other parties). Policy responses thus reveal current policy preferences at the time of the speech. Here, our coding exercise ended with 12 codes for policy responses. Based on the discussion in Chapter 3, these can be heuristically grouped into three levels of overall electoral popularity: low, mixed, or high. Codes in the high-popularity group denote policies that

[5] This is also found when looking at the number of rpo topics per speech, which on average is 3.7 rpos in conservative speeches and 3.9 in leftist party speeches ($p = 0.79$).
[6] Party differences are mostly small for specific types of pressures. Compared to social-democrats, conservative candidates speak slightly more about labour market related rpos (11.9 per cent versus 8.3 per cent; $p = 0.24$) as well as slightly more about population change (4.9 per cent versus 2.4 per cent; $p = 0.32$), but slightly less about economic rpos (1.5 per cent versus 5.0; $p = 0.14$), and inequality theme (0.2 per cent versus 3.2 per cent; $p = 0.17$).
[7] We also ran exploratory OLS regressions with the three predictors: time, party family, and incumbent. None of which yielded significant coefficients.

can be assumed, or have been found, to be most welcomed by median voters. For active labour market policies (ALMPs), the situation is complicated by the existence of several distinct aspects that feature in the speeches. For this category, we therefore went through each coding and decided individually to which group particular statements belonged. Specifically, politicians sometimes address more popular aspects of ALMPs, such as the expansion of education programmes. From a social investment perspective, these are known as 'enabling' ALMPs (for a discussion see Fossati 2018). Such instances were coded as positive (13 instances). At other times, politicians propose greater duties, more benefit conditionality, and generally harsher demands on, individuals. Such more 'demanding' ALMPs (Fossati 2018) were coded as low popularity (four instances), leaving a residual category of ALMPs with mixed or otherwise unclear signals (four instances). Finally, we assume that the following six policy types belong to the group of comparatively high-popularity policy responses: defence of the status-quo; social investment; expansion; efficiency gain and cost containment of existing programmes; vague improvements; and enabling ALMPs.

The policy responses that can be regarded as popular come out clearly towards the top and middle of Table 5.3 (ranks 1–3, 6–8 out of 13). The salience of defence of the status-quo, social investment,[8] and expansion of existing programmes have the highest salience at 5.1 per cent, 5.0 per cent, and 4.4 per cent respectively, followed by vague promises of improvements (2.5 per cent), active labour market policy-opportunities (2.4 per cent), and cost containment (2.0 per cent). At the bottom of the table, we find retrenchment (0.5 per cent). The demanding version of active labour market policy is slightly more common at 1.5 per cent. The mixed-popularity policy responses range from other organizational reforms (3.2 per cent), privatization and market reforms (2.8 per cent) in the upper half of the table, to structural public sector reforms (1.1 per cent), active labour market policy, mixed signals (1.0 per cent), and recalibration (0.5 per cent).

How are policy responses coupled with reform pressures (rpos)? To answer this, we check whether each rpo coding instance is linked with a policy response and if it is, we code its type. Such links are established when the respective codes are either directly overlapping or are in adjacent paragraphs.

---

[8] ALMP and social investment overlap as conceptual categories, but are not the same. ALMP has labour market integration by activation as the central objective, regardless of any long-term implications for human capital, whereas the social investment code refers to the improvement of human capital itself with perhaps the implicit objective of better labour market integration.

Table 5.3 Salience of types of policy responses in the context of the welfare state

Type	Definition	Overall electoral popularity	Salience as % of all words
Defence of the status-quo	Speaker defends existing welfare state policies.	High	5.1
Social investment	Welfare state policy used as instrument for the creating, preserving, or making better use of human capital/competence to generate economic benefit for the individual or society.	High	5.0
Expansion	Expansion of existing welfare state provision as manifested in more public resources, lower user fees or more tax deduction of fees, lower contributions, or in increasing generosity and better coverage or higher pay to public employees.	High	4.4
Other organizational reforms	Reforms of welfare state programme institutions that are less than a fundamental change of the institutional landscape.	Mixed	3.2
Privatization and market reforms	Some aspect of services/protection at least partly transferred to non-public agency/providers, or market-like competition between several providers is created or increased.	Mixed	2.8
Vague improvement	Quality, delivery, services, protection etc., 'will improve', or 'have improved' without any details about how this will be or was done (i.e. not even 'expansion').	High	2.5
Active labour market policy—opportunities	Policy that aims to increase employability by offering train-ing/education or by lowering the hurdle for companies to get to know the individuals and consider them for further employment, or in-work benefits to increase incentives to get into work with just opportunities mentioned and no sanctions.	High	2.4

Continued

Table 5.3 *Continued*

Type	Definition	Overall electoral popularity	Salience as % of all words
Cost containment and efficiency gain	The self-proclaimed will and ability to lower costs while keeping welfare generosity or service quality intact.	High	2.0
Active labour market policy—duties	Policy that aims to increase employability of the unemployed by offering training/education or by lowering the hurdle for companies to get to know the individuals and consider them for further employment or in-work benefits to increase incentives to get into work with just duties mentioned. Usage of sanctions and conditionality.	Low	1.5
Structural public sector reforms	When state/public bodies/agencies are merged, split, or when entirely new public organizational bodies are created.	Mixed	1.1
Active labour market policy—mixed signals	Policy that aims to increase employability of the unemployed by offering training/education or by lowering the hurdle for companies to get to know the individuals and consider them for further employment, or in-work benefits to increase incentives to get into work with opportunities and duties mentioned in the same instance.	Mixed	1.0
Recalibration	Retrenchment in one area or aspect of the welfare state, compensated by the simultaneous expansion or prioritization of another.	Mixed	0.5
Retrenchment	Existing welfare state services or benefits are cut back, i.e. the inverse of 'expansion'.	Low	0.5

Note: A residual 'Other' category captured another 0.5 per cent.

Table 5.4 shows that there are 85 instances where at least one rpo code was used. Thirty-four of these were linked with a policy response of high electoral popularity, 13 with mixed popularity, and 6 with low popularity. Thus, roughly two-thirds of all pressures (53 out of 85) are linked with a policy response, whereas roughly one-third lack a clear policy solution. Moreover, 40 per cent of all reform pressures are linked with a positive policy response, 15 per cent with a mixed response, and 6 per cent with an unpopular response. Expressing the same pattern per speech, we found an average of 4.7 codings of rpos per speech. An average of 1.9 are linked with a high-popularity policy response, 0.7 with a mixed policy response, and 0.3 with a low-popularity policy response. In sum, then, the politicization of reform pressures does not always come with a clearly discernible policy response. And when it does, it is the more popular policies that take centre stage.

Table 5.4 allows us to compare subgroups of speeches. On the left-hand side of Table 5.4, we see the means for each subgroup defined by the row variable. For example, leftist parties have a mean of 4.8 instances of rpos in their speeches, 2.8 instances of linkage with high-popularity responses, 0.6 instances for mixed-popularity responses, and 0.1 for low-popularity responses. On the right-hand side, we see the conditional proportions as a percentage. For example, left-leaning parties have 102 per cent of the mean for rpos in their speeches. Given the number of instances of rpos in their speeches, 58 per cent are linked with high-popularity policy responses, 13 per cent with mixed-popularity responses, and 2 per cent with low-popularity responses. This can be compared with the percentages of right-leaning parties. Their mean of rpos is exactly the mean overall (100 per cent), but only 21 per cent of their rpo instances are linked with high-popularity policy responses, 19 per cent with mixed-popularity responses, and 13 per cent with low-popularity responses.

These examples show that, whereas right- and left-leaning parties show similar levels of reform pressure talk, leftist party speakers are clearly more prone to coupling pressures with any sort of policy response, and in particular to high-popularity responses (pressures yes, but no painful reforms). Conservative speakers display a more balanced pattern when policy is mentioned. Crucially however, they are much less likely to bring up discernible policy in the first place; this omission happens in roughly 50 per cent of conservative pressure messages. Thus, conservatives stay more balanced but also more silent on policy whereas social democrats engage more in the 'cherry-picking' of popular policy responses. This last conclusion is permissible as studies show that during this period social democratic governments are in fact equally likely

Table 5.4 Bivariate analysis of reform pressures and opportunities and their links to policy responses at different levels of electoral popularity

			Linked to policy response with electoral popularity			Conditional percentages			
						Overall mean of pressures	Mean of pressures in that subgroup		
		Pressures instances	High	Mixed	Low		High	Mixed	Low
Absolute N		85	34	13	6				
Means	Overall	4.7	1.9	0.7	0.3	100	40	15	6
Party family	leftist	4.8	2.8	0.6	0.1	102	58	13	2
	rightist	4.7	1.0	0.9	0.6	100	21	19	13
Incumbency	yes	5.2	2.0	0.9	0.4	111	38	17	8
	no	4.1	1.8	0.5	0.3	87	44	12	7
Election wave	2000–02	5.2	1.5	1.1	0.2	111	29	21	4
	2003–06	3.3	1.3	0.7	0.7	70	39	21	21
	2007–10	5.7	2.8	0.3	0.2	121	49	5	4
Countries	Germany	5.8	1.7	0.7	0.0	123	29	12	0
	Norway	3.7	1.5	0.8	0.5	79	41	22	14
	Sweden	4.7	2.5	0.7	0.5	100	53	15	11

to preside over retrenchment following elections where welfare state issues have been systemically salient (Jakobsson and Kumlin 2017).

Incumbency does not dramatically change linkage with high-popularity policy (38 per cent compared to 44 per cent). So, incumbents talk slightly more about pressures, but are no different in terms of the policy types pressures are linked with. Finally, as for the time dimension, the number of rpo instances per speech is lower in the middle period 2003–06 (70 per cent of the overall mean) compared with the early period 2000–02 (111 per cent of the overall mean) and the later period 2007–2010 (121 per cent of the overall mean). However, the later period has a higher relative percentage of high-popularity policy responses (49 per cent given the number of rpos in the speeches) with almost no links to other policy responses (5 per cent mixed, 4 per cent low). The middle period displays a more balanced coupling of high-popularity (39 per cent), with mixed-popularity (21 per cent), and low-popularity policy responses (21 per cent). Recall that the poor health of the economy was the most important rpo in the later period. We can now infer that the economic crisis led not only to a higher salience of rpos in general, but also to a stronger focus on coupling with high-popularity responses. Crisis means more pressure talk, but apparently also more 'cherry-picking'. In fact, across all the speeches, we find that a stronger emphasis on reform pressure is associated with a higher connection with high-popularity policy responses ($r = 0.30$).

This last observation is illustrated by the country differences. Chapter 1 emphasized that Norway must be seen as the least pressured welfare state of the three. It is therefore understandable that we see less pressure talk in Norwegian speeches (79 per cent of the overall mean). At the same time, however, Norwegian politicians display the most balanced pattern in policy coupling. Only 46 per cent of rpo instances are linked to high-popularity policy responses, whereas 22 per cent are linked to mixed-popularity, and 14 per cent to low-popularity policy responses.

Normative outcomes and values

Party messages about welfare state politics contain more than just concrete pressures and policies. They are also opportunities to provide voters with abstract ideological signals. To assess this, we created a third code family and called it 'normative values and outcomes' ('nvos'). In general, we defined these codes as instances of messages concerning desirable socio-economic outcomes and normative end states that the welfare state should contribute to.

These messages help us to further illuminate democratic linkage and leadership. In terms of linkage, they provide information about abstract left–right 'programmatic' choice. Looking for such abstract linkage becomes more important having learned that particularistic messages are not massively different across parties as well as partly flawed ('cherry-picking'). But perhaps the abstract cues in the nvo family offer complementary party differences, thus compensating for the partial shortcomings of particularistic messages? On democratic leadership, we have discussed the possibility that leaders also successfully legitimize welfare state change using 'normative arguments' (e.g. Stiller 2010). These are essential components in broader narratives about how *choosing* reform makes both economic 'cognitive' sense *and* has a certain normative pay-off. Such messages differ from entirely blame-avoiding storylines about how overwhelming pressures allow *no choice* but to implement essentially unwanted change.

Table 5.5 shows the presence of the 15 registered nvo types. A first observation is that collectively, they show a high level of salience. More precisely, 16.1 per cent of all words are coded with at least one nvo code. This is on par with the presence of reform pressures. Put differently, sending some cue about the desirable end states of welfare state policies (normative arguments) is roughly as common as bringing up some discernible reform pressure (cognitive arguments). Recall again that these are general speeches and that our coding only captures welfare state related statements. Nevertheless, roughly one-sixth of the speeches were associated with at least one instance of a normative cue about desirable values and outcomes in the welfare state domain.

One theme leads the pack in terms of salience: prime ministerial candidates frequently mention 'justice and fairness' (8.1 per cent of all words are associated with this category). It is interesting that this category is so frequent as it is arguably also among the more substantively 'empty' ones. After all, 'justice and fairness' are very general and contested terms that usually need further explanation to work well as ideological cues. Now, we cannot say for sure based on our data whether parties provide such additional information, or whether citizens manage to correctly 'fill in the blanks' left open by cues about justice and fairness. What we can say, however, is that these general normative cues cannot on their own make up for an absence of concrete policy information. On the contrary, they need more specific information (for example related to policy) to convey substantive programmatic stances and choices. As such, 'justice and fairness' is a normative parallel to the previously discussed policy category of 'vague improvements'. Of course, few would be against improvements, justice, or fairness without further specification. Still, quite a lot of welfare rhetoric in these speeches is devoted to such signals which—taken on their own—lack a very clear substantive meaning.

Most other codes in the nvo family have more substantive content. This is true for social equality (5.3 per cent), which is the second most salient code in the speeches. This category captures leaders talking negatively about income or wealth differences. Two other codes, which we show separately, also revolve around equality or the lack thereof: equal opportunities in society (3.0 per cent) and gender equality (1.5 per cent). All in all, hinting at how inequalities are problematic, or how greater equality is desirable, is a prominent feature of these speeches. Besides justice/fairness and equality topics (both around 8 per cent), there is a middle salience group with social cohesion (4.0 per cent), personal choice in access to services (3.7 per cent), and liberty/freedom (2.5 per cent). All other topics, such as universalism or poverty, are uncommon and we disregard them from now on.

Are normative cues also present in talk about reform pressures? To begin with, the number of pressures in a speech is only weakly correlated with the number of normative cues ($r = 0.19$). This is a very mild tendency indeed with

Table 5.5 Fifteen thematic codes related to normative values and outcomes

Thematic code normative values and outcomes ('nvos')	Code definition	Number of words	Relative % of all words
Justice or fairness	Any allusion to the concepts of justice or fairness even if only semantic	8071	8.1
Social equality	Equality in terms of income and or wealth in the general population	5244	5.3
Social cohesion or solidarity	Desired state of affairs in which individuals are willing to tolerate costs for others or give in favour of others within the realm of the welfare state, e.g. solidarity between the have and have-nots	4012	4.0
Personal choice	Personal choice in access to services, regulation or redistribution	3697	3.7
Equal opportunities	Equal opportunities in terms of access to material opportunities, such as education or jobs	2982	3.0
Security	Allusion to security, whether social or in the sense of security against crime	2758	2.8
Liberty or freedom	Any allusion to the concepts of liberty or freedom	2482	2.5
Gender equality	Equality in access or outcomes between gender groups	1480	1.5
Universalism	Universal access to welfare state services and benefits; this refers to material outcomes, not some kind of general notion of social equality	882	0.9
Poverty	Material poverty of individuals or social groups	881	0.9
Immigrant integration	Integration of immigrants into the majority population	620	0.6
Economic growth	Growth of the regional or national economy	466	0.5
Individual initiative	Progress initiation by individuals	385	0.4
Meritocracy	Situation in which achievement pays off materially	324	0.3
Individual responsibility	Moral or material responsibility of individuals	150	0.2
		15,980	16.1

Table 5.6 Codings of welfare state reform pressures, normative outcomes and values, and their links to policy responses

			Pressures WITH				
Pressure instances	Pressures WITH normative outcomes	Pressures WITH normative outcomes WITH policy response	'equality'	'justice or fairness'	'security'	'social cohe- sion'	'individ- ualistic values'
85	44	26	14	17	8	8	8
Per speech							
Overall	2.4	1.4	0.8	0.9	0.4	0.4	0.4
leftist	2.7	1.9	1.1	1.2	0.3	0.8	0.4
rightist	2.2	1.0	0.4	0.7	0.6	0.1	0.4

Note: The first row shows counts pressure instances. For example, 14 pressure instances have a co-occurrence with the normative outcome and value 'equality'. Rows 2 to 4 show means per speech. For instance, left-leaning prime ministerial candidates have on average 1.1 instances of reform pressure and opportunities that are linked to the normative outcomes and values code 'equality'.

only 18 cases. Nonetheless, it is interesting that there is at least no negative association (recall that policy solutions become more uncommon with more pressure talk).

Table 5.6 looks more closely at the 85 instances of pressure talk across the 18 speeches. Out of these, roughly half (n = 44) are linked with a normative cue. However, we also see that 26 out of the 44 instances of pressure talk that are combined with normative cues *also* provide policy information. In other words, it would be wrong to regard concrete policy information and normative cues as communicating vessels. More often than not general normative cues complement concrete information about policy rather than make up for its absence. What is more, further analyses (not shown) reveal that 63 per cent of all policy-connected normative cues appear in conjunction with high-popularity policy responses. As little as 5 per cent appear in conjunction with low-popularity policy. These observations do not square well with the idea that 'ideational leaders' motivate potentially unpopular reform by pointing, not only to economic realities, but also to a normative pay-off.

The right-hand side of Table 5.6 shows how pressures are linked with the more common nvo codes (In this analysis we collapse some of the smaller ones.[9]). Essentially, we see the same front runners as in Table 5.5 with equality

[9] Collapsed categories reflect the following codes. Equality: social equality, equal opportunities, gender equality; justice/fairness; individualist values (personal choice, individual initiative, individual responsibility).

and justice/fairness being the most common normative values and outcomes linked to reform pressures.

Differences between social democratic and conservative speakers exist, but are hardly massive overall. The most common theme ('justice and fairness') is, as we have discussed, probably less informative. This theme, moreover, is used by both parties, although more often on the left (a little over once per speech for the left, and a little less for the right). 'Social cohesion' has clearer substantive political meaning at the same time as it is mentioned almost once per speech by social democrats but basically never by conservatives. However, this theme is not very salient overall. By contrast, social equality cues (which are also more informative than justice and fairness) are only mildly divisive across the parties, with leftist speakers averaging around 1 equality theme per speech, whereas conservative speakers mention equality roughly every second speech. Finally, and perhaps surprisingly, normative cues related to physical security and personal choice are neither very divisive across parties, nor very common overall.

Conclusions

This chapter has examined if leading politicians put welfare state reform pressures on the agenda and if they link these pressures with concrete policy and abstract normative cues. The answers shed further light on the book's overarching concerns with democratic linkage and leadership.

We uncovered a sort of unfinished—or perhaps half-baked—coupling of welfare state reform pressures and policy responses. On the one hand, reform pressures are clearly salient: prime ministerial candidates in Germany, Norway, and Sweden spend significant shares of election-year congress speeches talking about reform pressures and the welfare state. At the same time, approximately one-third of all reform pressure talk is not associated with *any* discernible policy strategy. Thus, a sizeable share of welfare state rhetoric resembles 'issue ownership' conflict under which citizens are clearly informed about which problems (i.e. reform pressures) parties prioritize, but not about which concrete solutions parties have in mind.

In two-thirds of pressure messages we do find discernible policy directions. However, these tend to be popular strategies in our classification; the examples include expansion and social investment. Leftist parties are more prone to couple pressures with policy, in particular popular policy. Rightist parties, by contrast, talk almost as much about pressures but keep their policy cards more tightly pressed against the chest. Whenever conservative speakers link pressures with policies (still the most common outcome for them), they, too, focus on high-popularity responses, although to a lesser extent than leftist parties. Overall, the main left–right divide is *not* about daring to politicize pressures (both do), *nor* about daring to politicize unpopular policies (neither does), but rather about the extent to which reform pressures are linked to policy at all (the left is best at this) and in particular to the more popular policy responses. The latter is again more common on the left, whereas the right complements this strategy with that of remaining silent about policy. Neither of these patterns jibes well with a traditional left–right programmatic conception, which would suggest that the right attacks the welfare state by politicizing pressures and championing retrenchment. The left would downplay pressures while defending or expanding the welfare state. Neither do the patterns support the 'Nixon goes to China' logic suggested by Ross (2000a), under which the left has greater leeway in politicizing pressures and, in particular, unpopular policy like retrenchment. True, pressures are slightly more politicized on the left, but the left also remains more silent about painful reforms.

Beyond particularistic narratives about pressures and policies, we also analysed abstract normative cues. These turned out to be just as salient as reform pressures. However, rather than making up for the considerable absence of concrete policy information, normative cues quite often complement policy whenever such information is given. Moreover, there is only a mild and inconsistent left–right pattern in normative cues. For example, one common and relatively divisive type of cue (i.e. 'justice and fairness') is also less substantively informative. Other cues are more informative but mostly either uncommon or not very divisive. Just like particularistic messages about specific pressure and policies, then, normative/ideological messages do not necessarily provide the clear democratic choice that democratic linkage requires.

Our results also illuminate questions about democratic leadership. As noted previously, scholars have warmed towards models such as 'ideational leadership', under which top politicians openly legitimize the totality of welfare reform using cognitive as well as normative arguments. Cognitive arguments explain why reforms alleviate reform pressures. Normative arguments link them (also its unpopular aspects) to values like fairness and deservingness. Empirically, however, our results suggest that normative cues predominantly co-exist with policy that is already on the popular side.

More than this, we found clear support for blame avoidance theory. The devil is in the details, however, as the less subtle blame avoidance variants are not widely supported. This is true for the strategy of hiding problems away from public sight altogether. Additionally, similar to Chapter 4, we find little support for the idea of crisis as a catalyst for blame-avoiding 'no choice' narratives. Reform pressure talk became only marginally more widespread after the financial crisis and often concerns long-term pressures that are less suitable for arguing that a crisis leaves us 'no choice' here and now. Above all, we found a large amount of talk about welfare state challenges in our three welfare states, which are among Europe's most stable and affluent. Apparently, it takes neither immediate economic crisis, nor unusually severe pressures, to trigger debate about the challenges of mature welfare states.

Instead, we see evidence of a subtler blame avoidance type: 'cherry-picking' of popular policy solutions to reform pressures. This tendency, which becomes more pronounced as pressure talk intensifies, is observable for prime ministerial candidates who often propose social investment or active labour market policy of an expansive or enabling kind. Furthermore, they frequently defend the status quo, propose welfare state expansion, or simply hint vaguely at some sort of 'improvements' that will be made despite reform pressure. Rarely do prime ministerial candidates speak plainly about less popular retrenchment or punitive and demanding activation, although these policy directions have been part of the actual reform trajectory in these countries. In important ways, then, politicians 'cherry-pick' policy to be marketed electorally from what is, in reality, a complex and at least partly unpopular menu of actual ongoing reform.

PART III
PUBLIC RESPONSES

6

What Makes People Worry about the Welfare State?

The previous chapters studied the agendas and messages about welfare state reform pressures that citizens encounter in election campaigns. We learned that welfare state issues have become more 'systemically salient' over time and that reform pressures are politicized by major parties to the left and the right. However, parties mainly couple pressures with popular policy or debate pressure without referring to policy at all.

But how are citizens affected by messages about reform pressures? This is the main question in Chapters 6 and 7. Taken together, these chapters report three experiments on how 'reform pressure framing' affects perceptions of future welfare state sustainability. Recall from Chapter 3 that we already suspect that such perceptions are somewhat distinct from normative welfare state support. They also have behavioural consequences in that they dampen electoral punishment for unpopular welfare reform (Giger and Nelson 2013). Few studies, however, examine how such perceptions are formed in the first place. Can they be regarded as responses to actual information about pressures, with citizens drawing meaningful conclusions based on complex demographic and economic transformations? And if so, which type of information affects which citizens in which contexts?

The answers to these questions inform the book's broader research problems concerning democratic 'linkage' and 'leadership'. By example, do citizens' reactions match the linkage model's insistence on informed preferences? Or perhaps citizens are biased such that they ignore major pressures but are highly sensitive to less significant ones? As for democratic leadership, the experiments tell us something about whether citizens are able to engage with uncomfortable information that challenges the status quo. Overall, the findings help us assess whether election campaigns might plausibly contribute to explaining welfare state change through a process in which public opinion registers and adapts to growing challenges.

Election Campaigns and Welfare State Change. Staffan Kumlin and Achim Goerres, Oxford University Press.
© Staffan Kumlin and Achim Goerres (2022). DOI: 10.1093/oso/9780198869214.003.0006

The first experiment, which is examined in this chapter, was conducted in all three countries. We asked people about perceived welfare state sustainability while randomly varying the source of the supposed pressure (i.e. population ageing, low employment, global economic conditions, immigration from the EU or non-EU/non-Western countries). In this experiment, moreover, respondents did not learn about conceivable policy responses, thus emulating the 'policy-free' pressure messages that appear common according to previous chapters. As we shall also see, this experiment offers improvement over past studies on pressure framing, which have tended to focus on 'one pressure in one country'. This has made it hard to know if results are message-specific or reflect a more general tendency to react (or not react) to pressure information.

The next three sections formulate hypotheses about how influential various types of pressure framing might be. In doing so, we will use three theoretical perspectives on welfare state change that were discussed in Chapter 3. First, Pierson's influential 'new politics of the welfare state' framework (Pierson 1996, 2001) implies limited effectiveness for pressure framing. It is likely to be present and effective mainly in policy areas with weak initial support or when multiple pressures are used in a 'blame-avoiding' fashion, for example portrayed as so strong and immediate that obstacles related to self-interest and strong support for the status quo are overcome.

A second and more recent body of work analyses how accelerating welfare state change is not only due to blame avoidance but to 'credit claiming'. Reform-minded ideational leaders argue their case by publicly politicizing growing reform pressures (e.g. Levy 2010; Stiller 2010). Importantly, they mix cognitive arguments about economic pressure with normative arguments. Thus, the focus here is not on the blame avoiding argument that massive pressure leaves us with 'no choice'. Rather, serious but ultimately manageable pressures, together with a clear normative cue, are integral to the narratives offered by ideational leaders.

A third accumulation of studies comes from experimental work on welfare attitudes. Despite surging interest in experiments (Druckman et al. 2011), however, we largely lack studies about pressure framing as a broad phenomenon. Instead, a large number of studies show the importance of cues about how 'deserving' recipients are (Tyler et al. 1997; Slothuus 2007; Petersen et al. 2010). These studies complement work on welfare state change by convincingly specifying a plausible normative component of ideational leadership narratives. Having said this, 'deservingness' studies have typically left the question of economic sustainability aside. We know little about whether the framing of economic pressures can matter in the absence of deservingness cues and—crucially—how the two operate in combination: are citizens more susceptible to economic pressures if provided with the right deservingness cue? The experiment reported in this chapter gets at this by comparing effects of different types of economic pressures, some of which are linked to '(un)deserving' groups, whereas some are not linked to any groups. This gives a handle on whether group deservingness is, as it were, a normative key that opens the door to pressure framing effects.

The concluding section will emphasize that reform pressure framing is by no means universally consequential. In fact, several treatments yield none or only weak effects. As far as it goes, this fits with the 'new politics' depiction of institutions and citizens as change-resistant despite reform pressure. At the same time, certain treatments did trigger responses. This fits better with recent work on welfare state change, in that citizens are at least in principle capable of processing and reacting to pressures. However, such effects indeed depend on normative cues implicit in pressure frames: the framing strategy most clearly supported by our data is to 'zoom in' on pressures linked to groups seen as undeserving. Another possible framing strategy is to 'zoom out', making messages span a more diverse and broadly threatening set of challenges. This strategy, which is more in line with the 'new politics' emphasis on blame avoidance, shall receive some but clearly weaker support.

In addition to effect variation across messages, the results will reveal intricate patterns of country variation. The concluding section will use these for an inductive discussion about context-message interactions. This discussion is inductive as our one-shot experiment in 'only' three countries cannot, and was not, designed to firmly test contextual hypotheses. The discussion is also inductive because our results did not corroborate whatever initial expectations we had. We thought that pressure framing would be especially influential in contexts marked by more real and perceived unsustainability. And as Chapter 1 emphasized, our three countries are among the more economically stable and sustainable European welfare states, at the same time as there is variation among them. Norway, with its exceptional oil revenues, stands out economically and displays more policy stability (Bay et al. 2010). Hence, we initially thought that pressure framing would be the least consequential there. But results revealed a more complicated or even the opposite cross-country pattern. This begs for new explanations and the concluding section will identify two broad lessons about country variation in pressure framing effects. The first one concerns immigration. Recent work raises the possibility that immigration related pressure frames are generally important, but particularly so in Scandinavia. The second lesson is that effects may grow with systemic salience. Reform pressure frames make a greater impression in policy areas where pressures have been recently and massively salient in the public sphere. The concluding section illustrates this lesson by juxtaposing key findings with key developments in each country.

This last discovery is especially important to this book as it connects the chapters on public responses with those on campaign contents. More precisely, the implication is that systemic salience of welfare state pressures is not only indicative of *how much* information and debate citizens are exposed to. More than this, systemic salience may enhance reactions to a given piece of information. This salience-based account of contextual variation has the important implication that pressure framing can 'pave the way for its own success'. That is, it contributes to an overall context in which future messages of the same type work better, at least for a period of time.

Theory recap: 'new politics' versus work on welfare state change

Paul Pierson's 'new politics' framework implies welfare state stability in the face of considerable reform pressures. Mature welfare states have generated their own support, partly through large, self-interested and risk-averse constituencies defending their benefits. However, broader mechanisms of institutional inertia are also invoked to explain why even non-beneficiaries see the status quo as more rational, natural, and even desirable. Several implications seem to follow. For example, fear of electoral punishment makes office-seeking actors think twice before they visibly propagate welfare reform; they prefer to use a menu of blame avoidance techniques to conceal reforms and responsibility for them. Moreover, if it is true that a risk-averse public supports a strongly institutionalized status quo, then a reasonable implication is that citizens are also predisposed against information suggesting that the welfare state is unsustainable. Conversely, one would expect them to be more open to positive messages that, as it were, 'deny' pressures or claim that they are not very severe.

As was discussed in Chapter 3, the new politics framework has been amended and partly questioned in recent research on welfare state change. Significant reforms have occurred (Hemerijck 2013; Beramendi et al. 2015), and to explain these changes, scholars have reassessed the strategies that actors employ to make change electorally feasible. Of course, under the new politics framework, reform is difficult but occasionally possible through blame avoidance. Increasingly, however, there is also evidence of more offensive credit claiming and 'ideational leadership' strategies (Levy 2010; Bonoli and Natali 2012). From this vantage point reform may be electorally feasible if visibly and publicly legitimized. Scholars in this vein demonstrate a number of reoccurring features (Stiller 2010; Elmelund-Præstekær and Emmenegger 2013). One is 'pro-active agenda-setting' of reform pressures. Political actors put reform pressure on the agenda explaining in public why it makes the search for alternatives sensible. Among other things, this allows politicians to make a positive point out of exercising daring leadership and accusing opponents of sweeping problems under the rug. A further feature is legitimization of visible reform using *both* 'cognitive' and 'normative' arguments. Cognitive arguments explain the economic logic behind proposed solutions, that is, why reform alleviates pressure. Normative arguments link solutions to values such as fairness and deservingness (Cox 2001; Schmidt 2002). This stance, too, is different from the archetypal blame avoidance storyline that somebody else or, say, a massive economic crisis *forces* us to do what is 'all bad'. In sum, then, actors are not necessarily afraid to put pressures on the agenda and publicly argue that *choosing* seemingly unpopular reform is both economically sensible and can have a normative pay-off.

We know surprisingly little about how citizens respond to the types of information at the centre of this debate. Most available experimental studies examine how citizens react to different types of exposure to immigration. A reoccurring finding and/or interpretation is that effects exist and are not only due to perceived 'cultural threat', racism, and the like, but also to the notion that immigration is an economic reason to worry about welfare state sustainability (e.g. Bay and Pedersen 2006; Aalberg, Iyengar, and Messing 2012; Bay, Finseraas, and Pedersen 2016; Hjorth 2016; Fietkau and Hansen 2018). Only a handful of experimental studies have considered the impact of reform pressure beyond immigration. Naumann found that experimental subjects in Germany exposed to detailed quantitative facts about demographic pressures become more accepting of a raised retirement age (Naumann 2017). By contrast, Brooks reported that information emphasizing a global economic crisis did not sway welfare support in the USA (Brooks 2011; see also Jerit and Barabas 2006). Kangas, Niemelä, and Varjonen operationalized both 'moral sentiments' and 'factual viewpoints' on costs of administrative social assistance reform in Finland and found that the former especially built reform acceptance (Kangas et al. 2014).

These pioneering studies are valuable. Still, they are limited in two ways. First, most are single-country studies that cannot reveal whether results are context-specific or signal a more universal (in)ability to process sustainability problems. A second limitation is more crucial to our endeavour: these studies generally examine only one category of reform pressure (i.e. population ageing *or* immigration). Thus, we know little about whether effects vary across conceivable ways of framing the message that the welfare state is pressured.

Framing generally means that certain aspects of reality are highlighted, and others ignored, to promote a problem definition (Entman 1993: 52). Moreover, while framing can generate entirely new beliefs it is likely to be more effective when it triggers and strengthens considerations already encountered and rehearsed. However, this cannot happen so frequently that it eliminates competing considerations or crystallizes attitudes completely. Thus, people are seen as ambivalent and malleable, being potentially open to emphasis on competing considerations (Zaller 1992), with attitudes varying depending on which ones are accessible in short-term memory. 'Framing effects', then, occur when changes in emphasis produce opinion change (Chong and Druckman 2007: 104). The reform pressure framing studied in this chapter concerns variation in emphasis on how pressured the welfare state is, and what it is pressured by. The next section presents hypotheses about the nature of and conditions for this phenomenon, drawing especially on the new politics framework and deservingness theory. As it turns out, these frameworks have useful and partly contrasting implications for what the ingredients of successful pressure framing are.

Which pressures matter?

Which specific reform pressure frames are likely to matter? One possibility is that most or all of them matter. Much research has demonstrated that citizens from most social and political groups are 'sociotropically' concerned with the overall health of the economy. This is seen most clearly in research on economic voting, showing that concerns about the entire country's economy matters more than personal pocketbook concerns (for an overview see Lewis-Beck and Stegmaier 2007). Macroeconomic concerns are also widely seen as the ultimate valence issue. While there is disagreement over policy the underlying goal is valued in all social and ideological camps (Stokes 1963). Thus, one might reasonably formulate the baseline prediction that references to cost-inducing reform pressures generally make citizens worried about welfare state sustainability.

H1: Citizens will be more concerned about welfare state sustainability when exposed to reform pressure framing.

This hypothesis is a useful starting point, and one that certainly fits with the broad emphasis on leadership and generally pressure-aware citizens in research on welfare state change. But already at the outset there are reasons to believe things are more complex. We now use the new politics framework and research on deservingness theory to develop more curtailed expectations.

Insights from the new politics framework

The new politics framework assumes that welfare state institutions have built strong support for the status quo. This is partly due to the rise of self-interested constituencies that defend their own benefits and services. Also, the framework relies on institutional theory to explain why the status quo often seems both more rational and normatively desirable beyond immediate beneficiaries. These assumptions suggest limited room for reform pressure framing, particularly among self-interested and status quo-supporting citizens, but also among the many with more generalized support for social protection and redistribution. Such groups are assumed to punish incumbents for unpopular policy changes prompted by reform pressures. By implication, we expect them to resist messages about pressure and sustainability problems, and formulate two hypotheses:

H2: Generalized welfare state support diminishes reform pressure framing effects.

H3: Support for a specific welfare state policy area diminishes framing effects concerning an associated reform pressure.

It may not show at first sight, but new politics assumptions do allow for more effective reform pressure framing of a certain kind. Strong vested interests and normative support for the status quo make blame avoidance strategies necessary for reforming politicians. Of special interest here is the notion that politicians can argue that reform pressure is so massive and ubiquitous that we have 'no choice' but to implement the necessary changes. Probably, the best-documented version of this storyline is that a big economic crisis, with high unemployment-related budgetary strains, perhaps coupled with galloping debt and poor credit ratings of the state, necessitate policies that neither citizens nor decision makers prefer (Kuipers 2006; Starke 2008). But one can also imagine that politicians simultaneously bring up several pressures in a single argument, implying exceedingly strong pressure from multiple angles. In these situations, self-interested and risk-averse citizens may feel it is no longer possible to postpone painful reforms. The distinction between immediate self-interest and vague long-term collective interests (not prioritized by citizens under the new politics framework) becomes smaller. Additionally, broader references to encompassing pressure make it harder to discern which policy/group will suffer. Overall, we hypothesize:

> H4: Reform pressure frames that invoke a larger number of reform pressures, or are otherwise more encompassing and broadly threatening, matter more for perceptions of welfare state sustainability.

In sum, then, the 'new politics' framework implies limited effectiveness for pressure framing. It is likely to be present and effective mainly in areas with weak initial support or when multiple pressures are portrayed as so strong and immediate that obstacles related to self-interest and support for status quo are overcome.

Insights from 'deservingness' theory

Deservingness theory implies a different answer to what increases sensitivity to economic messages about reform pressures. Here, the key to stronger effects is to 'zoom in' on specific pressures that make citizens think about particular undeserving groups (rather than 'zooming out' on general or multiple pressures).

Much past research shows that welfare state-related attitudes are sensitive to perceived deservingness. Deservingness-oriented reasoning is regarded as a deep-seated, perhaps genetic, tendency that is emotionally based, automated, and chronically salient. It is thought to matter as soon as there is any information about deservingness (Slothuus 2007; Petersen et al. 2010; Petersen et al. 2012; van Oorschot, Roosma, and Reeskens 2017b). Deservingness theory is related to a broader class of models suggesting that people evaluate the political world in terms of *social justice* just as much as in terms of personal gain (Tyler et al. 1997). To convey the idea, theorists have used terms like 'dual utility function' (Rothstein 1998), 'contingent consent' (Levi 1997), or 'moral economy' (Mau 2003).

There are at least two general ways for citizens to judge deservingness. The more direct one involves the application of specific deservingness criteria. Van Oorschot distilled five such criteria from a large number of previous studies (van Oorschot 2000). First, people are thought to assess 'control over neediness', where those who cannot help their predicament are more deserving. Second, the greater the 'level of need', the greater the perceived deservingness. Third, identity is thought to matter, that is, mainly needy people who 'belong to us' are 'deserving'. A fourth criterion taps the attitudes of beneficiaries, while a fifth one concerns the reciprocal relationship between benefactors and beneficiaries; the solidarity of the former is thought to be contingent on whether the latter adhere to behavioural norms.

Lacking the facts needed to apply these criteria, citizens can instead use general stereotypes about groups. Van Oorschot finds that Europeans share a common deservingness culture: the old are perceived as the most deserving of public welfare, followed by the sick and disabled, and then the unemployed (van Oorschot 2006). Immigrants are more or less universally seen as the least deserving of all. Our experiment draws on this universal hierarchy. It has implications for reform pressure framing, as some (but not all) reform pressures are implicitly linked to specific groups. This is the case for three of the pressures included as treatments in the experiment. Population ageing, for example, concerns a group universally regarded as 'deserving', whereas the opposite is true for immigration. Pressure emanating from high unemployment/low employment concerns groups that are more mixed and where deservingness is evaluated somewhere in between.

Importantly, we extend deservingness assumptions to also cover economic messages about the welfare state. The idea to be tested is that pressure framing is more effective if information about costs is mixed with cues about which groups are involved, allowing respondents to see mounting economic pressure through a normative deservingness lens. The suspicion is that deservingness provides the key normative ingredient in credit claiming narratives that also incorporates cognitive arguments about economic pressure (Esmark and Schoop 2017; Slothuus 2007). Two psychological mechanisms may be at play here. First, deservingness-related processing is widely seen as affective and automated and so the evaluation about reform pressures themselves may be shaped by a quick 'transfer of affect' preceding, and subsequently shaping, more elaborate thinking about the plausibility of costs. Second, a further mechanism arises from the fact that deservingness criteria themselves are linked to issues of reciprocity, contributions, and even belongingness. Thus, a pressure linked to a less deserving group may seem a more plausible generator of costs, perhaps due to welfare abuse or lack of taxpaying contributions. We formulate the following hypothesis:

> H5: Reform pressure frames associated with groups perceived as 'undeserving' (i.e. immigration/immigrants) elicit stronger effects than pressure associated with 'deserving' groups (i.e. population ageing/the old).

Note that H5 has similarities with H3, which predicts stronger effects with weaker concrete policy support. The overlap arises as policy support correlates with the deservingness perceptions of associated groups. A crucial nuance, however, is that the deservingness perspective predicts the *strongest* impact for very concrete frames that single out specific undeserving groups. New politics assumptions imply at least as strong effects when pressures are big and scary (and hence useful in blame-avoiding and 'no choice' narratives, see H4). From a deservingness viewpoint, by contrast, such encompassing frames should be less effective as they are by definition less clear about groups. Hence, frames that mix many pressures should impact less as it becomes harder to extract deservingness information.

Experiment 1: A three-country experiment

We carried out three identical survey experiments in Germany, Norway, and Sweden. The German experiment was embedded in an online survey of 1860 respondents fielded in April 2015 by Yougov. The sample is a quota sample based on census data about region, age, gender, and education from its pool of volunteers. The Norwegian experiment was embedded in a nationally representative survey of 2,836 respondents carried out in late March 2014 by TNS Gallup. The sample is based on TNS Gallup's pre-recruited panel consisting of 50,000 individuals, an online sample of volunteers originally recruited by random sample from the national register. The Swedish experiment was embedded in the citizen panel of the Laboratory of Opinion Research (LORE), University of Gothenburg, and fielded in early spring 2015 including 3,729 respondents. It uses a non-random quota design as in Germany.[1]

---

[1] We do not have a response rate for Germany and Sweden as the sampling follows the logic of a nuanced quota design without a random component. In a quota sample, respondents in a certain group are recruited until the quota is filled. Non-willing volunteers are not counted towards the quota. For Norway, the response rate was 50.1 per cent.

Experimental design

The treatments were randomly assigned at the individual level.[2] We opera-tionalized five types of pressure: 'the ageing population', 'the high number of people at an employable age not working', two types of immigration ('EU' and 'non-Western'),[3] and the 'financial crisis'. We also developed a frame that included all these pressures (see Table 6.1). Finally, we designed a frame that highlighted the relatively favourable economic situation of these countries with positive implications for the welfare state. This left us with seven treat-ment groups.[4] These are compared to a control group which did, like everyone else, receive an opening statement saying that there is some debate about welfare state costs. This is in itself a weak reminder about reform pressures. The control group, however, did then not receive any additional information telling them what it is specifically that pressures the welfare state or why 'many people' think so. Since all respondents learned that there is some debate about pressures, the experiment becomes a conservative but well-controlled test cap-turing the impact of receiving additional information about specific pressures in various combinations. More exactly, the experiment was embedded in the following question:[5]

There is some debate about [reform pressure, text fragment A] (see Table 6.1) the costs associated with social security systems and public services in [coun-try]. [explanation, text fragment B (see Table 6.1). Thinking ahead 10 years from now, for each of the following social security and public services, where would you place yourself on a scale from 1 to 7, where 1 means that [coun-try] will not be able to afford the present level of social security and public services, and 7 means that [country] will be able to afford to increase the level?

Dependent variable

The dependent variable comes from a subsequent battery on sustainability perceptions in seven policy areas: public health care, old age pensions, sickness

---

[2] In Germany, the random assignment was stratified by region of residence (East/West) with 20 per cent of all individuals in a treatment group living in the East.

[3] We used non-western immigration in Norway and Sweden, and non-European immigration in Germany.

[4] The assignment was random with regard to gender, education, and age.

[5] The question is an adapted version of an item included in the 2008 wave of the European Social Survey.

Table 6.1 Treatments and experimental groups

- EXPERIMENT GROUP 1: 'THE GRAY WAVE'
  - A= how an increasingly aging population affects
  - B= Many people believe that this 'gray wave' generates costs that eventually will make it difficult to maintain the current levels of social security and public services.
- EXPERIMENT GROUP 2: 'TOO FEW PEOPLE WORKING'
  - A= how the high number of people at an employable age who are not working in [country] affects
  - B= Many believe that the high proportion of people on various social benefits generates costs that will eventually make it difficult to maintain the current levels of social security and public services.
- EXPERIMENT GROUP 3: 'HIGH LEVEL OF IMMIGRATION FROM THE EU/EEA'
  - A= how immigration from the EU/EEA area affects
  - B= Many people believe that labour migration from the EU/EEA area generates costs that will eventually make it difficult to maintain the current levels of social security and public services.
- EXPERIMENT GROUP 4: 'HIGH LEVEL OF NON-WESTERN IMMIGRA-TION'
  - A= how non-western immigration affects
  - B= Many people believe that non-western immigration generates costs that will eventually make it difficult to maintain the current levels of social security and public services.
- EXPERIMENT GROUP 5: 'ECONOMIC CRISIS IN EUROPE AND THE WORLD'
  - A= how the deep and prolonged economic crisis in the world and Europe affects
  - B=Many people believe that the economic crisis will also affect [country]'s economy and generate costs that will eventually make it difficult to maintain the current levels of social security and public services.
- EXPERIMENT GROUP 6: 'FAVOURABLE SITUATION' (6A does not contain the last part of the opening sentence in the head question, only the part that comes before the addition)
  - A= how [country]'s favourable economic situation affects the country's opportunities with regard to social security systems and public services
  - b= Many people believe that this favourable economic situation will eventually make it possible to maintain or increase the current levels of social security and public services
- EXPERIMENT GROUP 7: 'ALL REFORM PRESSURES AT ONCE'
  - A= Is blank
  - B= [country] faces a number of challenges that may contribute to increasing these costs and reducing revenues. These challenges include an aging population, and the fact that a large and growing proportion of people at an employable age are not working. In addition, different types of immigration increase, and the world economic crisis affects the [country's] economy. Many people believe that these challenges generate costs that will eventually make it difficult to maintain the current levels of social security and public services.

---

benefits, unemployment benefits, social welfare benefits, elder care, and child-care. These items are combined in an additive 'sustainability index', comprising all these items. Principal component analysis shows that all items load strongly on one underlying factor. Cronbach's Alpha for the index is 0.96, being almost the same across all countries.[6]

Results

Table 6.2 gives an overview of the seven sustainability items and the index. As expected, Norwegians clearly worry the least about welfare state sustainabil-ity. In contrast, Germans are the most worried with Swedes falling exactly in between. The order of countries in terms of levels of worry is the same across policy areas.

We now proceed in two steps to test the five hypotheses. In a first step we investigate the main effects of reform pressure framing, testing H1, H4, and H5; we analyse these experimental effects through simple OLS regressions model with dummies for countries.[7] In a second step we examine modera-tion effects arising from both general welfare state support (H2) and support for government responsibility in specific policy areas associated with a given frame (H3).

Table 6.2 Means for all respondents on the seven sustainability items, and the sustainability index

	Sustainability index	Health	Pensions	Sick pay	Unemployment benefits	Social welfare	Elder care	Child care	N
Norway	30.1	4.7	4.3	4.1	4.0	4.0	4.5	4.6	2754
Sweden	27.2	4.2	3.6	3.8	3.8	3.7	3.9	4.2	3207
Germany	24.3	3.5	3.1	3.6	3.5	3.4	3.3	3.8	1859

Note: See main text for question wording and scale. Explicit 'don't know' answers recoded to the neutral category. Only for respondents who answered all items.

[6] The items varied in the proportion by which respondents indicated 'don't know'. The likelihood of giving an answer other than 'don't know' is unrelated to the revealed attitude. 'Don't know' respondents were recoded to the central category of 4.

[7] We report R^2 values, but as the purpose is to estimate the causal impact of the frames and not a full model to explain the variance of the dependent variable, high R^2 is not the main goal.

Main direct effects on sustainability perceptions

Table 6.3 reports two series of regressions.[8] One shows the impact of receiving any kind of information about a negative pressure, alongside that of the one positive frame. On average, receiving any of the negative frames reduced belief in sustainability by about 0.83 scale points compared to the control group ($p = 0.03$).[9] This effect across the three countries is about 7 per cent of the standard deviation. Interestingly, there is no corresponding positive effect of the largely positive storyline that the welfare state is in good shape despite some talk about costs. Breaking down these results by country yields a further observation: effects are only significant in the two Scandinavian countries; indeed, the p-value of an F-test comparing models with and without experimental variables is highly insignificant at 0.76 in Germany. So overall, hearing about these pressures does so little in Germany that the variation may be due to chance.

Models 5–8 further unpack the effects of negative frames. Already the pooled model 5 suggests considerable variation between treatment groups. The strongest effects, relative to the control group, come from the two immigration-related stimuli. Individuals informed about EU migration pressure are on average 1.36 scale points lower on the sustainability index compared to the control group ($p = 0.005$). Pressure emanating from non-Western (Scandinavian formulation)/non-European (German formulation) has a somewhat stronger estimate of -1.86 ($p = 0.000$). This corresponds to about 16 per cent of the standard deviation. The third biggest effect stems from the 'all pressures' treatment containing all the negative pressures used elsewhere ($b = -.85; p = 0.08$). All other treatments have non-significant effects with population ageing performing the worst, and 'too few working' only approaching significance in the pooled analysis ($b = -.72; p = 0.14$). Consistent with H5, then, the uncovered hierarchy of effects reflects what we know about Europe's deservingness culture (van Oorschot 2006). Effects indeed appear to

---

[8] For the analysis that includes data from all three country surveys, we weigh the data so that each country–time context is equally relevant for the estimates, thus discounting the differences in population size.

[9] Most of our hypotheses are directional, implying that a one-sided significance test would be appropriate rather than the often-reported two-sided tests. However, the multiple comparisons of different treatment groups in a one-short experiment requires adaption of significance levels to multiple testing. Since the number of comparisons differs by our models given a multitude of hypotheses, the calculation of the appropriate levels, for instance, by means of the very conservative Bonferroni method is lengthy. Also, there is considerable disagreement in the literature as to the appropriate methods of adjustment (Shaffer 1995). We thus decided to report the unadjusted p-values of the two-sided tests as a kind of middle ground between the two approaches of multiple testing and one-sided tests of directional hypotheses.

Table 6.3 OLS regression models of the perceived welfare state sustainability index (b-coefficients with p values in brackets)

	(1) Three countries	(2) Germany	(3) Sweden	(4) Norway	(5) Three countries	(6) Germany	(7) Sweden	(8) Norway
Experimental treatment								
Negative pressure frames	-0.83*	0.10	-1.40*	-1.17*				
	[0.03]	[0.89]	[0.03]	[0.05]				
Favourable situation	-0.53	-0.44	-0.77	-0.44				
	[0.27]	[0.63]	[0.36]	[0.57]				
p-value: F-test[a]	0.07	0.76	0.07	0.09				
Experimental treatment (baseline=control group)								
Grey wave					-0.02	0.23	-1.12	0.80
					[0.97]	[0.80]	[0.18]	[0.29]
Too few working					-0.72	-0.380	-1.62	-0.01
					[0.14]	[0.68]	[0.05]	[0.99]
EU Immigration					-1.36*	-0.024	-1.13	-2.98*
					[0.01]	[0.98]	[0.17]	[0.00]
Non-European)/non-Western immigration					-1.86*	-0.48	-1.98*	-3.11*
					[0.00]	[0.60]	[0.02]	[0.00]
Financial crisis					-0.20	0.93	-1.01	-0.54
					[0.68]	[0.31]	[0.23]	[0.48]
Favourable situation					-0.53	-0.44	-0.77	-0.45
					[0.27]	[0.63]	[0.36]	[0.57]
All pressures					-0.85	0.28	-1.51	-1.34
					[0.08]	[0.77]	[0.07]	[0.08]

Continued

Table 6.3 Continued

	(1) Three countries	(2) Germany	(3) Sweden	(4) Norway	(5) Three countries	(6) Germany	(7) Sweden	(8) Norway
F-test[b]					0.001*	0.81	0.40	0.000*
Constant	30.62*	23.83*	28.26*	31.16*	30.61*	23.83*	28.26*	31.15*
	[0.000]	[0.000]	[0.000]	[0.000]	[0.000]	[0.000]	[0.000]	[0.000]
Country dummies (Norway=baseline) and weights	yes	no	no	no	yes	no	no	no
Observations	7820	1859	3207	2754	7820	1859	3207	2754
McFadden R^2	0.049	0.013	0.002	0.004	0.051	0.014	0.003	0.020
Adj. McFadden R^2	0.048	0.010	0.001	0.003	0.050	0.009	0.000	0.017

Notes: [a] p-value of the F-test that all coefficients of broad experimental groups equal to zero.
[b] p-value of the F-test that all coefficients of single experimental groups equal to zero.
All regressions include a control variable indicating whether the value of the dependent variable has been imputed. Models with German data include a control variable for region of residence (West, East). Additional models with extra control variables for gender, income, age, and education do not differ much in the estimated experimental effects. Models that are fitted separately for East and West Germany do not yield statistically significant differences.

depend on whether information about reform pressure 'zooms in' on pressure associated with a particular group, and how deserving that group is regarded to be.

It is interesting that the encompassing pressure frames matter less than the immigration frames. Specifically, the international crisis message is wholly inconsequential while the 'all pressures at once' effect is just under a half and two-thirds, respectively, of the estimates of the immigration frame. These observations are not very consistent with H4, which expects multiple and encompassing reform pressure framing to be especially effective. Note also that the immigration information is part of the 'all pressures' information. Thus, *only* hearing about immigration produces stronger effects than hearing about immigration *as well as* ageing, low employment, and a financial crisis. These observations fit well with deservingness theory in that citizens react more to information that singles out supposedly undeserving groups. They are less consistent with the blame avoidance-inspired notion that citizens are especially sensitive to ubiquitous and overwhelming pressure.

At the same time, the 'all pressures' frame is not wholly inconsequential. Thus, while H4 is not strongly supported, it is also the case that encompassing pressure framing adds something over and above deservingness. Apparently reform pressure framing can play some role even though it is confusing about deservingness (i.e. mixing pressures linked to 'deserving' and 'undeserving' groups, and with some pressures unconnected to groups), at the same time as it is clear and dramatic on the multiple sources of rising welfare state costs.[10]

Breaking down the results by country (models 6 to 8) again reveals no effects in Germany, stronger effects with significant coefficients in Sweden, and the strongest single effects in Norway.[11] The non-Western immigrant treatment has a significant impact in both Scandinavian countries, but is more influential in Norway ($b = -3.11$; $p = 0.000$, whereas $b = -1.98$; $p = 0.02$ in Sweden;). Only in Norway, moreover, does the EU immigration treatment matter ($b = 3.0$; $p = 0.000$). Further, the estimates for 'all pressures' in the two Scandinavian countries are -1.51 and -1.34, respectively, with p-values around 0.07. Finally, only in Sweden do we see an effect of the 'too few working' frame (-1.62; $p = 0.05$). Overall, we can say that Swedish effects are slightly stronger but also more

---

[10] The influential work of Zaller (1992) suggests that political awareness often interacts with information processing. However, we find no interaction effects between reform pressure framing and political awareness (operationalized using an additive index based on political interest (0–3), political discussions (0–3), and political news consumption (0–3)).

[11] Indeed, Norway is the only country where the F-test has a clearly significant p-value, meaning that only in Norway is the statistical model clearly improved by the experimental set-up in its entirety.

dispersed across frames. By contrast, Norwegians react most strongly to immigration with the non-Western frame causing a decline in the belief in long-term sustainability of about 30 per cent of the standard deviation.

To summarize, we have unearthed considerable heterogeneity and limitations in reform pressure framing effects, both across frames and contexts. Contrary to H1, there is little in the way of generally present effects. Instead, H5 receives a good amount of support in that deservingness cues matter. Also, and somewhat consistent with H4, a frame that 'zooms out' and encompasses many pressures at once (but is unclear on 'deservingness') made some impression in two of the three countries.

Finally, it is clear that the results suggest variation not just across frames. There also seem to be interactions between country context and specific frames. The obvious example is the strong immigration effects in Norway, but one can also mention the importance of low employment in Sweden. This last observation about Sweden is underscored by further analyses of specific components of the sustainability index (not shown Table 6.3). While in general the experimental treatments have similar effects on all components of the sustainability index, items related to the labour market behave differently in Sweden. The 'too few working' stimulus affects sustainability perceptions in all policy areas in Sweden, but effects are clearly stronger (and statistically significant) in the two areas most directly linked to this pressure: unemployment benefits (−0.25) and sick pay (−0.28). In Sweden, moreover, sick pay perceptions are affected by reform pressure framing of all kinds. Put differently, *all conditions* impact significantly on Swedes' sustainability perceptions in this particular area. The concluding section will discuss possible explanations and avenues for further research on these discoveries about country-policy area interactions.

Moderated effects?

H2 and H3 predict that people with high levels of welfare state support are less affected. However, we find no support for H2 stating that *general* welfare state support hinders pressure framing. We ran a series of regressions involving interactions between seven treatments and general welfare state support, on the seven policy items and the sustainability index, in two countries.[12] We

---

[12] The moderating variables were only included in the German and Norwegian surveys.

found no significant interactions.[13] Further, H3 states that those with stronger *support for a specific related policy area* are less affected by an associated reform pressure. Here, we ran four regressions for Germany and Norway respectively to check whether support for government responsibility conditions effects. As moderators, we used well-known items on government responsibility to provide a reasonable standard of living for the old, for the unemployed, and for migrants (0 to 10, with higher values indicating more support).[14] Specifically, three items are relevant for four corresponding frames: ensure a reasonable standard of living for the unemployed ('too few working'); ensure a reasonable standard of living for the old ('grey wave'); ensure a reasonable standard of living for immigrants (the two immigration treatments).

We find only some support for H3. F-tests comparing models with and without 'treatment X specific support' interactions suggest no model fit improvement for the population ageing and low employment treatments. However, for the strongest effects in our analysis—that is, those of immigration—we find interactions with support for government responsibility in this area. This provides a modicum of support for H3 in the area where pressure framing matters the most.

Figure 6.1 illustrates marginal effects of the two immigration frames, relative to the control group, in Germany and Norway. The horizontal X-axis represents the moderator variable, that is, support for the government providing a reasonable standard of living for immigrants.

The EU immigration frame is not significantly moderated here as illustrated by a rather flat gradient in the first row both for Germany and Norway. When individuals are confronted with the non-Western immigration frame, however, their reaction is clearly contingent. In Norway, those at scale values 8 to 10 (about one-third of the sample) are not estimated to be significantly affected by the non-Western frame compared to the control group. Those who indicate a value of 0 to 7, however, react significantly. In Germany, we see a similar pattern, although the effect estimates are actually positive for values of the moderator variable of 6 and higher (about 45 per cent of the sample). Only for those with very low support for the government's responsibility for immigrants is the estimated negative effect close to being statistically significant.

---

[13] Detailed results available upon request.
[14] The moderator items were placed after the treatments with varying amounts of survey time between them, but the levels of the moderators were not influenced by the experimental treatment.

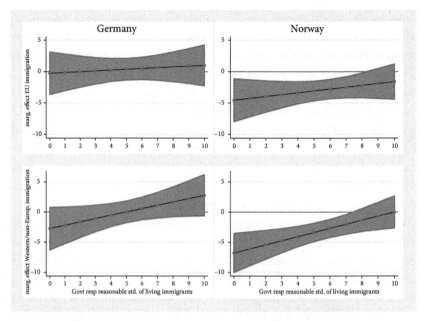

Fig. 6.1 Predicted marginal effects of the EU immigration frame versus control, and non-European/non-Western immigration, across levels of support for government responsibility for providing a reasonable standard of living for immigrants.

Note: The graphs show the point estimates of the marginal effect of the immigration frames compared to the control group at all 11 values of the third variables (government should provide a reasonable standard of living for immigrants). The band stands for the 95 per cent confidence interval.

Conclusion: One or two paths to effective pressure framing?

We conducted an experiment in three countries, testing whether exposure to 'policy-free' welfare state reform pressure frames triggers concern about the long-term financial sustainability of the welfare state. We formulated hypotheses using three bodies of research (i.e. new politics, welfare state change, and deservingness). As explained below, all three have implications that receive some support, at the same time as none of them provides the full story of the empirical results.

Perhaps the best way to summarize is to say that pressure framing has a clear causal potential that is not always realized. In fact, exposure to several major cost-inducing welfare state challenges—most notably population ageing—did *not* make people more worried about sustainability. This observation, together with the fact that most significant coefficients are moderately sized, fits the new politics depiction of welfare states and citizens as change-resistant despite heavy reform pressure. Other observations, however, are less consistent with the implications we teased out of the new politics framework. For example, we found no positive effects of a positive message saying the welfare state is in good shape. So even though 'pressure framers' may struggle to sway the public they may not need to worry about 'pressure deniers' (as could be expected on the assumption that people are biased towards the status quo). Furthermore, we found that whenever 'policy-free' framing matters it usually does so across broad attitudinal groups. Here, the migration frames worked differently with clearer interactions with attitudes towards redistribution to immigrants. But overall, and mostly inconsistent with H2/3, successful 'pressure framers' may not risk indifference, and certainly not backlash, among groups predisposed against their message. Thus, whatever obstacles exist for pressure framing, the results in this chapter would suggest that strong welfare state support will, for the most part, not be one of them. At the same time, we ask the reader to hold the verdict on this matter until Chapter 7. There, we will investigate if interactions with political predispositions grow when frames also include information about policy and the party behind the message.

Some treatments yielded stronger effects. Before getting into detail, the very existence of such effects fits recent work on welfare state change. Here, some scholars observe that welfare reforms have come with open 'ideational leadership'. Others report that citizens have economic perceptions of the welfare state that are rather unrelated to normative support, showing how perceptions moderate electoral punishment for unpopular reform. We add evidence suggesting that citizens are at least in principle perfectly able to draw key conclusions about welfare sustainability from brief reminders about reform pressures. This is consistent with the view that successful pressure framing can at least in principle be part of an explanation for why significant reforms have not triggered electoral punishment despite strong support for status quo.[15]

Crucially, however, effects vary greatly across the negative pressure frames. Consistent with deservingness theory, they elicit stronger effects if pressure is linked to groups generally seen as 'undeserving'. Linking immigration and, to a lesser extent, low employment rates with costs boosts effects compared to population ageing. This hierarchy of effects suggests deservingness theory is also key to understanding *economic* messages about the future of the

---

[15] Of course, our experimental data cannot determine whether this inference to real-world politics is valid. But overall, evidence is mounting that 'new politics'-inspired blame avoidance does not provide the full story behind accelerating welfare state change.

welfare state. Relatedly, it suggests deservingness theory is useful for specifying the normative components of successful ideational leadership, which has increasingly been seen as a factor in welfare state change.

There may, however, be another path to effective pressure framing. Consistent with ideas taken from the new politics framework, we found some impact of a broader stimulus that was dramatic and clear about reform pressure, but confusing about deservingness. Although its effect was clearly weaker compared to immigration frames, this 'all pressures' treatment did play some role in two of three countries. Overall, these results suggest that reform-minded politicians who want to take their case to the public are left with a choice. Either they 'zoom in' on pressures linked to 'undeserving' groups, or they 'zoom out', making messages span a broader mix of multiple challenges.

Two lessons about country variation

We found clear country differences in pressure framing effects. This section identifies two possible explanations that may be examined in future research. They grow directly out of the empirics, but it must be said that they were mostly not theoretically anticipated. We treat them as inductive insights and emphasize that they require future deductive testing.

One lesson concerns the importance of immigration. Our data indicate that especially Norwegian respondents in particular, but also those from Sweden, are more prone than the Germans to react to immigration as a cost-inducing reform pressure. This is consistent with several single-country studies showing that exposure to immigration-related stimuli affects welfare state-related attitudes in Scandinavia (Aalberg et al. 2012; Bay et al. 2016; Hjorth 2016; Fietkau and Hansen 2018). What is more, our results fit with a recent two-country experimental comparison in which Fietkau and Hansen (2018: 17) found that:

> Danes react more strongly to immigrants' educational and qualification background than do Germans. We argue that because of Denmark's larger welfare state and significantly larger social benefit spending, Danes are more afraid that immigration will pose a threat to their universal welfare system. Danes may perceive immigrants as exploiting welfare benefits more than natives and thus as bearing a high economic cost.

In sum, then, current evidence is consistent with an institutional explanation of country variation: citizens in larger and more universal welfare states, whose services and benefits are more generous (and possibly easier to access) are more sensitive to immigration as an alleged reason to worry about welfare state sustainability.

At the same time, our three-country study of multiple reform pressures uncovered a more complex contextual pattern indicative of a second lesson. It seems that effects grow where reform pressures have been recently and massively debated in the public sphere. This 'salience explanation' is consistent with standard assumptions in political psychology where recently activated 'cognitive schemas' are more likely to be applied again than those rarely used. Zaller (1992: 48) drew on this idea in his 'accessibility axiom', stating that 'the more recently a consideration has been called to mind or thought about, the less time it takes to retrieve that consideration or related considerations from memory and bring them to the top of the head for use'. Similarly, scholars working specifically on framing often assume, or find, that people 'embrace the frame they hear most often and that most easily comes to mind' (Chong and Druckman 2007: 104).

One can see the relevance of salience when juxtaposing key results with recent developments in each country. Beginning with Norway, we find that the strongest effects in our data concern both kinds of immigration. This is logical from a salience perspective, given that the populist right had recently entered the government in 2014, and given that an influential government task force had for several years forcefully drawn the attention of policy-making elites, and the wider public, to the welfare–immigration nexus (Brochmann and Grødem 2013; NOU 2011). Importantly, this debate concerned immigration from the EU/EEA as much as it concerned refugee immigration from outside Europe.

Looking to Sweden, the 2006–14 centre-right government's main winning narrative was *arbetslinjen*. The idea was that employment levels were too low to sustain the welfare state and the economy, and that incentive-oriented tax reforms, activation, tightened conditionality, and some retrenchment were needed. Employment issues were highly salient among voters in the 2006 and 2010 elections. The centre-right coalition took over issue ownership in this area (Oscarsson and Holmberg 2013). Because *arbetslinjen* dominated Swedish politics for several years, and because some of the most controversial reforms involved sick pay and unemployment benefits, it is logical that pressure framing effects in Sweden arise for both stimuli and dependent variables related to these topics.

The non-Western immigration frame (but not EU immigration) also matters in Sweden. From a salience perspective this makes sense. In the summer of 2014, the conservative Prime Minister Fredrik Reinfeldt held a massively debated speech, and a press conference, to kick off the election campaign. He forcefully put the increase in refugees after the Syria crisis on the campaign agenda. Although he famously asked his fellow citizens to 'open their hearts' to refugees he also used the occasion to be frank about budgetary implications, arguing there could now be no expansive election promises. In the subsequent election, the populist radical right Sweden Democrats received what was then an eye-popping 13 per cent. The prime minister was widely interpreted as, and often blamed for, pitting immigration against the welfare state and making this a defining campaign feature. Overall, it makes sense that some six months later we find that Swedes are sensitive to pressure framing concerning especially non-western immigration.

The German data threw up little impact and hence fewer clues. At the same time, the largely absent effects in Germany could be explained by declining overall attention to welfare sustainability. This drop might in turn have happened partly because major reforms addressing reform pressure were implemented in an earlier phase. Of course, Germany's Bismarckian social insurance systems, with their emphasis on status maintenance principles, were long seen as impervious to reform. This perception, however, has changed, with public agenda attention at its peak during the *Reformstau* debate of the late 1990s and early 2000s (Palier 2010). This debate eventually produced reforms of pensions, unemployment benefits, and family policy. After that, Zohlnhöfer notes, debates about pressures and reforms declined markedly with subsequent governments being 'unwilling to pursue further some of the reform projects they themselves had embraced ... and talk about a German employment miracle began. This meant that reforms appeared less urgent for the time being, while it would have become particularly difficult to communicate the reforms as necessary and appropriate to the voters' (Zohlnhöfer 2015: 13–14).

The salience perspective has an important implication: reform pressure framers can, as it were, pave the way for their own success. That is, if pressure frames accumulate in a somewhat concentrated period they contribute to an overall context in which further opinion formation on the same topic works smoother. A momentum is created in which pressure awareness builds at the same time as the conditions for future framing effects of the same kind improve. Of course, Chapter 4 suggested that the period around the turn of the millennium saw such a peak in systemic salience of welfare state issues. From the point of view of explaining welfare state change, it is interesting that past research also singles out this period as particularly reform intense (e.g.

Hemerijck 2013). What is more, policy change during this period is partly explained by the salience of, and public discourse about, welfare state issues (Schmidt 2002; Jakobsson and Kumlin 2017). This chapter has added that such discourse triggers not only policy change but also eases the transmission of pressure awareness among citizens.

Of course, as Chapter 4 also made clear, the reform momentum created as welfare state pressures climb the agenda is unlikely to last. Eventually even the most salient issues will wane, in part due to ever-changing 'issue attention cycles' (Downs 1972), or by more sudden and dramatic 'punctuated equilibrium' (Baumgartner et al. 2009). Moreover, such agenda shifts may be especially likely whenever politicians change actual policy in the process (Soss and Schram 2007). In such cases, 'thermostatic' reactions to actual reforms may quickly take citizens back to a more sceptical stance (Soroka and Wlezien 2010; Naumann 2014), thus contributing further to a closing of the reform window that pressure framing initially helped to open.

7

Who Persuades and Who Responds?

Chapter 6 culminated in several generalizations about how and when citizens respond to reform pressure framing. Negative pressure frames were more consequential than 'pressure-denying' messages, especially when connected to 'undeserving' groups and under conditions of 'systemic salience'. Moreover, and despite theoretical reasons to the contrary, effects did not seem variable across broad attitudinal groups.

The Chapter 6 experiment was valuable in that its 'many-pressures, several countries' design allowed progress over the 'one-pressure, one-country' nature of extant research. On the critical side, however, the treatments are somewhat remote from the messages citizens receive in the real world of democratic politics. There, citizens do not respond to variable keywords veiled inside survey questions, but to overt persuasion attempts by identifiable politicians. These represent a political party with an ideological stance and a policy agenda. In this chapter we therefore analyse an experiment from Norway (experiment 2) and one from Germany (experiment 3) with specific stimuli that better capture such realistic features.

More exactly, these experiments introduce three types of realism. First, they increase message complexity. Real-world pressure frames are typically longer and involve nuances, vagueness, and semantic complexity. Do the Chapter 6 generalizations hold for the 'messier' information provided by real-world party politicians? Second, real-world pressure frames quite often provide policy cues about how pressure is to be alleviated. Of course, we found in Chapter 5 that leaders sometimes ignore policy, such that the policy-free messages in Chapter 6 capture a realistic variant. But more often than not, according to our findings, politicians provide policy hints—particularly 'vague improvements' that are hard to oppose, defence of the status quo, or 'social investment' expansion. Most treatments in this chapter hint at such policies whereas others tap more unusual types such as retrenchment. Finally, a third realistic feature is that the treatments clarify which party actually says the welfare state is pressured. This again points to a somewhat artificial feature of

Election Campaigns and Welfare State Change. Staffan Kumlin and Achim Goerres, Oxford University Press.
© Staffan Kumlin and Achim Goerres (2022). DOI: 10.1093/oso/9780198869214.003.0007

Chapter 6, one that it incidentally shares with much past research. As Slothuus and de Vreese (2010: 630) observe, for a long time, framing research ignored political parties as providers of frames and instead focused on the mass media. Meanwhile, political party scholars have showed less interest in subtle framing variations of party messages. Consequently, Slothuus and de Vreese explain:

> [...] we still know very little about how citizens actually react towards much of the everyday political discussion wherein political parties develop and pro-mote issue frames in attempts to win support for their policies. Thus, whereas there is now a widespread understanding of the importance of elite framing to public opinion [...] it has been virtually overlooked what it means that issue frames are sponsored by political parties or partisan candidates.
> (Slothuus and de Vreese 2010: 630)

We follow a number of recent studies that have taken these remarks onboard (e.g. Druckman, Peterson, and Slothuus 2013). Specifically, experiment 2 will use excerpts from Norwegian election manifestoes for alternative tests of most of the pressures studied in Chapter 6. In addition to party cues, most messages introduce hints of the more common and popular policy responses mentioned above, but also in some cases retrenchment and privatization. This helps to reveal consequences of politicians' tendency to 'cherry-pick' less controversial reform for electoral marketing.

Experiment 3, by contrast, was conducted in Germany and concentrates entirely on dual-earner policy as an example of expansive social investment. This issue area gained in systemic salience in the 2000s but did not feature in Chapter 6; as we will discuss, this may have attenuated effects in Germany. Moreover, this experiment compares actor-free treatments with treatments containing political statements (using excerpts from the congress speeches analysed in Chapter 5). Finally, it gauges the impact of Social Democrat and Christian Democrat messages separately, but also the joint impact of major parties simultaneously providing similar frames.

Overall, the results will speak to two broader questions of relevance for the book. First, they illuminate consequences of varying the party behind func-tionally similar narratives. We can thus continue to assess the 'Nixon goes to China' hypothesis discussed in Chapter 3 and partly examined in Chapter 5 (where we saw no evidence that Social Democrats are more frequent 'pres-sure framers'). In this chapter, we assess another facet of the Nixon storyline. Are social democrats more persuasive as pressure framers? We also consider the alternative view that messages are actually more persuasive if they fit with the party's ideological pedigree and 'issue ownership' record (see chapter 3 in Schumacher et al. 2013; Vis 2016).

A second broader theme is *who reacts how* to pressure frames. As we discuss in the next section, frames with clearer party- and policy cues may trigger resistance and counter-arguing among those predisposed against sender/content. Resistance implies that effects are weaker or non-existent among those groups. Counter-arguing goes one step further and implies polarization effects—rather than net negative persuasive effects—such that different groups react in different directions to the same message.

Who reacts how? Resistance and counter-arguing against pressure framing

Notions of contingent reactions to information are as old as political behaviour research.[1] In *The People's Choice* Lazarsfeld, Berelson, and Gaudet (1944) argued that selective psychological mechanisms allow some citizens to withstand persuasion that is inconsistent with their political predispositions. Since then, most successful theories of mass preferences have incorporated some notion of selectiveness and resistance (for an introduction, see Eagly and Chaiken 1993: 595–9). Thus, in the 'Michigan' model '[i]dentification with a party raises a perceptual screen through which the individual tends to see what is favourable to his partisan orientation' (Campbell et al. 1960: 1333). More recently, scholars have emphasized how predispositions such as political values function as 'informational shortcuts' (Popkin 1991; Sniderman, Brody, and Tetlock 1991; McGraw and Hubbard 1996), allowing politically unmotivated citizens to quickly process information. Finally, Zaller (1992: 44) incorporated into his theory the 'axiom' that: '[p]eople tend to resist arguments that are inconsistent with their political predispositions'. Taking a relevant example, a social democratic voter that hears a social democratic leader saying the welfare state is pressured is more likely to buy the message than if a conservative says exactly the same. Taking another example, supporters of general welfare state spending are less likely to accept a pressure frame if it is coupled with retrenchment and privatization, compared with an identical pressure frame that lacks a policy solution.

In recent years, scholars drawing on a framework known as 'motivated reasoning' have taken these ideas one step further. They see predispositions as

---

[1] This section builds on Kumlin (2004, ch. 4).

more than just 'rejection filters' that regulate how strong effects are in a given direction. Individuals predisposed against a message may also counter-argue such that information is cognitively reshaped or even replaced with something that better suits predispositions. This may produce effects in a direction not intended by the messenger or logically motivated by content alone.

These constructivist ideas have long been around in political psychology. Still, the 'empirical pedigree of this classic expectation is even more dubious than the various selectivity hypotheses' (Taber and Lodge 2006: 756). Hence, it will be interesting to see if counter-arguing processes seem to produce polarizing patterns. For example, do pressure frames ever backfire and evoke *less* worry about welfare sustainability among those predisposed against messenger and content (Taber and Lodge 2006)? Taking a reverse example, 'pressure-denying' messages may create *more* sustainability worries among those predisposed against messenger and content.

Crucially, resistance and counter-arguing can only occur if messages convey cues about how a message fits a predisposition. In Zaller's (1992: 44) formulation, 'The key to resistance ... is information concerning the relationship between arguments and predispositions'. Such cueing information is often, but not always, available as partisan information, as well as ideological or policy-related signals (i.e. 'we in party X want more individual freedom and choice'). The upshot is that the conclusion from Chapter 6—that reform pressures themselves are not very divisive—may be incomplete. Pressure framing effects may well be contingent on predispositions if clearer cueing information is provided, as is the case in this chapter.

Which *predispositions* are relevant to analyse? In general, these should be relevant for the treatments as well as be generally known to guide opinion formation in these countries. Quite obviously, we shall assess if party preferences act as a 'perceptual screen' for pressure framing (as messages have clear party senders). But we also examine political values, focusing on two crucial value dimensions that are widely regarded to structure ideological conflict in West European party systems (Kriesi et al. 2012). This means (1) generalized support for government spending and taxation (i.e. 'economic left–right' orientations), and (2) generalized attitudes towards immigration (often seen as tapping a cultural 'authoritarian–libertarian' dimension).[2]

---

[2] The party-political messages tested in this chapter are mostly 'one-sided'. Rather than presenting opposing views from different parties, messages come from 'one party at the time'. This is not because we regard two-sided messages as inconsequential. On the contrary, as Druckman et al. (2013: 57) have demonstrated 'polarisation stimulates partisan motivated reasoning, which in turn generates decision making that relies more on partisan endorsements and less on substantive arguments'. At the same time,

Experiment 2: Is immigration all that makes people in Norway worry about the welfare state?

In order to find suitable and realistic statements about welfare state pressure in Norway we consulted the election manifestoes of the Social Democrats (AP) and the Conservatives (Høyre) at the time of the 2013 Norwegian parliamentary election. As could be expected, given our conclusion that pressure statements are common on campaign agendas, several examples of such messages were found. Table 7.1 displays the ones used in experiment 2. These were selected on the basis that they are (1) close to the substance of the experiment in Chapter 6 that was conducted in three countries while (2) deemed succinct enough such that they could form the basis for survey experiment stimuli.

As can be seen in Table 7.1, the manifestoes offer alternative tests of real-world messages in most areas that we recognize from Chapter 6. Moreover, two pairs of messages capture different parties speaking largely about the same reform pressure: population ageing and immigration/benefit export. Looking more closely at these statements reveals that the social democrats speak about the population ageing challenge in a rather vague fashion, in particular when it comes to intended policy. If anything, there is a hint of expansion ('increased need for manpower'). However, this interpretation rests on the assumption that it is in fact possible to meet this expansion need. If not, then the need for manpower can be read as a backhanded admission that there may be cuts and service deterioration. The conservatives, in contrast, discuss population ageing while clearly emphasizing individual freedom of choice and wanting to

---

Chapter 5 found that public party conflict concerning welfare state pressures and policy solutions is at best moderate, with several aspects being quite similar between the major parties of these countries. It would therefore be somewhat unrealistic to expose citizens to strongly two-sided messages. These would almost certainly reveal stronger partisan and ideological divisions in reaction to treatments but, based on Chapter 5, it arguably becomes especially interesting to expose respondents to mild or no polarization. Thus, in the Norwegian experiment we exposed subjects to one-sided party messages in a context where messages often resemble those championed by other major parties without our intervention. The German experiment, instead operationalizes a depolarized context by having the major parties, quite realistically, saying roughly the same thing to the same subjects. Overall, the interesting question is how much resistance and counter-arguing there is under these arguably realistic circumstances. Finally, note that elite-level polarization is not the only thing that inflates counter-arguing. Scholars also argue that caring about and being knowledgeable about an issue area, matter. Personal importance makes individuals more motivated to 'protect' their priors, whereas knowledge provides them with 'greater ammunition with which to counter-argue incongruent facts, figures, and arguments' (Taber and Lodge 2006: 757). Our goal is not to test all these possible interactions. But there is a link between these variables and our emphasis on systemic salience as we can expect personal salience and knowledge to correlate with systemic salience (which Chapter 4 finds to be high in the political systems under study, albeit with issue variations). Overall, one might depict the empirical setting as one with at best moderate polarization but relatively high salience. These off-setting contextual features make it interesting to examine empirically just how much resistance and counter-arguing there is for welfare state reform pressure framing in these political contexts.

Table 7.1 Treatment groups in experiment 2 in Norway in 2015

SOCIAL DEMOCRATS	CONSERVATIVES
Grey wave	
Arbeiderpartiet has the following statement in its party manifesto: 'The elderly are the major consumers of health and care services in the municipalities. The number of elderly will begin to increase from 2020. We must prepare for changing demographics, and develop new and future-oriented health and care services for the elderly, as well as for others who require good services in the municipalities. In the years to come the need for health and care services will increase, and there will be a great need for manpower in this sector'.	Høyre has the following statement in its party manifesto: 'Our health service will not be sustainable if the development in the scope and extent of lifestyle illnesses continues. The increase in life expectancy and the higher number of young people needing nursing and care requires greater capacity and quality in the nursing and care sector. Enhanced competence and changes in the care service's working methods aim to help more individuals to live at home and to choose their activities themselves. Freedom of choice in care extends individuals' opportunities to run their own lives'.
Immigration and benefit export	
Arbeiderpartiet has the following statement in its party manifesto: 'Persons who earn National Insurance benefits in Norway may be eligible to take these benefits with them when they relocate to another country. With today's relocation flows, it is necessary to take a closer look at whether the regulations are in step with the new reality. In the development of our welfare society, we put more emphasis on services rather than cash transfers. We would also like to link obligations to benefits'.	Høyre has the following statement in its party manifesto: 'New patterns of migration are bringing pressure to bear on today's welfare schemes. Høyre wants to assess whether part of the welfare schemes that are in the form of cash payments today should be replaced by services and new measures. We also want to consider measures that can limit the export of social assistance, but within the frameworks of international agreements that Norway is bound by'.
Too few working	
	Høyre has the following statement in its party manifesto: 'The welfare society rests on our joint work effort. This finances the welfare state. The fact that a large number of people drop completely or partly out of working life—or have never had a job—is a negative trend. We must ensure that those who are able to work do actually work. A stronger focus on work is necessary to ensure the future of the welfare state. Høyre wants to scrutinize current tax and welfare schemes to ensure that they stimulate activity and work—it must pay to work'.

Continued

Table 7.1 *Continued*

SOCIAL DEMOCRATS	CONSERVATIVES
Welfare state as economic advantage	
Arbeiderpartiet has the following statement in its party manifesto: 'A fair distribution of good welfare services contributes to increased productivity. The most developed welfare societies are therefore among the most productive. Giving priority to tax cuts rather than to welfare weakens collective solutions. If fundamental welfare services are made dependent on the market, this may weaken support for the welfare society, because it can undermine the common interest of the people to jointly support collective solutions. We believe that cooperation is a more important prerequisite for development than competition.'	

give some elderly people the opportunity to live at home, receiving home help, presumably instead of institutional care.

Moving to the immigration messages, both parties bring up the specific problem of 'benefit export', whereby Norway sends welfare benefits abroad to former residents and their families although these former residents no longer contribute to the tax base. The issue of benefit export was clearly salient in Norwegian politics in 2014 when these experiments were run. The populist right had entered the government and an influential government-appointed task force had drawn the attention of elites and the public to the welfare–immigration nexus. A cornerstone of the immigration debate concerned European Union/European Economic Area immigration in general, not least the specific possibility of 'social tourism' whereby EU migrants accumulate social rights that must be honoured by Norway after workers and/or families return home (NOU 2011; Brochmann and Grødem 2013).

Certainly, both parties are cautious about how the alleged benefit export is to be addressed. Social democrats want to 'take a closer look' at the problem and, like the Conservatives, emphasize services rather than portable cash benefits for migrant groups. Additionally, the Conservatives will 'consider' limiting the export of social assistance while honouring Norway's commitment to international agreements (among them, surely, the EEA agreement).

Two pressures that featured in Chapter 6 were only coherently addressed by one of the parties. For example, the challenge of 'too few working' motivates the conservatives to propose making tax and welfare schemes ensure that 'it must pay to work'. Also in this case, there is a certain vagueness but it is not far-fetched to read into this message the possibility of lowered benefits and/or tax cuts for the employed. Meanwhile, the social democrats were largely alone in making another argument akin to the positive pressure frame found in Chapter 6, which said that the welfare state is in good economic shape. Here, the social democrats even argue that good welfare services and social equality is also good for the economy.

After having been randomly exposed to one of these treatments, respondents were asked about the extent to which they agreed with the message. This is another realistic feature compared to the previous experiment where respondents were unaware that they were exposed to a survey-embedded message. Respondents then clicked to a battery of survey items prefaced by the head question: 'Here are some further questions about social security systems and public services in Norway. To what extent do you agree or disagree with the following statements'. The first item was: 'In the long term, Norway will not be able to afford the current levels of social security and public services'. Respondents used a 7-point scale, which we reverse so that 1 means agree and 7 disagree, with don't know answers recoded to the midpoint. Thus, higher values denote the perception that the welfare state is more affordable.

Table 7.2 reports an OLS regression analysis where sustainability perceptions were regressed on treatments captured by dummy variables. The reference category is the control group, in which respondents went straight to the survey battery. As far as they go, these simple results are largely consistent with observations made in Chapter 6. Thus, the only treatment with an overall net negative effect is an immigration treatment (the one from the Conservatives). This information increased pessimism by −0.31 on the 7-point scale. In contrast, the population ageing treatments did not trigger sustainability worries at all; in fact, the social democratic ageing statement has a slight and insignificant (0.17; $p = 0.21$) positive effect. We will get back to this tendency. Finally, the results do not lend any support for the 'Nixon goes to China' hypothesis. If anything, the conservatives have the upper hand as pressure framers in that the only net imprint is made by the conservative immigration treatment.

Of course, our focus is not only these net effects but also interactions with predispositions. We start by analysing the role of partisan leanings as tapped by a recall question about voting in the previous election. Does the

Table 7.2 Effects of experiment 2 treatments on perceptions of welfare sustainability in Norway in 2015

Grey wave (conservatives)	0.178
	[0.210]
Grey wave (social democrats)	0.0112
	[0.936]
Too few working (conservatives)	−0.0206
	[0.879]
Welfare state as advantage (social democrats)	−0.0920
	[0.499]
Immigration/benefit export (conservatives)	−0.308*
	[0.023]
Immigration/benefit export (social democrats)	−0.124
	[0.358]
Constant	3.497*
	[0.000]
Observations	2576
R^2	0.005
Adj. R^2	0.003

Notes: In brackets p-value of a two-sided test that coefficient = 0,
*$p \leq .05$.

clear identification of party messengers, and to some extent policy responses, make effects more conditional on party preferences and political orientations? To answer this, we added to the model multiplicative interaction terms between treatments and voting for either of the two major parties in the previous election. Here we are content to graphically display these interactions in Figure 7.1.

A first observation concerns the 'welfare state as economic advantage'. Similar to the 'pressure-denying' frame in Chapter 6, this message does not evoke significant positive reactions. This fits previous conclusions in that messages saying the welfare state is in good economic shape, or else generates economic advantages, do not make much of an impression. Instead, we see again that it is negative, problematizing pressure frames that matter. Crucially however, effects differ across groups. Looking first at those not voting for either party we see that most treatments create greater worries about sustainability, although only the two migration treatments have statistically significant effects (−.52 and −.34). Conservative voters resemble neutrals in their mainly negative reactions. The difference is that they reject the social democratic message about benefit export, while they indeed develop greater sustainability worry when exposed to a comparable message from their own party.

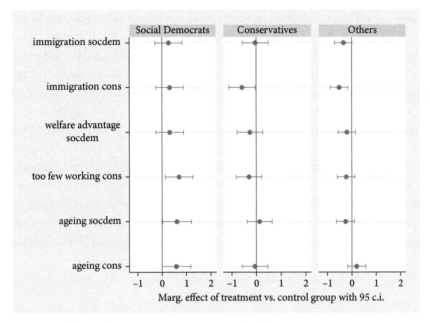

Fig. 7.1 Effects of experiment 2 treatments in different voter groups.

Meanwhile, social democratic voters show clear signs of counter-arguing against pressure framing. For instance, they become *less* worried about sustainability when conservatives tell them 'too few are working' and that this motivates adjusting benefits and taxation to 'make work pay'. This frame even appears to trigger a polarization effect as conservatives and others do become more worried. (These negative effects approach significance when the two groups are collapsed (b = −.23; p = 0.14).

Moving to population ageing, we see again that social democratic voters get *less* worried about sustainability, in this case when conservatives tell them population ageing should motivate more choice and more elderly living by themselves. Here though, there are no effects in any direction in other groups. Finally, it is interesting to note the same backlash when social democratic voters get a similar but more cautious narrative from their own party, stressing ageing and the need for manpower. From this we can infer that counter-arguing is not necessarily only triggered by party cues but also by content. Exactly which content is hard to say here, not least as the social democrat message does not contain much controversial content beyond the idea of population ageing as reform pressure. Perhaps people interpret the seemingly harmless 'need for manpower' negatively as a growing need that will not be met.

As discussed, contingent reactions can arise either because people take cues from trusted actors or because different voter groups hold different substantive values. To assess this, we move on to interactions with generalized welfare state support and support for immigration/immigrants, respectively.[3] As measure of welfare support, we use a question about how to trade-off tax and service cuts against raised taxes and service improvements. Initial analyses show that the ageing treatments had insignificant effects at all levels of this variable. In contrast, two other treatments did indeed interact with such support, namely the conservative 'too few working' frame and the social democratic frame defining 'the welfare state as an economic advantage'. Furthermore, as a measure of immigration attitudes we employ responses to the statement that 'we have enough immigrants and asylum seekers in this country'. Initial analyses show that the effects of both immigrant treatments depend on this variable. Figure 7.2 plots these interactions.

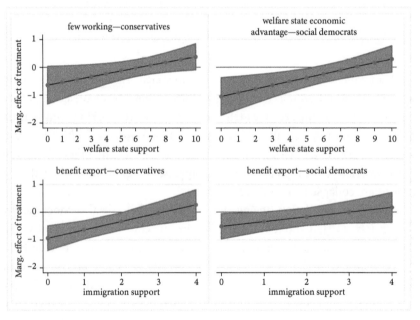

Fig. 7.2 Treatment effects compared to control group and moderating political attitudes.

The band represents the 95-confidence interval.

---

[3] Here, we will no longer pursue interactions with attitudes in specific policy areas. As we saw in Chapter 6 such attitudes did not interact greatly with treatments in the comparative experiment and further analyses (not shown) show that this conclusion also holds here.

The graphs in Figure 7.2 further illustrate how consequences of overt persuasion attempts depend on predispositions. We see statistically insignificant tendencies towards positive effects—that is, worrying less about sustainability at high values of these variables. Conversely, there are corresponding negative effects at low values. Clearly, however, the latter are generally stronger and more statistically significant. The 'too few working' message comes closest to a genuinely polarizing effect: at minimum welfare state support there is a negative effect ($b = -.64$; $p = 0.06$) that gradually turns positive and approaches significance at maximum levels of support ($b = 0.38$; $p = 0.12$).

The social democratic message about the welfare state as an economic advantage displays the most curious pattern. This message arouses no strong positive effect among people who are favourably predisposed towards the welfare state (0.30; $p = 0.22$). At the same time, the message backfires among those who are more in favour of cuts (mid-point and lower; 44 per cent of the sample). Among these groups, hearing social democrats arguing that 'A fair distribution of good welfare services contributes to increased productivity' and that 'the most developed welfare societies are therefore among the most productive' elicits *more* worry about welfare state sustainability. This result further underlines that positive messages that either deny pressure or, as here, suggest the welfare state is an economic advantage, are not received well even in Europe's arguably most affluent and sustainable welfare state.

The immigration treatments again suggest stronger negative rather than positive effects. Thus, suggestions that benefit export pressures the welfare state increase worries among anti-immigrant respondents but elicit no significant positive effect among immigration supporters. Interestingly, the conservative message clearly has a stronger effect, one that is also statistically significant among those on the mid-point. In contrast, a similar social democratic message is only effective in the negative direction among people who are very opposed to immigration.

Experiment 3: Are people in Germany really 'pressure-resistant'?

We now turn to Experiment 3, which was conducted in Germany and focused on a dual-earner policy. This experiment is interesting as it is about expansive social investment. As discussed in Chapter 3, expansive social investment reforms are typically regarded as popular, and Chapters 4–5 showed that political leaders often 'cherry-pick' them for public promotion. We might expect, then, that dual earner policy cues make for an effective type of pressure framing, especially among those predisposed towards welfare state spending.

Another interesting feature is that economic pressure emanating from low female labour participation became systemically salient in Germany throughout the 2000s. The three-country experiment in Chapter 6 suggested that Scandinavian respondents are more susceptible to pressure frames than German ones. We tentatively explained this with the fact that the systemic salience of welfare state issues had remained high in Scandinavia but dropped in Germany for some time in the years preceding the experiment. Relatedly, Chapter 4 showed that the systemic campaign salience of welfare state issues has tended to be high over a long historical period in Scandinavia. This could explain why Scandinavians would engage naturally with, and react more strongly to, reform pressure framing.

But the three-country experiment may have stacked the cards against German effects by ignoring family policy. This area grew important in Germany in the wake of the 'Hartz reforms' in the early 2000s while welfare state salience writ large dropped. During this time, family policy emerged as a domain in which German parties sought new voter groups in an era of accelerated de-alignment. In the second Schröder cabinet (2002–05), Renate Schmidt (SPD) led the ministry of family affairs with a strong emphasis on the reconciliation of family and work. A former president of the German Organisation for Families (*Deutscher Familienverband*) (Blum 2012), Schmidt engaged a host of actors, not least the Employers' Association, to create an alliance around the macroeconomic benefits of reconciliation of children and paid work. Ultimately, however, this process did not result in red-green reform as it was short-circuited by an early 2005 election. Quite unexpectedly, 'In the SPD-CDU grand coalition that then came to power, the CDU grabbed the limelight in tackling the country's inadequate work-family policy regime' (Morgan 2013: 96). Meanwhile, the SPD was perceived to make relatively moderate proposals that still catered to a conventional understanding of family in order not to antagonize traditionalist voters (Morgan 2013; Blome 2014). The CDU sought to 'steal themes—as well as young, urban, and female swing voters—from the SPD, and modernising family policies was one way to achieve this' (Morgan 2013: 97). Crucially, The CDU now led the federal ministry for family affairs through Ursula von der Leyen, an embodiment of expectations for the new role as a career physician and mother of seven. It was under this leadership that a number of pathbreaking dual-earner oriented reforms were enacted by the CDU/CSU/SPD government in 2007–08. Several analysts suggest that it was the CDU that was most successful in visibly taking credit for these changes, thus rapidly building issue ownership in an area where Germany had until recently lagged behind (e.g. Morgan 2013).

This alleged CDU success will serve as an interpretative backdrop as we analyse which party is the most potent pressure framer. There are in fact two reasons to expect a conservative advantage here. On the one hand, a newly gained issue ownership may ease the transmission of reform pressure argumentation. Meanwhile, the situation also resembles the 'Nixon goes to China' scenario in an important sense: while this theory was formulated for retrenchment a similarity arises as the CDU's dynamism deviated from the party's Christian conservative legacy in family policy, instead promoting dual-earners to alleviate reform pressure.

After this initial intense period of reform, the CDU and the SPD (together in a grand coalition after 2013) have gradually adopted similar family policy goals and solutions. As for policy goals, the major objectives of family policy had the families with pre-school children at their focus, seeking to increase fertility, female paid labour participation, as well as household income and so reduce the poverty risks for such families (Rainer et al. 2013b; Rainer et al. 2013a).[4] The by now considerable similarities between the parties will be exploited in several of the experimental treatments that we discuss next.

Table 7.3 contains the treatments of Experiment 3. All respondents (including the control group) were first informed that family policy is currently being discussed in Germany. The treatment groups then differed in what further information they received. It is useful to therefore subdivide the treatments into two further groups.

The first group consists of three 'neutral' messages that do not convey a clear party-political sender; thus, they are akin to the Chapter 6 treatments. Specifically, a first treatment group *only* received some facts about the pressure itself and a suggestion that the situation is problematic. This message resembles the Chapter 6 treatments in the sense that it says nothing about policy. Nonetheless, it is probably the most cognitively demanding pressure information as it contains a series of statistical facts and is rather long. The second treatment contains the same information but adds a sentence on how some politicians favour a certain policy response (expand kindergartens for small children and school pupils). This information is retained in the third treatment, where it is

---

[4] Taking one example, the federal ministry of family affairs commissioned a large report from leading German economics institutes in 2012, asking for an assessment of the more than 150 different family policy programmes in place to determine their effectiveness (Rainer et al. 2013b; Rainer et al. 2013a)

Table 7.3 Treatment groups related to concrete pressures in experiment 3 (family policy) in Germany in 2015

	Text elements in the treatment text							
	A	B	C	D	E	F	G	H
Experimental groups								
Control group	√							
Pressure facts	√	√						
Facts + policy response	√	√	√					
Facts + policy response + CDU sender	√	√	√	√				
Facts + policy response + SPD sender	√	√	√		√			
Facts + policy response + CDU/SPD sender	√	√	√			√		
Facts + policy response + coalition sender	√	√	√				√	
Facts + policy response + no choice	√	√	√					√

Text elements

A   In Germany, there are currently discussions about family policy. We would like to know your thoughts on this political matter.

B   In Germany, women are currently having an average of 1.4 children. To maintain the size of society, 2.1 children would be necessary. At the same time, only 60 % of mothers are in work, of those two thirds part-time, whereas 84 % of all fathers are in work, of those only one twentieth part-time.
Many believe that the low fertility rate and the low labour market participation of mothers represent challenges to the economy.

C   Some politicians say that the childcare services for pre-school and school children have to be expanded.

D   For example, a leading politician of the CDU/CSU once said: 'I know how difficult it is for young parents to balance family and work. In many places, there are long waiting lists for a place in a nursery, with a nanny or in an after-school club (Hort). Therefore, we need better childcare provisions. We are currently already doing a lot to expand services, more than many SPD-run state governments.'

E   For example, a leading politician of the SPD once said: 'The big challenge of the coming years is to invest in all-day childcare. This will help families and will be in the interest of our children. But it will also be good for women in Germany. This is exactly what we want. The others – evidently – do not.'

F   For example, a leading politician of the CDU/CSU once said: 'I know how difficult it is for young parents to balance family and work. In many places, there are long waiting lists for a place in a nursery, with a nanny or in a after-school club (Hort). Therefore, we need better childcare provisions. We are currently already doing a lot to expand services, more than many SPD-run state governments.'
A leading politician of the SPD said about the same topic: 'The big challenge of the coming years is to invest in full-day childcare. This is exactly what we want. The others – evidently – do not.'

G   Some politicians say that the childcare services for pre-school and school children have to be expanded. CDU/CSU and SPD said in a joint statement: 'We want to successively expand all-day services in kindergarten/nurseries. We want to make the 36 months of paternal leave more flexible. We want to make sure that the rules correspond better to the needs of parents.'

H   and that there is no alternative but to make these changes.

also said that a lot of politicians think that there is 'no alternative' to reforming services and benefits for families with children.

In the second group, there are four treatments that add real-world statements from party politicians or political parties. Here, all treatment groups receive the same basic information about pressure and policy response; the varying parts are which political partie(s) are behind the message and the details of their statements. Specifically, three treatments incorporate excerpts from the congress speeches analysed in Chapter 5. Here, we identified the parties but were content to inform respondents that the statements came from a top candidate in said party (the statements were made in election-year congress speeches in 2002 by chancellor Gerhard Schröder and chancellor candidate Edmund Stoiber.). The party-specific messages were given to two groups, while a third group was exposed to both party messages. One interesting feature of these messages is that SPD and CDU largely agreed about pressure and policy responses while also—to our mind realistically—signalling severe conflict through overbidding, each accusing the other of being too defensive and modest. The fourth treatment turns this situation on its head and exposes respondents to a more harmonious joint statement put forward by the grand coalition governing between 2005 and 2009.

After random exposure to one of these treatments, respondents clicked onto a battery of survey items, asking respondents to disagree–agree on a 1–7 scale. Our main interest here lies with three items that tap attitudes towards expansive family policy. These include 'parental leave benefits and the regulations of the parental leave scheme should be more generous, even if it means higher taxes', and 'the coverage of kindergarten/nurseries services, parental leave and parental leave income replacement should all be expanded, even if this means higher taxes', and finally that 'working parents deserve a better provision of kindergarten/nurseries, parental leave and parental leave income replacement'. Here too, we analyse an additive index of the individual's mean response on these three items.[5] The created index has a mean of 4.6, a minimum of 1, and a maximum of 7.

The take-away is simple: there were no significant net effects of any treatments on the dependent variable. Again however, our focus is not so much net effects as the possibility of predisposition-dependent effects. We therefore proceed to analyse the interactive role of partisan leanings.[6] Specifically, Figure 7.3 shows predicted effects based on a regression model with multiplicative

---

[5] We have imputed don't knows with the sub-scale mean. Here, we deleted from the analysis 87 respondents who said don't know to all questions.
[6] This was tapped by a recall question about voting in the previous election.

Table 7.4 Treatment effects on family policy support index (1–7).

	Coef./p-value
Control group	0.000
	[.]
Pressure facts	0.086
	[0.533]
Facts + policy response	0.079
	[0.567]
Facts + policy response + CDU sender	−0.110
	[0.426]
Facts + policy response + SPD sender	−0.001
	[0.995]
Facts + policy response + CDU/SPD sender	0.017
	[0.899]
Facts + policy response + coalition sender	0.001
	[0.996]
Facts + policy response + no choice	−0.087
	[0.527]
Constant	4.571*
	(0.000)
N	1920
R^2	0.002
Adj. R^2	−0.002

Notes: In brackets p-value of a two-sided test that coefficient = 0,
*$p \leq .05$.

interaction terms between treatments and voting for either of the two major parties in the previous election.

The striking finding is that mainly CDU voters are affected. This voter group became significantly more supportive of expansive family policy after reading only facts about female labour market participation and fertility rates, as well as after reading those facts in combination with the notion that Germany has no choice but to expand dual-earner policies. Moreover, comparable effects in this group are achieved (significantly or near-significantly) by several party-political messages. This is marginally truer for messages involving their own party. But the SPD statement also aroused a near-significant effect among CDU voters (leaving, ironically, a weaker impression on SPDs own voters). Overall, while we cannot confirm the 'Nixon goes to China' implication that CDU would have the upper hand as pressure framers, their own voters are especially susceptible almost regardless of the source and nature of the message.

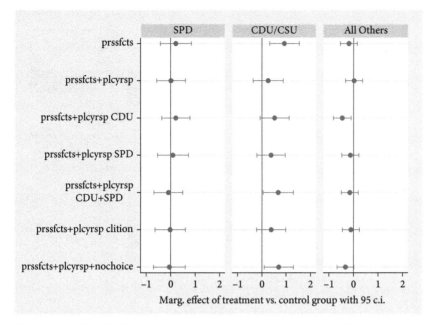

Fig. 7.3 Predicted effects of treatment on attitudes towards family policy
(1–7) moderated by party choice at the previous Bundestag election.
Prssfcts= pressure facts, plcyrsp = policy response, cltion=coalition

What could explain these tendencies among CDU voters? The most plausible explanation, we think, is that the CDU had played a leading symbolic role during the most reform intensive years, such that CDU voters had come to regard this area as owned by, or at least strongly connected with, their own party. Put differently, the notion of expansive family policy as a modern economic strategy for alleviating reform pressure had become a 'cue' for CDU voters telling them that these ideas are compatible with their political predispositions.

Looking at other voter groups reveals little in the way of significant differences. Importantly, there is no impact among SPD voters. However, a couple of treatments appear to have triggered counter-arguing processes among those with no recent history of supporting any of the major parties. There we see falling levels of family policy support as a result of exposure to the CDU message, as well as to a pressure message saying there is 'no alternative' to expansion.

Figure 7.4 shows how treatment effects interact with general welfare state support. Here, most treatments tell a similar story: welfare state supporters increase their policy support somewhat as a result of reform pressure framing

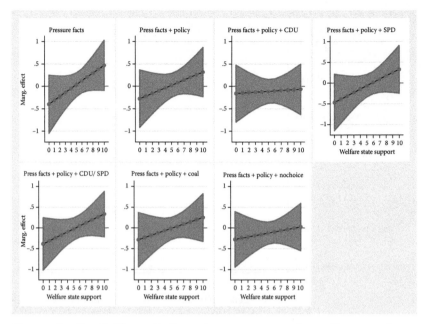

Fig. 7.4 Predicted effects of information treatment moderated by general welfare state support, DV: support for families themselves.

in this area, whereas those prioritizing benefit and tax cuts become somewhat less supportive. Although these effects are surely modest, they are interesting as they reverse the patterns we saw previously in the chapter. There, retrenchment cues made welfare state supporters resist frames whereas welfare state opponents embraced them. Here, the pattern is turned around in an issue area where the implied policy response is expansive.

Conclusions

In this chapter we have analysed two further experiments on reform pressure framing. Unlike Chapter 6, most treatments were real-world political messages from a clearly identified sender and with hints about intended policy. We initially wondered if findings from Chapter 6 would resurface with such realistic treatments. In this regard, experiment 2 from Norway is especially informative as it contained alternative operationalizations in most areas present in Chapter 6. Overall, this second experiment vindicates previous findings whenever comparisons can be made. Importantly, it provides further support that people can process reform pressures, this time by engaging with realistic but at times complex and demanding information.

Going into specifics, we learned once more that a 'positive' pressure frame—this time stating that a generous and egalitarian welfare state is an economic advantage—elicits no positive effects on perceptions of welfare sustainability. Thus, we have one more piece of experimental evidence suggesting that upbeat 'pressure denying' messages are not effective. A further similarity with Chapter 6 is that immigration—now in the form of messages about 'benefit export'—remains the most potent ingredient of pressure framing. Even though benefit export is of marginal importance to Norwegian public finances it evokes broad worries about the future of the welfare state. Meanwhile, population ageing—a reform pressure seen by experts as a crucial fiscal challenge—remains unable to evoke such worries. These differences across pressures fit Chapter 6 and expectations extracted from 'deservingness' theory. Stated generally, there is further evidence that economic pressure immediately linked to groups seen as more undeserving sparks greater worries that the welfare state is not affordable.

These similarities with Chapter 6 indirectly lend further support to the suggestion that pressure framing matters more when the subject is 'systemically salient'. What is more, this chapter has yielded a further observation that underscores this contention. The three-country experiment in Chapter 6, we noted, stacked the cards against German effects by ignoring an area—family policy—that grew systemically salient after the Hartz reforms. This area, then, should be more benevolent to pressure framing effects and the data bear this out. Whereas the Chapter 6 stimuli unearthed almost no impact at all in Germany, the family policy experiment revealed positive effects on reform support among CDU voters. That said, effects are not overwhelming, often barely significant and slightly inconsistent across treatments. Perhaps there are also more generic differences between Scandinavia and Germany even under benevolent systemic salience conditions? If so, this could conceivably be explained by the long-term salience differences across welfare regimes uncovered in Chapter 4.

We also raised two new broad questions. One addressed the consequences of varying the party behind similar frames. Of course, the 'Nixon goes to China' hypothesis suggests social democratic politicians are more persuasive. Against this, one can pit the view that deviations from ideological heritage and established issue ownership breed confusion and suspicion among voters. Overall, our findings lend little support for the Nixon idea. If anything, the results testify to a comparative weakness of social democratic parties in getting pressure framing across; the clearest support here is that Norwegians react less to the social democratic message on benefit export. Then again, similar comparisons for population ageing in Norway and family policy in Germany suggested parties are equally good or poor persuaders. The prudent conclusion is that while the 'Nixon goes to China' hypothesis does not work well its opposite is not strongly supported either.

A second broader question was *who reacts how* to pressure frames. While Chapter 6 surmised that frames had largely similar effects across groups, the conclusion is clearly different in this chapter. Specifically, the messages examined now included party- and policy related 'cues'. Helped by relevant work in political psychology, we expected these cues to structure reactions through resistance or even polarizing counter-arguing.

Starting with party cues, we found as expected that reactions to several statements from identified party messengers were contingent on the respondent's recent voting history. Thus, Norwegian conservative voters are unaffected when social democrats talk about benefit export, but get more worried about sustainability by reading a similar message from their preferred party. We also saw examples of backlash reactions among individuals not supporting the sender: Norwegians voting social democratic become *less* worried about sustainability when conservatives say employment levels pressure the welfare state, making it necessary to adjust taxes and benefits in order to make work pay. Similarly, Germans not favouring any major parties become less supportive of a dual-earner policy when either the CDU or many politicians claim fertility and female labour levels pressure us to spend more.

Several treatments also differed from Chapter 6 by including policy cues. There are several indications that such cues matter. Norwegian social democrats become less worried about welfare sustainability *regardless* of whether their own party or the conservatives imply (in different ways and with different degrees of clarity) that population ageing implies cost containment and even cuts. And German CDU voters embrace most positive dual earner messages, almost regardless of whether the sender is CDU, SPD, or both.

The key observation, however, is that reactions to policy-impregnated frames depend on whether destructive retrenchment/cost containment is on the table. The effects of 'too few working' and 'population ageing' in Norway are instructive examples. These frames had weak and evenly spread effects in their policy-free Chapter 6 versions. But when combined with hints of retrenchment and with a conservative sender we find more contingent patterns. Social democratic voters tend to counter-argue against frames and become *less* worried about sustainability while conservatives, welfare state opponents, and others tend to become more worried (though usually not significantly so). Meanwhile, our German respondents received pressure frames pointing firmly in an expansionary social investment direction. The results showed a consistent (but not quite significant) pattern where if anything it was now welfare supporters who reacted positively to pressure framing.

Overall, this analysis of policy cues suggests that the frequent absence of (controversial) policy in real-world campaign messages previously uncovered does matter. Our results suggest that this absence is likely to produce more acceptance and less division in the electorate compared to a political leadership that is clearer and upfront about (all) the policies reform pressures will likely trigger.

8

Do People Adjust Policy Preferences to Reform Pressures?

In Chapters 6–7 we found that people—at least under certain realistic conditions—seem able to comprehend and react to information about 'reform pressures' by changing their perceptions of welfare sustainability. This is an important finding as we know from past research that such perceptions have political consequences. Giger and Nelson (2013) find that negative perceptions of economic welfare state consequences moderate electoral punishment for unpopular welfare reform such as retrenchment. Citizens who support the welfare state on an abstract level, but who nonetheless worry about troublesome welfare state effects on the economy, are less likely to punish reforming incumbents, compared to welfare supporters who see smaller sustainability problems.

This chapter adds a central element to our knowledge of how sustainability perceptions can have political consequences. We ask if negative perceptions also hurt welfare state support itself? A broadly affirmative answer would mean that such perceptions do more than temper a key electoral expression of policy demands (i.e. electoral punishment). More fundamentally, sustainability perceptions would then appear to reshape policy demands themselves.

As dependent variables, we employ some of the most used and oft-repeated indicators of welfare state support: attitudes to government responsibility in various policy areas, generalized support for redistribution in society, and generalized support for service and tax cuts. As independent variables, we use the overall index of sustainability perceptions familiar from Chapter 6. In terms of the statistical design, we use our panel data collected in Germany and Norway, to estimate cross-lagged panel models. These models allow the estimation of causal paths across time, giving a handle on whether initial sustainability perceptions affect the subsequent development of welfare state support, but also the reciprocal possibility, that is, whether initial welfare support shapes sustainability perceptions. Relatedly, we can study if the effects of perceptions on

Election Campaigns and Welfare State Change. Staffan Kumlin and Achim Goerres, Oxford University Press.
© Staffan Kumlin and Achim Goerres (2022). DOI: 10.1093/oso/9780198869214.003.0008

preferences are attenuated among those more supportive of the welfare state at the outset.

These questions are important for the book's overall research problems concerning welfare state change and democracy. Without any evidence of preference adjustment in the light of sustainability worries, one can more easily question the idea of democratic leadership as a mechanism through which welfare states have been able to change with public consent. Similarly, the notion that welfare state change becomes legitimate through democratic linkage processes becomes more problematic if citizens' prospective policy demands are never adjusted in the light of underlying pressures for change.

The next section sets the scene by discussing past research, after which a number of theoretical issues are considered. These involve, in turn, the psychological processes through which preference adjustments might occur, the types of policy inferences that might be drawn, and finally the role played in these processes by pre-existing policy preferences. We then discuss measurement and statistical modelling, after which it is time for empirical results, and eventually the concluding section.

Preliminary findings in past research

To our knowledge, there are few extant studies drawing on individual-level panel data to study the perception–preference interplay that we are concerned with here. However, a handful of studies have approached the related question of whether increasing real-world reform pressure affects welfare state attitudes. Naumann (2014), for example, studied the relationships between ageing populations, the acceptance of pension reforms, and actual reforms over time. Using a difference-in-difference design and aggregate data from a large number of time points and European countries, he found that Europeans adjusted their retirement age preferences to the new reality produced by population ageing.[1] In a similar vein, Jensen and Naumann (2016), treated the outbreaks of influenza epidemics in Europe as a natural experiment on how increasing pressure on public health care affects its support. A regression discontinuity analysis suggested that average support for public health care decreases in the wake of such events. Importantly, effects were more pronounced and long-lasting among people with a self-designated rightist political ideology. Leftists, largely, did not adjust their preferences.

---

[1] Naumann (2014) also found that after actual policy adjustments of the retirement age, support for further increases has decreased, demonstrating that people also adapt to the new policy environment.

Extant research, then, provides some evidence that growing actual (and presumably perceived) reform pressure generates downward adjustments in demand on specific support for related policies (at least in groups not strongly predisposed against such inferences). Still, we cannot be certain that what we are seeing in these studies is preference adjustment as they do not directly measure perceptions of welfare state sustainability. By implication, these studies (strong as they are on causal inference) have not been able to gauge the reciprocal possibility that existing policy preferences are also a cause of such perceptions. A better assessment of this interplay is one of the chapter's main contributions. More than this, however, there is also reason to develop and nuance the theoretical underpinnings of the subject matter. The following sections do this and present hypotheses concerning the preferences that are most likely to be affected, as well as individual and contextual contingencies of such effects.

Our analysis uses data where both perceptions and preferences are repeatedly measured for the same individuals with intervals of roughly a year. Thus, a year or so later, we can assess if more negative perceptions produced greater deviations from initial preferences in a hypothesized direction. Now, such preference adjustments cannot be taken for granted. For example, social-psychological research on 'cognitive consistency' has long emphasized that people can live with considerable perception–preference inconsistency, especially in situations where perceptions and the problem situation they refer to, are not seen as important (Krosnick 2002) or where there is uncertainty about whether perceptions are true. Moreover, preference adjustment requires an ability to understand policy implications of sweeping societal problems and this cannot be taken for granted. Alternatively, the motivation to engage in preference adjustments may be lacking, such as in cases where the policy preference will likely not be of future psychological or behavioural use (Lavine 2002). In general, then, one can say that this chapter provides a test of whether sustainability perceptions are seen as important and true enough, with clear- and useful-enough policy implications, such that they trigger adjustments in policy demand.

How could the adjustment process work, more precisely? Research in political psychology has often made a useful distinction between 'memory-based' and 'on-line' attitude formation.[2] In memory-based processes, the immediate cause of an attitude is the information about the attitude object that can be remembered at the time of forming the attitude. An attitude is the outcome

---

[2] This section draws on Kumlin (2004: ch. 4).

of the particular mix of *pros and cons* or *likes and dislikes* one can recall when reporting or using an attitude. Hence, policy preferences are not formed before being put to use in, say, an election or when a pollster asks for them. Respondents form preferences 'on the spot' using information that is immediately available in memory (Zaller 1992).

Memory-based models are attractive as they make no heroic assumptions about people's ability to hold many crystallized attitudes, or about their ability to handle large swathes of information. Relatedly, they clarify that almost any attitude can be affected by whatever information people can currently recall. On the downside, for our purposes, these processes operate within the narrow constraints of short-term memory. Thus, a memory-based account of how initial sustainability perceptions affect welfare support a year later would depend on subsequent repetition and reinforcement of the initial perception throughout the one-year process.

The on-line model, by contrast, does not demand of citizens that they store and then recall information at some distant point in time (see Lavine 2002 for an overview). It rather states that citizens immediately update (some) preferences as relevant information is encountered. After this extraction of evaluative content, people forget the information and even the perceptions that caused it. Only the evaluative imprint on preferences lingers on. When a researcher after some time asks why a person holds a certain opinion, she will hardly come to think of long-forgotten information. Still, such information and perceptions have played a role in the past although its political connotation is now gone. This model, then, can explain why we would find a correlation between past perceptions and later attitudes without continuous reinforcement.

The on-line model describes an efficient process through which citizens might learn from potentially large swathes of information. On the downside, for our purposes, the model is likely to be relevant for a small subset of attitudes which the individual is motivated to update. Such attitudes should be of special importance to the individual or have a clear expected future psychological and behavioural relevance.

This discussion has two implications for our undertaking. One has to do with the dependent variables that may be affected. Given that we also wish to capture on-line updating, we are well-advised to include preferences that tap into broader dimensions of persistent psychological and behavioural relevance. In our case, this requirement is fulfilled as we include generalized attitudes towards redistribution as well as attitudes towards immigration. As noted in Chapter 7, these aspects of welfare state policy preferences are intimately related to the two major conflict dimensions that now structure most West European party systems.

The second implication has to do with context. More exactly, both memory-based and online accounts of preference adjustment suggest we are well-advised to continue our analysis of 'systemic salience' entertained elsewhere in the book. Chapters 6 and 7 concluded that 'reform pressure framing' effects depend on pressures having been recently debated in the public sphere. In this chapter, we will entertain the possibility that similar predictions can be made for preference adjustment. In general, one would expect more prefer-ence adjustment in contexts where sustainability issues have been 'systemically salient' throughout the analysed period. Greater political and media attention raises perceived importance and makes perception–preference inconsistency more disturbing to individuals. Meanwhile, memory-based processes become more realistic as complements to on-line processes in that sustainability con-cerns are likely to be more available in short-term memory throughout the examined period.

This basic contextual condition is, we argue, met in both Germany and Norway. In fact, both countries experienced rather dramatic events involv-ing changing welfare state reform pressure and intensified debate about them. Beyond this general characterization, however, the experiences of the two countries were very different.

The German data were collected between April 2015 and April 2016. The former, 2015, was the year of the so-called 'refugee crisis'. The number of migrants who entered Germany, especially from Syria and African countries, rose more per capita than in most other European countries (except Sweden). In total about 900,000 individuals immigrated into Germany in 2015, 27.7 per cent more than in 2014.

In Norway, the data were collected between March 2014 and June 2015. Between the two waves, Norway's exceptional and oil-fuelled economic prospects were negatively and unexpectedly hampered by a sharp and seem-ingly structural drop in oil prices. As discussed by Kumlin and Haugsgjerd (2017), this sparked a significant political and public debate over Norway's general economic future. Most political actors and parties agreed that the economic prospects for Norway had fundamentally changed (but naturally disagreed over the correct policy adjustments). In addition, migration flows increased to Norway, but the major increase was yet to come after the second wave had been completed.

These differences between the countries may affect which preferences citizens adjust. In an overview of research on information processing and public opinion, Lavine (2002: 238) argues that 'the formation of policy attitudes is ... more likely to occur on-line when a policy domain occupies center stage in the political debate'. The underlying mechanisms include a greater likelihood that citizens form a more crystallized attitude that can be updated, but also better practice at extracting evaluative implications of new information for preference dimensions that are salient. This implies somewhat different expectations about which preferences might be adjusted in the two countries. In Germany, with the salience of inflows of migrants, a debate concerning possible negative effects for Germany, and the eventual rise of the radical populist right AfD party, one can expect preference adjustments to be especially present for so-called 'welfare chauvinism' (i.e. attitudes towards migrants' social rights). In Norway, by contrast, rising pressures were of a more diffuse macroeconomic kind and one might thus expect preference adjustments in this period to concern welfare state support more broadly.

Which inferences?

Based on existing studies, the baseline hypothesis is that more negative perceptions of sustainability undermine support for redistribution and government responsibility. If you are worried about the long-term financial viability of the welfare state, you are likely to gradually draw the conclusion that the state should become smaller and less ambitious. We call this the 'retrenchment inference' hypothesis.

Of course, this is not the only possible or logical inference. At least three alternatives exist. For example, we will consider an 'expanded funding' hypothesis, that is, the possibility that support for higher taxation, personal contributions, and fees is also, or even mainly, boosted. Those worried about sustainability then become sterner supporters of raised taxation, fees, and so on, rather than (only) retrenchment. Now, while this is theoretically and logically possible it may still not be plausible. It is only rarely advocated among political elites in these countries except on the radical left. Still, one of the indicators of welfare state support does address a trade-off between raised taxation and retrenchment, thus allowing us to assess this type of reasoning.

Another possibility is that those concerned with poor sustainability have by now begun to draw 'social investment-type' inferences. This would entail a more diversified set of effects weakening some demands (i.e. accepting retrenchment in old social policy) but boosting demands for expansion of human capital generation through childcare, education, and active labour market policy. Thus, worried citizens would become more likely to support retrenchment in old social policy areas, while increasingly supporting priorities inherent in the 'social investment/activation turn' discussed in previous chapters. This inference is given some credibility by the fact that it resembles actual, ongoing welfare reform in Europe, as well as the rhetoric citizens often face (see Chapters 4 and 5). What speaks against it is the complexity and sophistication inherent in the idea that citizens manage to separate between expansion and retrenchment responses along two separate dimensions.

A third and final hypothesis makes continued use of 'deservingness' theory (see Chapter 6). According to a deservingness inference hypothesis, poor perceived sustainability functions as a reason to reinforce the long-standing hierarchy in welfare state support, such that demands weaken more for groups seen as undeserving (i.e. immigrants and the unemployed but not so much for the old). Of course, we found previously that information about different kinds of reform pressures affected sustainability perceptions differently. Reform pressures associated with 'less deserving' groups were more consequential. The extension tested here is that support for redistribution to less 'deserving' groups might be more easily withdrawn in the light of poor perceived economic sustainability.

The role of initial preferences in adjustment processes

The cross-lagged models allow analysis of the causal role of pre-existing policy preferences at the start of the process. Two functions can be distinguished. The first and crudest is that pre-existing preferences affect the subsequent development of sustainability perceptions. People solve cognitive inconsistency by adjusting perceptions to preferences, not the other way around. This phenomenon, often known as 'projection' (see Krosnick 2002, for an overview), involves a rationalization effect whereby, say, welfare state supporters are more likely than others to develop more positive perceptions of sustainability over time. Conversely, welfare state opposition leads to greater worries.

A second and subtler function is that initial welfare state preferences *regulate the impact* of sustainability perceptions on the subsequent development of preferences. There are two variations on this theme. One is that initial preferences moderate the *strength* of preference adjustment. People with, say, stronger initial welfare state support—but who nonetheless see sustainability problems—may handle this inconsistency psychologically by downgrading perceived sustainability problems as less important or more uncertain. This will result in weaker preference adjustments effects at higher levels of initial welfare state support. As discussed, Jensen and Naumann (2016) found support for this possibility in their study of health care pressure and health care support. The other variation on this interactive theme is that pre-existing support even moderates the *nature* of policy inferences. If so, we would find effects running in different directions depending on how initially supportive prior attitudes are. There are multiple possibilities in this scenario. However, given the findings in Chapter 5—where most leading politicians, but especially social democrats, politicized pressures but 'cherry-picked' popular policies—we hypothesize that strong initial welfare supporters who perceive sustainability problems are more prone to social investment inferences, while more strongly resisting retrenchment inferences.

Models, data, and measures

We collected the first wave of panel data in Norway in March–September 2014[3] and the second in April–June 2015. In Germany, the first wave was fielded in March–April 2015, the second in April–May 2016. Panel data, of course, are often called for in research on welfare attitudes but usually hard to come by. They are valuable here for several reasons. One is that they provide insights into the longevity of opinion formation processes involving welfare sustainability perceptions. Since waves were collected roughly one year apart they indicate if such perceptions matter over a longer timespan than the short-term or even instantaneous impact typically gauged in experimental research. Moreover, the fact that we can study the impact of sustainability perceptions at t−1 on subsequent developments in preferences is also significant because perceptions and policy preferences may be correlated for reasons other than citizens having adjusted preferences to perceptions. For example, the correlation may have been generated by long-standing third variables, such as early socialization, that affected both some time ago. By controlling for the dependent variables at t−1 we reduce (but do not eliminate) the threat to causal

---

[3] The relatively long field period was due to a time-consuming effort to collect e-mail addresses by immigrants and to collect a sufficient number of interviews even in the smallest communities.

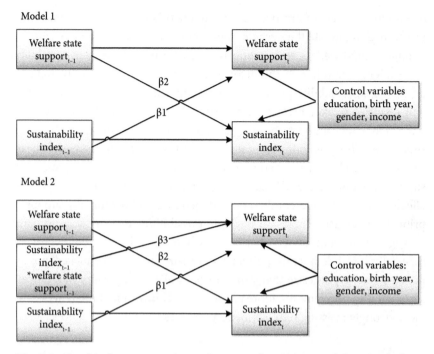

Fig. 8.1 Graphical representations of structural equation models estimated in the chapter.

inference posed by such confounders. Finally, the correlation may be due to reciprocal causality. Here, the data allow us to gauge whether perceptions drive preferences or whether already held preferences drive perceptions (or both).

Figure 8.1 graphically illustrates two different cross-lagged structural equation models that will be estimated. Model 1 is the standard 'cross-lagged' model described by Finkel (1995) and others, containing both welfare state support and the sustainability index, both at timepoint t as well as at t−1. Additionally, each of the equations contain a series of basic socio-economic control variables.[4]

In these models there are two regression coefficients of special interest. $\beta 1$ expresses the impact of initial sustainability perceptions on subsequent welfare state support in the second wave, controlling for initial welfare state support plus control variables. Conversely, $\beta 2$ captures the impact of initial welfare state support on subsequent sustainability perceptions, controlling for initial

---

[4] The parameters of these models were simultaneously estimated using Stata's structural equation 'SEM' command. Finally, in addition to the parameters shown in the simplified graphs, the models also contain residual covariances of error terms at t.

Table 8.1 Sustainability index, means, and standard deviations at two time points in Norway and Germany

	Mean		Standard Deviation	
	t−1	t	t−1	t
Germany	**24.2**	**23.2**	9.9	10.5
Norway	**30.2**	**28.9**	10.0	10.0

Note: t−1 2014 for Norway and t−1 2015 for Germany, t 2015 for Norway and t 2016 for Germany, estimates are based on each cross-section. Changes of means are significant at 0.05.

sustainability perception plus control variables. Model 2 adds a multiplicative interaction term containing initial levels of welfare state support and sustainability perceptions. Its associated coefficient, $\beta 3$, gauges whether the impact of initial sustainability perception on subsequent welfare state support depends on the initial level of welfare state support.

Moving on to measurement, sustainability perceptions are measured by the same index that we used as the dependent variable in Chapter 6.[5] Since the constituent items vary between 1 and 7, the additive index varies between 7 and 49.

Table 8.1 shows the variation of the mean of this index across the two waves and across the two countries. Recall that higher numbers means a perception of more positive sustainability. At both time points, Norwegian residents were on average more convinced of long-term sustainability of their welfare state compared to German residents. In both countries there has been a small decline. Sustainability perceptions declined in Norway from 30.2 to 28.9 compared to a decline from 24.2 to 23.2 in Germany. The negative direction of change is as expected given the two shocks to the welfare state system (the decline in oil price and the 'refugee crisis'). However, the magnitude of these approximate one year changes is not dramatic (roughly 10 per cent of a standard deviation), but still statistically significant. Overall, the modest decline provides non-experimental evidence that sustainability perceptions can respond to rising real-world pressure (of very different kinds) in these two countries.[6]

---

[5] To reiterate, the index is an additive, unweighted sum of sustainability perceptions in seven different areas of welfare state policy (health, social assistance, pensions, childcare, sickness benefits, elder care, and unemployment).

[6] The heterogeneity of attitudes remained fully unchanged in Norway with standard deviations staying put at 10.0. In Germany, the heterogeneity increased slightly from 9.9 to 10.5. This means that the

Dependent variables

We use six dependent variables, all measured on a scale between 0 and 10, where higher values denote more welfare state support. For five out of six items the head question was: 'For each of the following tasks, can you indicate on a scale from 0 to 10 how much responsibility you think the public sector should have?' We use the following specific items:

- Implement measures to reduce income inequality.
- Ensure a reasonable standard of living for the old.
- Ensure sufficient child care services for working parents.
- Ensure a reasonable standard of living for the unemployed.
- Ensure a reasonable standard of living for immigrants.

Finally, we use the following question to measure attitudes towards raising taxation: 'Many social benefits and services are paid out of tax money. If the state had to decide between two alternatives, which should it take? Either raise taxes and spend more money on social benefits or decrease taxes and spend less on social benefits and services? 0 means that the state should cut taxes and spend less on social benefits and services. 10 means that the state should raise taxes and spend more on social benefits. With the numbers in between, you can grade your opinion.'

Table 8.2 shows the variation across time and across countries. Across all five variables and all constellations, individuals support the notion of the state providing a decent standard of living for the old most highly and for the immigrants least, just as studies on deservingness demonstrate (see Chapter 6). Moreover, aggregate support is largely stable. Thus, whereas we saw a certain negative trend in sustainability perceptions, there is no systematic decline in these aspects of more normative welfare state support. These aggregate comparisons may seem to initially call into question the notion of a causal link between sustainability perceptions and normative support. However, what we shall test is whether individuals who initially see sustainability problems are found a year later to be less welfare state supporting than is predicted by their initial support level.

---

perception of a sustainable German welfare state decreased in that one year, but the variance in attitudes increased as well, meaning that the decrease was not equally shared across the full spectrum of values of the scale.

Table 8.2 Aggregate changes in five aspects of welfare state support in Norway 2013–15 and Germany 2015–16

	Mean		Standard deviation	
	t–1	t	t–1	t
state should reduce income differences				
Germany	6.9	7.2	2.8	2.8
Norway	6.0	5.9	2.7	2.9
state should provide decent standard of living for the old				
Germany	8.0	8.1	2.2	2.2
Norway	8.5	8.6	1.7	1.7
state should provide sufficient childcare services				
Germany	7.7	7.8	2.5	2.4
Norway	8.0	7.8	2.2	2.3
state should provide decent standard of living for unemployed				
Germany	6.0	6.2	2.7	2.7
Norway	7.0	7.3	2.3	2.3
state should provide decent standard of living for immigrants				
Germany	5.1	5.0	3.0	3.1
Norway	5.9	6.3	2.8	2.8

Note: estimates are based on all respondents, panellists or not.

Intra-individual stability in perceptions and attitudes

The panel data make it possible to check how stable attitudes are over roughly a year in these two countries. Change within an individual can have at least two very different reasons: the actual latent attitude may have changed, or the measurement of a stable latent attitude may not be very reliable. Be that as it may, it is helpful to look at the levels of intra-individual stability in our data through intra-individual correlations (see Table 8.3).

Starting with sustainability perceptions, the correlation coefficients stand moderately high at 0.48 (Norway) and 0.42 (Germany). Of course, if it stood at 1.0 the later response could be perfectly predicted using the initial response. But this is not the case and we can rather say that there is a relatively high, but certainly not perfect, level of stability. Turning to the five other welfare state support variables, the correlations in both countries are mostly somewhat higher (ranging from 0.39 to 0.62). Thus, most aspects of welfare state support display somewhat more individual-level stability over a one-year period than sustainability perceptions.[7] Overall, having learnt that subsequent welfare state

[7] A descriptively interesting finding is the fact that welfare state support for immigrants in Norway increases at the same time as support for other aspects is more stable in the aggregate.

Table 8.3 Intra-individual correlations on the sustainability index and five attitudes towards the welfare state in Norway 2014–15 and Germany 2015–16

	sustainability index	reduce income diff	Std. living for old age	sufficient childcare services	Std. living for unem- ployed	Std. liv- ing for immigrants
Germany 2016–2015	0.42	0.54	0.39	0.47	0.45	0.53
Norway 2015–2014	0.48	0.62	0.44	0.56	0.56	0.6

Note: estimates based on panellists only.

support responses can only be imperfectly predicted from initial support we now turn to the question of whether individual level change in this regard can actually be explained by initial sustainability perceptions.

Empirical analysis

We start by looking at structural equation estimates of the cross-lagged panel models for Germany (Table 8.4). Looking first at model 1, one sees that initial welfare state sustainability perceptions trigger significant change in three of the six dependent welfare state support variables.

Specifically, such effects are significant for generalized attitudes towards income inequality, the taxation item, as well as for specific government responsibility for immigrants. In all these three cases the coefficients are positively signed such that more upbeat perceptions increase normative support while negative perceptions reduce it. This is consistent with the retrenchment inference prediction discussed previously. The fact that this is also true for the taxation item casts doubt on what we called the 'expanded funding' hypothesis. Likewise, there is little support for the complex social investment inferences whereby some aspects of support may grow stronger in the face of perceived sustainability problems. Rather, all significant coefficients are negative, whereas the insignificant ones concern both old social policy (i.e. support for the unemployed and for the old), as well as new social policy (represented here by the item 'childcare').

The strongest single preference adjustment effect in Germany concerns immigrants. Here, the standardized regression estimate suggests that a one standard deviation reduction in sustainability perception reduces support for

Table 8.4 Model 1, cross-lagged path models of six welfare state support variables, Germany 2016–15

	reduce income differences	std. living old age	sufficient child-care services	std. living unemployed	std. living immigrants	trade-off benefits and taxes
β_1: Sustain. index$_{t-1}$ → Welfare state support$_t$	**0.05** [0.04]	−0.02 [0.40]	0.03 [0.27]	0.03 [0.24]	**0.13** [0.001]	**0.09** [0.0001]
B_2: Welfare state support$_{t-1}$ → Sustain. index$_t$	**0.06** [0.004]	−0.003 [0.92]	**0.05** [0.04]	**0.09** [0.0001]	**0.14** [0.0001]	**0.16** [0.0001]
R^2: Welfare state support$_t$	0.296	0.202	0.229	0.202	0.277	0.293
R^2: Sustain. index$_t$	0.194	0.190	0.192	0.198	0.216	0.212
Overall R^2 of the path model	0.432	0.352	0.376	0.353	0.403	0.417

Note: N = 1412, control variables: education, household income, gender, birth year, p-values in brackets, coefficients highlighted if $p < 0.05$

government responsibility for immigrants by 13 per cent of a standard deviation, over roughly a one-year period. The fact that this is the strongest single effect in Germany is consistent with the 'deservingness inference' hypothesis, under which bleak sustainability views provide a reason to reinforce the long-standing hierarchy in welfare state support, such that support drops more for 'undeserving' groups. Additionally, the finding is also consistent with the suspicion that the systemic salience of migration issues in Germany in 2015 would help to direct preference adjustment processes to this particular area.

So far, then, we do see support for preference adjustment. Importantly however, there is even stronger support for the reverse possibility that people 'project' preferences onto sustainability perceptions over time. This support is stronger in two ways. First, it applies to all but one of the welfare state measures (whereas preference adjustment is significant for half of the tests). Second, for one important case where both processes are at work (the general trade-off between taxes and services) the standardized coefficient for projection is significantly larger (as evidenced by a significant p-value (0.03) for a test comparing models with and without an equality constraint on the two parameters.

Model 2 (Table 8.5) adds information about how preference adjustment varies depending on initial values of the dependent variables. Such interactions are significantly present for three of the six dependent variables. One of these—'support for the unemployed'—is especially interesting in that model 1 showed no significant overall preference adjustment, whereas model 2 reveals adjustment among respondents with low initial support ($b = 0.16$; $p = 0.008$). In contrast, it is insignificant among respondents at the mean and higher. A slightly different interactive pattern is present for support for immigrants and for the tax–service trade-off. For these two dependent variables, preference adjustment again weakens with stronger initial support but is also significant among people at the mean. Overall, these interactions show that strong initial welfare state support blocks subsequent downward adjustment in normative support. Having said this, it is equally important that there is no support for the idea that adjustment effects have different signs in different sub-groups.

Tables 8.6 and 8.7 shows the corresponding structural equation results for Norway. Here, preference adjustments are present for all five dependent variables available in Norway. And for one important variable (generalized support for reducing income differences) the standardized effect is almost three times stronger compared to Germany (0.14 versus 0.05). The direction of adjustment, however, is generally the same such that it is still the 'retrenchment inference' hypothesis that receives support. In other words, those who see greater sustainability problems generally withdraw normative welfare state support, rather than advocate 'improved funding' or 'social investment'-style recalibration. In Norway, moreover, it is hard to discern traces of 'deservingness' inferences as most coefficients are about the same. Instead, as mentioned, we see significant effects on all items and the strongest effects on support for redistribution in general.

The coefficients tapping initial support effects on sustainability perceptions are mostly insignificant. There is one important exception, however, as initial support for government responsibility for immigrants does affect subsequent sustainability perceptions. This is the only case where 'projection' (0.14) dominates over preference adjustment (0.08). In all other cases there is significant preference adjustment without any significant reciprocal effect running in the opposite direction. Moving to model 2, moreover, there is little evidence of the subtler possibility that initial support interacts with preference adjustment. None of multiplicative product terms contributes to model fit. In other words, the preference adjustment effects in Norway are of largely similar magnitude regardless of the initial policy preference.

Table 8.5 Model 2, cross-lagged path models of six welfare state support variables with moderating effect, Germany 2015–16

	reduce income differences	std. living old age	sufficient childcare services	std. living unemployed	std. living immigrants	trade-off benefits and taxes
β_1: Sustain. index$_{t-1}$ → Welfare state support$_t$	**0.13** [0.05]	-0.07 [0.40]	0.14 [0.05]	**0.16** [0.008]	**0.24** [0.0001]	**0.24** [0.0001]
β_2: Welfare state support$_{t-1}$ → Sustain. index$_t$	**0.06** [0.004]	-0.003 [0.92]	**0.05** [0.04]	**0.09** [0.0001]	**0.14** [0.00001]	**0.16** [0.0001]
β_3: Sustain. index$_{t-1}$*welfare state support$_{t-1}$ → Welfare state support$_t$	-0.11 [0.21]	0.06 [0.53]	-0.15 [0.10]	**-0.2** [0.02]	**-0.21** [0.01]	**-0.27** [0.001]
Tabling moderating effects where $p < .05$ marginal effect of sustain t−1						
at Welfare state support$_{t-1}$ = Minimum				**0.16** [0.008]	**0.24** [0.0001]	**0.24** [0.0001]
at Welfare state support$_{t-1}$ = Mean				0.04 [0.126]	**0.13** [0.000]	**0.09** [0.000]
at Welfare state support$_{t-1}$ = Maximum				-0.04 [0.338]	0.03 [0.591]	-0.04 [0.412]

Note: N = 1412, control variables: education, household income, gender, birth year.

Table 8.6 Model 1, Cross-lagged path models of five welfare state support variables, Norway 2014–15

	reduce income differences	std. living old age	sufficient childcare services	std. living unemployed	std. living immigrants
β_1: Sustain. index$_{t-1}$ → Welfare state support$_t$	**0.14** [0.000]	**0.08** [0.002]	**0.09** [0.005]	**0.09** [0.002]	**0.08** [0.04]
β_2: Welfare state support$_{t-1}$ → Sustain. index$_t$	0.04 [0.22]	−0.07 [0.11]	0.03 [0.40]	0.07 [0.05]	**0.14** [0.000]
R^2: Welfare state support$_t$	0.359	0.269	0.296	0.340	0.350
R^2: Sustain. index$_t$	0.248	0.250	0.249	0.251	0.275
Overall R^2 of the path model	0.501	0.446	0.459	0.485	0.501

Note: N = 719, control variables: education, household income, gender, birth year; *p*-value in brackets.

Table 8.7 Model 2, cross-lagged path models of five welfare state support variables with moderating effect, Norway 2014–15

	reduce income differences	std. living old age	sufficient childcare services	std. living unemployed	std. living immigrants
β_1: Sustain. index$_{t-1}$ → Welfare state support$_t$	0.07 [0.42]	−0.01 [0.95]	0.08 [0.41]	0.04 [0.65]	0.03 [0.65]
β_2: Welfare state support$_{t-1}$ → Sustain. index$_t$	0.04 [0.22]	−0.07 [0.11]	0.03 [0.40]	0.07 [0.05]	**0.14** [0.000]
β_3: Sustain. index$_{t-1}$*welfare state support $_{t-1}$ → Welfare state support$_t$	0.12 [0.32]	0.10 [0.52]	0.01 [0.96]	0.08 [0.48]	0.07 [0.49]

Conclusion

In both Germany and Norway, citizens seem to draw policy conclusions based on their perceptions of welfare state sustainability. Whenever such effects are found, they run in the same direction, such that bleaker views of financial sustainability undermine normative welfare state support. Conversely, we find that perceived unsustainability *does not* drive up support for, say, improved funding or for expanded social investment to address perceived problems. This would have been empirically and intellectually possible, but it is not what the data imply.

These findings add some key components and nuances to the rather limited extant research. One is the realization that negative sustainability perceptions do not *only* moderate the electoral expression of stable normative policy demands, as convincingly shown by Giger and Nelson (2013). Sustainability perceptions may *also* affect those demands themselves. A second contribution to past research concerns the reciprocal causation in the relationship between perceptions and preferences. A small number of studies have used convincing causal designs and found that larger reform pressures hamper normative welfare state support (Naumann 2014; Jensen and Naumann 2016). While our results lend further support to this contention they also demonstrate how pre-existing welfare state support can shape the development of perceptions of reform pressures. In Germany, but not in Norway, such 'projection' processes are if anything stronger and more common than preference adjustment. This finding in fact also constitutes a key addition to our own experimental findings from previous chapters. While these suggest that perceptions of sustainability are affected by reform pressure information, we now see that it would be wrong to portray such information as the only potent factor. Pre-existing welfare state support does seem to frequently shape sustainability perceptions, alongside actual information about real-world reform pressures.

There are similarities and differences between the two countries. A fundamental similarity is the very existence of significant preference adjustment effects. As for differences, preference adjustment is more consistently present in Norway at the same time as initial preferences play a smaller causal role. In contrast, in Germany preference adjustment effects are only present for some dependent variables. Also, initial support is more important in Germany in terms of direct projection and in regulating the strength of retrenchment inferences.

The most important country difference, however, is that the targets for preference adjustment vary in ways that are predictable given the context. This suggests that one must theorize contextual factors in order to fully under-stand the nature of preference adjustment. Consistent with theory and results from previous chapters, we suggested that policy conclusions may mainly be drawn for topics that are 'systemically salient'. And while both countries under-went momentous and relevant events that could trigger preference adjustment, throughout the data collection period there were also notable differences cor-responding well with our findings. The German data were collected during the year of the 'refugee crisis'; it thus makes sense that the strongest effect of sustainability perceptions concerns 'welfare chauvinism'. In Norway, the data were collected largely before the refugee crisis, which affected Norway to a comparatively small extent. Instead, between the two waves, Norway's excep-tional oil-fuelled economic prospects were challenged by a drop in oil prices followed by an extended period of significant debate about the country's eco-nomic model. Because these events were of a more general macroeconomic kind it makes sense that preference adjustments in this context involve wel-fare state support more broadly than in Germany. Of course, one cannot draw firm conclusions from only two cases. However, these conclusions are also broadly consistent with those of the previous chapters. Taken together, they suggest that 'systemic campaign salience' has increased over the long haul in Europe's pressured welfare states. What is more, however, such salience affects the nature of democratically relevant political-psychological processes. The concluding chapter will discuss this democratic relevance in greater detail and revisit implications for how we should understand welfare state change.

PART IV
CONCLUSIONS

9

Democracy and Welfare State Change Revisited

The previous chapters have presented a series of investigations into how political leaders publicly debate welfare state reform pressures and reforms in election campaigns, and how citizens respond and draw political conclusions from such debate. Underlying these investigations is the ambition to address two intertwined research problems: how to evaluate representative democracy in an era of fiscal challenges, and how to understand the role of campaign communication in welfare state development. This concluding chapter discusses what the totality of our results implies for these big questions.

We continue to use the notions of democratic 'linkage' and 'leadership' as structuring devices for the discussion. As explained in Chapter 1, these models provide yardsticks of how democracy could and should function as welfare state pressures mount and as policies change. Linkage and leadership also alert us to distinct ways in which election campaigns, and the reactions they evoke among citizens, might help to explain the reform trajectories seen in mature welfare states.

The two upcoming sections will discuss linkage and leadership in overarching terms. We then bring the book to a close by analysing linkage and leadership in the context of two specific mismatches between how campaigns and party-politicians debate welfare state change and how citizens reason about it. The first mismatch concerns how elites and citizens think about reform pressures, and in particular the topic of immigration. A second mismatch relates to how elites and citizens treat welfare reform, in particular the 'social investment/activation' paradigm.

Democratic linkage

Democratic linkage is about the process of forming and translating citizen policy preferences into post-election policy. Political parties present distinct policy platforms, addressing which problems they prioritize and which

Election Campaigns and Welfare State Change. Staffan Kumlin and Achim Goerres, Oxford University Press.
© Staffan Kumlin and Achim Goerres (2022). DOI: 10.1093/oso/9780198869214.003.0009

policies will solve them. Citizens develop 'informed' preferences concerning problems and policies and vote for the party that is closest to them. After the election, parties and governments translate the mandates they have asked for into actual policy.

Does democratic linkage also work in times of growing fiscal challenges and policy changes? The more optimistic voices in the party decline debate outlined in Chapter 2 think so. They argue that even old mass parties have stayed relevant by showing an ability for policy development addressing new societal challenges, while at the same time successfully communicating these to citizens in election campaigns. These positive tendencies are believed to offset negative aspects related to party membership/identification decline, and corroding links with civil society and organized interests. Citizens, according to this upbeat narrative, are able to use the resulting information about pressures and reforms to develop informed policy preferences. After elections, in which citizens have voted for parties matching their well-considered views on pressures and reforms, governments let the policy mandates they asked for in the campaign translate into actual policy.

The linkage model implies an explanation of welfare state change where campaigns and parties have increasingly put reform pressures on the agenda as these have grown severe. Parties have told citizens about the existence of severe pressures and, crucially, about the policy changes they propose to handle those challenges. What is more, the problem/solution packages offered by various parties are distinct, thus allowing 'choice' in an era of challenges and change. Citizens, for their part, use the information they receive to update perceptions about welfare state reform pressures and—crucially under the linkage model—adjust prospective policy preferences.

We investigated three key aspects of this chain of events. We found in Chapter 4 that 'systemic salience', that is, the extent to which welfare state issues dominate campaigns overall, has increased over time. In other words: the party-political attention paid to welfare state issues grew during what most scholars agree was a period of increasingly problematic challenges. This finding does not support the most drastic versions of 'blame avoidance', where political parties are believed to keep uncomfortable challenges off the agenda altogether. On the contrary, according to our data, welfare state issues have neither been hidden away from public sight as pressures grew severe, nor did they surface only in times of exceptional economic crisis, as some blame avoidance theories suggest. Overall, the political systems that we studied appear to have collectively responded to reform pressures by increasing public sphere campaign attention to the welfare state domain. These observations fit well with those that emerged in Chapter 5, where we looked closely at the election-year messages of major parties in Germany, Norway, and Sweden in the first decade of the 2000s. This analysis yielded a similar story in that prime ministerial candidates spend significant shares of election-year congress speeches talking about reform pressures and the welfare state.

Bear in mind some limitations and caveats, however. Not all potential reform pressures have become more salient: the systemic campaign data revealed that population ageing-related themes in particular became more salient in Western Europe (see Green-Pedersen 2019, for a similar finding), whereas the party leader data for our three countries registered much salience of labour market related themes.

Another caveat is that the uncovered agenda shifts were neither linear nor permanent. Europe's welfare states did *not* react to increasing reform pressure from the 1970s and onwards by gradually paying more attention to the welfare state. Rather, it was mainly some 15–20 years into the 'era of permanent austerity' that we saw a marked attention spike appear during the years before and after the turn of millennium. This 'up and down' pattern is not totally consistent with the 'gradual change' framework discussed in Chapter 2, but fits better with the 'punctuated equilibrium' and 'attention cycle' theories discussed in Chapter 4. In addition, it is likely that the severe series of economic crises starting around the end of our empirical window helped to put at least a temporary end to the millennial period of intense attention to welfare state issues.

Nonetheless, our findings with respect to salience are satisfying. Chapter 2 emphasized that systemic salience is an understudied but crucial precondition for most aspects of democratic linkage. The fact that the political systems and actors under study have not hidden serious challenges as pressures have mounted and as policy change has accelerated, may be the single best democratic news reported in this book. And none of this was self-evident, as illustrated by the party decline debate and by influential theories of blame avoidance.

But democratic linkage requires more than issue attention and debate. It also presupposes that citizens get to choose between distinct and coherent platforms, and that these differences are clearly communicated to the citizenry. Our results in this regard testify to some fundamental shortcomings. Take the leader speeches analysed in Chapter 5. Here, as much as one-third of messages about welfare state reform pressures contain no discernible policy directions. Moreover, the analysis revealed only a modest and incomplete left–right structuration of pressure-policy messages. Of course, a traditional left–right programmatic conception is one where the right criticizes the welfare state by politicizing pressures/problems and proposing retrenchment. The left downplays pressures while defending the status quo or even advocating expansion. Empirically, however, we find that both the left- and right-leaning parties politicize welfare state reform pressures to a roughly equal extent. Social Democrats, moreover, are more prone to couple pressures with policy, in particular policy defined as popular in our classification. Rightist parties generally talk as much about pressures but keep their policy cards more tightly pressed to their chests. Whenever they link pressures with policies, they also focus mainly on high-popularity responses, although to a lesser extent than leftist parties. Overall, the uncovered left–right divide is *not* about politicizing pressures (both party families do to a roughly equal extent), *nor* about suggesting contentious and unpopular reform types (neither party family does this despite contributing to such policies, see Jakobsson and Kumlin (2017)). Instead, the communicated left–right division concerns the extent to which pressures are at all coupled with (popular) policy. The caveat here, of course, is that we have focused on the two major party families. While this is a limitation, Chapter 1 also emphasized that these parties are especially interesting as they provide citizens with the two main ideological centres of gravity for the governments that are likely to form after elections. Thus, they are arguably the most important (but not the only) providers of democratic choice and linkage.

Chapter 5 also analysed more abstract and ideological 'normative cues' as an additional vehicle for communicating party differences. Such cues, which signal desired end states and outcomes of welfare state policies, were very present in our data. Nonetheless, they seem to mostly fall short of communicating the clear choice that democratic linkage envisions. The few cues that were both common and divisive across parties tended to be unspecific and universally appreciated constructs such as 'justice and fairness'. Most other normative signals were either uncommon or used by both leftist and rightist leaders. Consistent with these results, Chapter 4 detected no increase over time in the systemic salience of abstract and ideological campaign themes, despite the rise in attention to welfare state issues writ large.

Perhaps clearly communicated party differences exist but no longer follow traditional left–right programmatic patterns. This is a real possibility given that a fragmented landscape of multiple reform pressures and multidimensional reform polices has emerged. In this potentially bewildering environment, parties may increasingly promote concrete and particularistic pressure–policy combinations, with parties stressing specific solutions to specific problems. Actually, Chapter 2 discussed two models for such competition.

First, under 'issue ownership' conflict parties put specific problems on the agenda where they are perceived as competent (while remaining largely silent on policy). That as much as one-third of party messages about reform pressures come without discernible policy supports the issue ownership model. However, the fact that we also find negligible party differences in the extent of reform pressure talk suggests a further way in which parties seem to fail to communicate a clear choice.

The other model of particularistic competition grew out of the 'multiple streams' framework associated with Kingdon (2011 [1984]). From this vantage point, real-world reform pressures only enter the agenda once 'coupled' with a new policy idea that can credibly solve problems and be marketed electorally. This model is attractive as it seems also to secure information about the actual policy solutions to problems. A potential drawback discussed in Chapter 2, however, receives clear support from our data: the menu of policy choice may be severely restricted if parties focus on a similar set of popular policy ideas. Towards the end of this chapter, we discuss the special role played in this regard by the social investment–activation paradigm.

The third aspect of democratic linkage examined concerns citizens. The optimistic voices in the party decline debate argue that political representation remains effective, partly because political parties engage in policy development, that is, adjust their problem–policy packages to new societal problems. Crucially, they manage to communicate their stances to citizens who are assumed to learn from the information and develop 'informed' preferences. This is in turn what allows people to choose between distinct party platforms in an era of significant pressure and policy change.

Several findings suggest that citizens can indeed perform the key 'tasks' necessary for maintained linkage in an era of rapid welfare state change. We found, for example, that citizens can adjust perceptions of welfare sustainability in light of reform pressure information. This seems to happen especially under conditions of systemic salience (a more common condition over time). Interestingly, Chapter 6 reported that this also happens for information that lacks policy cues. In other words, policy-free issue ownership style messages can affect citizens.

Moreover, while people respond to negative pressures, they seem resistant to 'pressure-denying' messages saying that welfare pressures are negligible. This suggests a capacity for differentiation. If we are willing to assume that pressures are in fact objectively speaking mostly negative (cf. Vis and van Kersbergen 2013; van Kersbergen and Vis 2014), then the uncovered pattern of reaction among citizens would seem to qualify as objectively 'informed'. Put differently, there is no evidence in our data that you can fool citizens by telling them that the welfare state is not under pressure. A caveat here—one that we shall return to later—is that citizens may still be disproportionally impressed by minor pressures associated with 'undeserving' groups. Judging from experimental results in Chapters 6 and 7, we find this to be especially true for messages saying that immigration pressures the welfare state.

In Chapter 8, we concluded that people also adjust policy preferences to perceived sustainability problems. We hasten to add, however, that there were several instances of reciprocal causation: weaker initial welfare state support also fosters more negative sustainability perceptions over time. Still, the interesting point is that such well-documented 'projection' coexists with genuine preference adjustment. It would be hard to explain welfare state change in terms of democratic linkage if there were no trace of policy preference adjustment to pressures among citizens.

An important qualification here is that preference adjustment is in itself not highly differentiated. Effects on normative support, whenever found, always seem to be negative such that bleaker views of sustainability undermine normative welfare support. The fact that we did *not* find more complex adjustment patterns involving both support for retrenchment and the new social investment/activation paradigm is discussed separately towards the end of this chapter.

In conclusion, how should we assess democratic linkage in an era of welfare state pressures and transformations? Certainly, we have uncovered several positive findings. The agendas of party systems and political parties have responded in several ways to welfare state challenges such that overall attention to welfare state issues and pressures has risen. This is a precondition for most aspects of linkage and representation, including informed preference formation, issue voting, and mass–elite congruence in opinions and in policy. Equally important, citizens appear perfectly able to respond to information about reform pressures. More than this, they manage to update their policy preferences after having heard that the welfare state is under pressure.

These positive aspects notwithstanding, we would still argue that the totality of our findings have sobering implications for how we think about the quality of democratic linkage. The 'linkage' metaphor is instructive here as it evokes the notion of a chain of related aspects that must all function for the overall system to perform. And a chain, according to the cliché, is never stronger than its weakest link. The weak link exposed in this book concerns the distinctiveness and coherence in the democratic choice communicated to voters in campaigns.

Now, we are not making the simplistic assertion that there are no differences anymore between parties in ideology or policy. Quite clearly, recent research theorizes and finds systematic party differences in both old and new social policy, and also between the old and large mass parties under study here (Beramendi et al. 2015; Huber and Stephens 2015; Manow et al. 2018). Our point, however, is to emphasize the difficulties parties seem to experience in clearly communicating distinct differences to voters in a complex landscape of multiple reform pressures and multidimensional reform. Certainly, one should bear in mind that our data have limitations concerning the period, parties, and countries covered. Bearing such caveats in mind, however, we would not feel justified in concluding that campaign information has secured the democratic legitimacy of welfare state change through a mandate given by citizens faced with coherent democratic choice. Welfare states are certainly changing but it remains to be proven that this is because parties, in election campaigns, have allowed citizens to fully choose one trajectory of change over the other.

Democratic leadership

The notion of democratic leadership entails courageous and honest leaders who defend potentially unpopular but sensible policies that are—so far as leaders can judge—in the interests of voters. Importantly, leaders argue their case in public, explaining to citizens' why their first preferences are not necessarily the most sensible ones. Citizens, for their part, are at least in principle and on occasion willing and able to accept such messages, that is, adjusting their views to become more congruous with those of the leaders. In cases where explanations fail to convince, democracy is ensured as voters can hold leaders to account in elections. Overall, democratic leadership and its impact on the public can allow even unpopular policy change, where parties did not allow much choice, to become more democratically legitimate.

Some have even suggested that top-down democratic legitimization will become ever more important in tandem with party decline in democratic linkage. Chapter 3 described how comparative welfare state scholarship has also moved towards a similar position. Before the accelerating and multidimensional policy changes of recent decades, much of the literature was focused on explaining policy stability with institutional theories and defensive communicative concepts such as 'blame avoidance'. Faced with increasing flux, however, scholars have developed theories that in effect put more emphasis on communicative legitimation using concepts such as 'credit-claiming' (see Bonoli and Natali 2012) and 'ideational leadership' (see Stiller 2010).

Before assessing these newer ideas, it is useful to recall that also institutional theory itself has evolved to better account for policy change. The book's findings also have relevance for these dynamic versions of institutional theory. For example, Chapter 4 made observations relevant for the 'gradual institutional change' framework (see Streeck and Thelen 2005). Under this model, welfare state change is a piecemeal and hardly perceptible—but eventually significant—'liberalization' of advanced political economies. Moreover, scholars in this tradition assign a limited or reactive role to electoral democracy in general and to public sphere communication in particular. Sweeping liberalization occurs largely under the radar of electoral democracy.

Empirical observations made in Chapter 4, however, suggested such explanations may not suffice. The data were more consistent with 'punctuated equilibrium' theory. This framework explains why long-standing reform pressures will—eventually—result in a 'late but large' outburst of time-limited political agenda attention. Moreover, our data suggest that the issue content of the attention outburst starting towards the end of the 1990s was not dominated by destructive liberalization, retrenchment, and similar reform types. If anything, it was dominated by expansive policies that we and others have defined as popular reform types. Many of them were related to the social investment/activation paradigm, which increasingly complemented retrenchment as the main reform trajectory during the period we investigated. If we also consider research showing that campaign attention triggers actual policy change (Schmidt 2002; Jakobsson and Kumlin 2017) it becomes hard to portray welfare state development as an entirely gradual and secretive process of liberalization. Rather, our findings testify to the importance of public sphere campaigns, and the role these have had in steering policy changes into a more multidimensional reform landscape where liberalization and retrenchment are not the only components.

Our evidence is more affirmative, though still mixed, for a second institutionalist theory of welfare state development discussed in Chapter 3, that is, Pierson's (1996, 2001) 'new politics' framework. On the one hand, our findings on party differences and linkage discussed above are consistent with new politics predictions concerning party depolarization. Having said this, we find no evidence of Ross's (2000a) more radical spin-off prediction. Her 'Nixon goes to China' hypothesis suggests that the left has greater leeway in politicizing pressures and, in particular, unpopular policy like retrenchment. What Chapter 5 found, however, was rather that while reform pressures are slightly more often discussed by social democrats these parties also remain more silent about the most painful reforms. Neither did Chapter 7 support the 'Nixon' implication that social democratic politicians are especially persuasive in their reform pressure talk. The experimental treatments mostly showed that the two major party families under study are equally good/poor persuaders. Overall then, our data seem inconsistent with the 'Nixon goes to China' claim that communicative blame avoidance is more prevalent and necessary on the path to success on the right.

We would rather conclude that blame avoidance remains important in voter communication among both the major party families studied in this book. The devil is in the details, however, and several reasonable blame avoidance permutations were not found throughout Chapters 4 and 5. There is little evidence for the 'agenda-controlling' strategy of hiding problems away from public sight altogether; again, welfare issues—including the specific politicization of uncomfortable pressures—register clearly both as systemic campaign themes and in leader speeches. Similarly, these chapters unearthed little support for the idea of crisis as a catalyst for blame avoiding 'no choice' excuses. Reform pressure talk became only marginally more widespread after the financial crisis and often concerns diffuse long-term pressures less suitable for arguing that we have no choice here and now. Above all, we found significant attention to welfare state challenges in Germany, Norway, and Sweden, countries that are among Europe's affluent and less challenged welfare states. Overall, it does not seem to take a massive crisis, nor unusually severe pressures, to spark election campaign attention to welfare state issues.

Instead, blame avoidance manifests itself in subtler ways. Throughout Chapters 4 and 5 we saw clear evidence of 'cherry-picking' of more popular policy solutions to reform pressures. Both systemic agendas of entire campaigns, as well as specific messages from prime ministerial candidates, appear lopsided in this regard. According to our findings, politicians often propose social investment and 'enabling' active labour market policy. They also frequently defend the status quo, propose expansion, or hint vaguely at some sort of 'improvements' that will happen despite reform pressure. Rarely do prime ministerial candidates speak plainly about less popular retrenchment or punitive and demanding activation, although these policy directions have also shaped reform in the studied countries. In important ways, then, politicians cherry-pick politically marketable policy responses from a complex and at least partly unpopular menu of actual, ongoing reform. More than this, Chapter 4 found that this imbalance may have become more pronounced. Chapter 5 added the finding that cherry-picking becomes more common as leader speeches emphasize reform pressures more. These tendencies do not reflect well on democratic leadership in an era of growing reform pressures in western welfare states.

Relatedly, our findings do not fit perfectly with explanations of welfare state change that emphasize how innovative 'ideas' are communicated to the public by 'ideational leaders' (Stiller 2010). This is not to say that these theories are without merit. Citizens have, after all, been exposed to debate over significant reform pressures, and they appear able to use this arguably limited information. In fact, the implication of the Chapter 6 experiment and the panel analysis in Chapter 8 is that citizens can partly 'connect the dots' themselves even when not informed about policy. We find that even policy-free pressure frames can leave an imprint on sustainability perceptions, which in turn trigger policy conclusions. Overall, some of the processes inherent to democratic leadership appear to be in place.

Nevertheless, Chapter 5 concluded that democratic leadership is at best 'half-baked'. It reported that about one-third of welfare pressure talk is not linked with *any* discernible policy. The remaining two-thirds expose citizens to the more popular aspects of welfare reform. In conclusion, then, while some aspects of democratic leadership processes are evident, the courageous leaders themselves—who supposedly champion tough but sensible polices—did not show up in our data.

Discrepancies between politicians and citizens in reasoning about pressures and reforms

We bring this book to a close by discussing two specific but important mismatches between how party politicians debate welfare state change and how citizens reason about it. These mismatches are relevant for, but not necessarily anticipated by, general theories of representative democracy. Neither are they well-accounted for by current welfare state scholarship. We discovered them as our research evolved and as our data gradually offered better opportunities to juxtapose findings on campaign contents and citizen reactions.

Immigration and the mismatch in how elites and citizens reason about pressures

A striking result from our experiments concerns the relative dominance of immigration-related pressure frames. In brief, Chapter 6 found that the

strongest negative effects on welfare state sustainability perceptions were triggered by suggestions that various immigration types create 'costs that will
make it difficult to maintain current levels of social security and public services'. Importantly, we also found country variation in the size and nature of
the effects, which appeared to follow patterns of systemic salience in country
contexts.

These patterns were hitherto largely unknown as past experimental research
rarely examined more than one reform pressure at a time. Moreover, they
become especially striking once juxtaposed with the relative emphasis of mainstream politicians. Chapter 5 reported that parties put less emphasis on immigration and globalization as reform pressures, compared to general economic
challenges related to (un)employment, the macroeconomy, and work–family
pressure. Overall, we seem to have uncovered a 'mismatch' between the pressures mainstream parties emphasize and the pressure information citizens are
most prone to react to. Whereas immigration-related pressures stand out in
their ability to evoke sustainability concerns among citizens, these pressures
are, at best, one of many secondary pressures for mainstream parties. It is hard
not to see this mismatch as a symptom of suboptimal democratic leadership
on the part of the major mainstream parties. Despite the very significant rise
in attention to welfare state issues (and pressures) major parties to the left and
right have apparently not conveyed their sense of proportion when comparing
welfare state challenges.

This mismatch, once it exists, creates a strategic dilemma for mainstream
parties in terms of how welfare reform is marketed. This dilemma may work
to the advantage of the populist right. Overall, our results suggest that reform-
minded politicians who want to take their case to the public are left with a
choice. The can either 'zoom in' on pressures linked to 'undeserving' groups, in
particular immigration or, alternatively, Chapter 6 found some evidence that
they can 'zoom out', making messages span a broad mix of multiple challenges.
The choice is not entirely easy. Especially when it comes to stressing immigration, there are obvious ideological and political obstacles for most party
families. Indeed, in some countries, only populist right parties are comfort-
able with making this connection. Immigration treatments were also the most
divisive ones in our experiments, even when frames lacked any policy and
party cues. Then again, our results also suggest that mainstream politicians
who do not want to play the immigration card, or are unable to formulate a
'deservingness-based' narrative, can still zoom out and formulate encompassing messages about multiple economic pressures. This may be palatable for
most party families in most democracies, and to some extent it is what the

parties under study here opt for in their messaging. However, judging from our results, this message is likely to make a weaker, if any, imprint. More research is needed here, however. As Chapter 6 explained, we tested only one possible permutation of the message that the welfare state is under multiple pressures.

A final implication concerns the 'informed' preferences assumed by democratic linkage models. Defining and measuring this concept is notoriously tricky. Nonetheless, Chapter 2 identified two possible perspectives. The 'objectivist/expert-driven' perspective is that preferences are informed if they comply with and are logically responsive to objective truths or at least totally consensual expert views. The 'subjective/deliberative' view is rather that informed preferences are secured through exposure to a procedurally legitimate information flow; it refers to whatever perceptions and preferences people develop with such exposure.

Is the disproportionate responsiveness of citizens to reform pressure linked to 'undeserving' groups, and to immigration in particular, a problem for these notions of informed preferences? As for the subjectivist notion, this book has little direct evidence to offer, as we have not studied the consequences of 'deliberation' or other types of procedurally legitimate information flows. Still, a small body of research raises serious questions to be answered in future work. In the USA, Gilens (1999) and others have shown that low support for welfare is rooted in exaggerated but adjustable misperceptions of the number of African Americans among welfare recipients (see Geiger 2018 for related results in the UK). A Swedish study used survey experiments as well as specific information about real-world TV campaign exposure and panel data (Kumlin 2014). Results showed that 'expert facts' about welfare state performance, as well as extensive exposure to political debate over these facts, more often than not generate meaningful adjustments in general evaluations of welfare state performance over time. Finally, Naumann (2017) found that Germans exposed to detailed facts about population ageing pressures are more prone to accept a raised retirement age. The totality of these findings raises key questions that have not been answered fully in this book: would citizens subjectively downplay the severity of immigration, and upgrade the severity of population ageing, after more intensive and procedurally balanced information?

From an objectivist perspective there may be other types of friction with the ideal of informed preferences. Take our findings for Norway as an example: here, population ageing elicited no—or in some cases even positive—consequences for sustainability worries. In contrast, immigration-related pressure information is almost the only thing that makes Norwegians worry about welfare sustainability, evoking the single strongest effects found anywhere. Meanwhile, questions can be raised as to whether citizens have got their proportions right. Certainly, leading experts in Norway emphasize, based on forecast calculations made by Statistics Norway, that population ageing and adjustments to lower oil prices are a significantly more severe fiscal pressure than immigration (NOU 2017: ch. 8). Compared with the objective pressures, citizens may subjectively be most reactive to the wrong pressures.

We do not possess special expertise or data allowing us to act as arbiters here. What we can say, based on our results, is that to regard the proportions citizens give to different reform pressures as 'objectively informed' one must likely argue that immigration is the most formidable fiscal reform pressure.

Social investment and the mismatch between how elites and citizens think about reforms

Throughout this book we emphasized that welfare reform is no longer a unidimensional conflict between the status quo and destructive retrenchment (Bonoli and Natali 2012; Häusermann 2012). Recent years have seen an ideational shift where parties, organizations, and experts embraced the notion of a social investment oriented welfare state. Concrete policy examples include expansive dual earner reforms and active labour market policies. This shift has made the welfare reform menu longer, less exclusively destructive, and seemingly more popular. Furthermore, the conflict structure around welfare reform has become multidimensional, as parties and voters position themselves along old and new policy dimensions in relatively uncorrelated ways.

These developments generated key questions for this book. Overall, we found that the social investment/activation turn has 'gone public', such that citizens have increasingly been exposed to information about key aspects of new social policy. Results reported in Chapters 4 and 5 mirror in no small measure Hemerijck's (2013) suggestion that the post-war era can now be fruitfully divided into three periods. A classic periodization, of course, starts with a 'golden' postwar age of expansion, followed by an era of 'neoliberal' retrenchment from the mid-1970s or early 1980s. Our results on campaign themes in Chapter 4 capture the transition from neoliberalism and retrenchment to a more recent epoch when aspects of social investment rose to prominence.

Now, the mere fact that social investment/activation themes are increasingly salient may be unsurprising to seasoned observers of welfare state politics. The flipside of this finding, however, is less obvious but significant. It seems that the new policy responses to reform pressures crowd out neoliberal retrenchment issues. Retrenchment was actually more salient in the early 1980s, when welfare issues rarely dominated campaigns. As a result, citizens have to a decreasing extent been exposed to the totality of welfare reform, that is, information that pays non-negligible attention to less popular policy changes.

Let us juxtapose these findings on campaign contents with results on citizen responses. This reveals two distinct discrepancies between how politicians present policy change and how citizens think about it. To begin with, politicians may have misread how citizens reason about links between pressure and policy. Chapter 8 found that citizens draw policy conclusions based on their perceptions of welfare state sustainability. Whenever such effects were found, they ran in the direction of retrenchment, such that bleaker views of sustainability undermine normative welfare state support. In no case or subgroup did we find that perceived unsustainability bolsters support for, say, improved funding or expanded social investment to address perceived problems. This would have been empirically and intellectually possible, but it was not what our data implies. So, there seems to be a mismatch between how citizens think about policy responses to reform pressures on the one hand, and how politicians *think that citizens think.*

Now, the fact that citizens can logically understand and apply the retrenchment logic does not necessarily mean they agree pressure is so heavy that it is needed. Far from it, acceptance of pressure messages depends on the policy cues people get. Past experimental studies have shown how general acceptance of welfare reform depends on the mix of retrenchment and expansion citizens are informed about. Thus, Busemeyer and Garritzmann (2017) confirmed that social investment is widely supported when not traded off against any retrenchment. Social investment support drops steeply, however, when such trade-offs are visible. Other studies observe how contentious reform may become more acceptable if 'packaged' with expansive compensation reforms (Lindvall 2017; Häusermann et al. 2019).

We have added to these studies by showing (in Chapter 7) that who embraces or counter-argues against pressure frames depends on whether retrenchment is on the table. Consider the effects of pressure messages concerning 'too few working' and 'population ageing' in Norway. These pressures had weak effects in their policy-free Chapter 6 versions. But when combined with retrenchment hints, and with a conservative sender, a more contingent pattern arises with welfare state opponents becoming increasingly worried about sustainability, and social democratic voters/welfare state supporters less so. Relatedly, German respondents were presented with pressure frames combined with social investment expansion. Those who in general favour social spending reacted positively, whereas adherents of welfare cuts reacted negatively.

Now juxtapose these results with findings on how social investment and other 'popular' reforms have come to dominate campaign information. We suspect that support for these reforms—and the parties responsible for them—is exaggerated by the fact that citizens are rarely invited to ponder the totality and trade-offs of welfare state change. The relative absence of controversial reform information may pacify the electorate compared to what we might see under a more balanced—dare we say truthful—democratic leadership.

Bibliography

Aalberg, Toril, Iyengar, Shanto, and Messing, Solomon (2012), 'Who is a "Deserving" Immigrant? An Experimental Study of Norwegian Attitudes', *Scandinavian Political Studies*, 35, 97–116.

Aardal, Bernt and van Wijnen, Pieter (2005), 'Issue Voting', in Jacques Thomassen (ed.), *The European Voter: A Comparative Study of Modern Democracies* (Oxford: Oxford University Press), 192–212.

Achen, Christopher M. and Bartels, Larry M. (2016), *Democracy for Realists: Why Elections Do Not Produce Responsive Government* (Princeton, NJ: Princeton University Press).

Adams, James, Ezrow, Lawrence, and Somer-Topcu, Zeynep (2014), 'Do Voters Respond to Party Manifestos or to a Wider Information Environment? An Analysis of Mass-Elite Linkages on European Integration', *American Journal of Political Science*, 58 (4), 967–78.

Alesina, Alberto, Carloni, Dorian, and Lecce, Giampaolo (2012), 'The Electoral Consequence of Large Fiscal Adjustments' (Working paper).

Allan, James P. and Scruggs, Lyle (2004), 'Political Partisanship and Welfare State Reform in Advanced Industrial Societies', *American Journal of Political Science*, 48 (3), 496–512.

Althaus, Scott L. (1998), 'Information Effects in Collective Preferences', *American Political Science Review*, 92 (3), 545–58.

Anderson, Christopher J. (2007), 'The End of Economic Voting? Contingency Dilemmas and the Limits of Democratic Accountability', *Annual Review of Political Science*, 10, 271–96.

Andeweg, Rudy B. (2003), 'Beyond Representativeness? Trends in Political Representation', *European Review*, 11 (2), 147–61.

Armingeon, Klaus and Giger, Nathalie (2008), 'Conditional Punishment: A Comparative Analysis of the Electoral Consequences of Welfare State Retrenchment in OECD Nations, 1980–2003', *West European Politics*, 31 (3), 558–80.

Armstrong, David, et al. (1997), 'The Place of Inter-Rater Reliability in Qualitative Research: An Empirical Study', *Sociology*, 31 (3), 597–606.

Arndt, Christoph (2014), 'The Electoral Consequences of Reforming a Bismarckian Welfare State', in Staffan Kumlin and Isabelle Stadelmann-Steffen (eds), *How Welfare States Shape the Democratic Public: Policy Feedback, Participation, Voting, and Attitudes* (Cheltenham: Edward Elgar Publishing), 132–55.

Asp, Kent (1983), 'The Struggle for the Agenda. Party Agenda, Media Agenda, and Voter Agenda in the 1979 Swedish Election Campaign', *Communication Research*, 10 (3), 333–55.

Baldwin, Peter (1990), *The Politics of Social Solidarity. Class Bases of the European Welfare State 1875–1975* (Cambridge: Cambridge University Press).

Banducci, Susan, Giebler, Heiko, and Kritzinger, Sylvia (2017), 'Knowing More from Less: How the Information Environment Increases Knowledge of Party Positions', *British Journal of Political Science*, 47 (3), 571–88.

Bartels, Larry M. (1996), 'Uninformed Votes: Information Effects in Presidential Elections', *American Journal of Political Science*, 40, 194–230.

Baumgartner, Frank R., et al. (2009), 'Punctuated Equilibrium in Comparative Perspective', *American Journal of Political Science*, 53 (3), 603–20.

Baumgartner, Frank R., Green-Pedersen, Christoffer, and Jones, Bryan D. (eds) (2008), *Comparative Studies of Policy Agendas* (London: Routledge).

Baumgartner, Frank R., Jones, Bryan D., and Wilkerson, John (2011), 'Comparative Studies of Policy Dynamics', *Comparative Political Studies*, 44 (8), 947–72.

Bay, Ann-Helén, et al. (eds) (2010), *De norske trygdene* (Oslo: Gyldendal).

Bay, Ann-Helén, et al. (eds) (2019), *Trygd i aktiveringens tid* (3rd edn, Oslo: Gyldendal).

Bay, Ann-Helén and Pedersen, Axel West (2006), 'The Limits of Social Solidarity: Basic Income, Immigration and the Legitimacy of the Universal Welfare State', *Acta Sociologica*, 49 (4), 419–36.

Bay, Ann-Helén, Finseraas, Henning, and Pedersen, Axel West (2016), 'Welfare Nationalism and Popular Support for Raising the Child Allowance: Evidence from a Norwegian Survey Experiment', *Scandinavian Political Studies*, 39 (4), 482–94.

Beramendi, Pablo, et al. (eds) (2015), *The Politics of Advanced Capitalism* (Cambridge: Cambridge University Press).

Blome, Agnes (2014), 'Politischer Wettbewerb und rapide Wechsel in der Familienpolitik', in Friedbert W. Rüb (ed.), *Rapide Politikwechsel in der Bundesrepublik: Theoretischer Rahmen und empirische Befunde* (1st edn, Baden-Baden: Nomos Verlagsgesellschaft mbH & Co. KG), 154–81.

Blum, Sonja (2012), *Familienpolitik als Reformprozess: Deutschland und Österreich im Vergleich* (Wiesbaden: Springer).

Blumler, Jay and Gurevitch, Michael (1975), 'Towards a Comparative Framework for Political Communication Research', in Steven H. Chaffee (ed.), *Political Communication: Issues and Strategies for Research* (Beverly Hills, CA: Sage), 165–93.

Bonoli, Giuliano (2005), 'The Politics of New Social Policies: Providing Coverage against New Social Risks in Mature Welfare States', *Policy and Politics*, 33 (3), 431–49.

Bonoli, Giuliano (2010), 'The Political Economy of Active Labor-Market Policy', *Politics and Society*, 38 (4), 435–57.

Bonoli, Giuliano and Natali, David (2012), 'Blame Avoidance and Credit Claiming Revisited', in Guiliano Bonoli and David Natali (eds), *The Politics of the New Welfare State* (Oxford: Oxford University Press).

Brochmann, Grete and Grødem, Anne Skevik (2013), 'Migration and Welfare Sustainability. The Case of Norway', in Grete Brochmann and Elena Jurado (eds), *Europe's Immigration Challenge. Reconciling Work, Welfare and Mobility* (London: I.B. Tauris), 59–76

Brooks, Clem (2011), 'Framing Theory, Welfare Attitudes, and the United States Case', in Stefan Svallfors (ed.), *Contested Welfare States: Welfare Attitudes in Europe and Beyond* (Stanford: Stanford University Press).

Brooks, Clem and Manza, Jeff (2007), *Why Welfare States Persist: The Importance of Public Opinion in Democracies* (Chicago: University of Chicago Press).

Budge, Ian and Farlie, Dennis J. (1983), *Explaining and Predicting Elections: Issue Effects and Party Strategies in Twenty-three Democracies* (London: Allen & Unwin).

Busemeyer, Marius R. and Garritzmann, Julian L. (2017), 'Public Opinion on Policy and Budgetary Trade-offs in European Welfare States: Evidence from a New Comparative Survey', *Journal of European Public Policy*, 24 (6), 871–89.

Busemeyer, Marius R., Franzmann, Simon T., and Garritzmann, Julian L. (2013), 'Who Owns Education? Cleavage Structures in the Partisan Competition over Educational Expansion', *West European Politics*, 36 (3), 521–46.

Butt, Sarah (2007), 'How Voters Evaluate Economic Competence: A Comparison between Parties in and out of Power', *Political Studies*, 54 (4), 743–66.

Campbell, Angus, et al. (1960), *The American Voter* (New York: Wiley).

Carmines, Edward and Stimson, James (1990), *Issue Evolution: Race and the Evolution of American Politics* (Princeton, NJ: Princeton University Press).

Carnes, Matthew E. and Mares, Isabela (2007), 'The Welfare State in Global Perspective', in Carles Boix and Susan C. Stokes (eds), *The Oxford Handbook of Comparative Politics* (Oxford: Oxford University Press), 868–87.

Castles, Francis G. (ed.), (2007), *The Disappearing State: Retrenchment Realities in an Age of Globalization* (Cheltenham: Edward Elgar).

Chong, Dennis and Druckman, James N. (2007), 'Framing Theory', *Annual Review of Political Science*, 10, 103–26.

Cohen, Bernhard C. (1963), *The Press and Foreign Policy* (Princeton, NJ: Princeton University Press).

Converse, Philip E. (1964), 'The Nature of Belief Systems in Mass Publics', in David E. Apter (ed.), *Ideology and Its Discontents* (New York: The Free Press of Glencoe).

Cox, Robert Henry (2001), 'The Social Construction of an Imperative: Why Welfare Reform Happened in Denmark and the Netherlands but Not in Germany', *World Politics*, 53, 463–98.

Cox, Robert Henry and Béland, Daniel (eds) (2011), *Ideas and Politics in Social Science Research* (Oxford: Oxford University Press).

Dahl, Robert A (1989), *Democracy and its Critics* (New Haven, CT: Yale University Press).

Dalton, Russell J., Farrell, David M., and McAllister, Ian (2011), *Political Parties and Democratic Linkage: How Parties Organize Democracy* (Oxford: Oxford University Press).

Damore, David F. (2005), 'Issue Convergence in Presidential Campaigns', *Political Behavior*, 27 (1), 71–97.

Delli Carpini, Micheal X., Cook, Fay Lomax., and Jacobs, Lawrence R. (2004), 'Public Deliberation, Discursive Participation, and Citizen Engagement: A Review of the Empirical Literature', *Annual Review of Political Science*, 7, 315–44.

De Vreese, Claes H (2003), 'Television Reporting of Second-Order Elections', *Journalism Studies*, 4 (2), 183–98.

Dearing, James W. and Rogers, Everett M. (1996), *Agenda-Setting* (Thousand Oaks, CA: Sage).

Downs, Anthony (1972), 'Up and Down with Ecology: The Issue–Attention Cycle', *Public Interest*, 28, 38–46.

Druckman, J.N., et al. (2011), *Cambridge Handbook of Experimental Political Science* (Cambridge: Cambridge University Press).

Druckman, James N., Peterson, Erik, and Slothuus, Rune (2013), 'How Elite Partisan Polarization Affects Public Opinion Formation', *American Political Science Review*, 107 (1), 57–79.

Eagly, Alice H. and Chaiken, Shelly (eds) (1993), *The Psychology of Attitudes* (New York: Harcourt Brace Jovanovich College Publishers).

Ellingsæther, Anne Lise (2014), 'Nordic Earner–Carer Models—Why Stability and Instability?', *Journal of Social Policy*, 43 (3), 555–74.

Elmelund-Præstekær, Christian and Emmenegger, Patrick (2013), 'Strategic Re-framing as a Vote Winner: Why Vote-seeking Governments Pursue Unpopular Reforms', *Scandinavian Political Studies*, 36 (1), 23–42.

Entman, Robert M. (1993), 'Framing: Toward Clarification of a Fractured Paradigm', *Journal of Communication*, 43 (4), 51–58.

Ervik, Rune and Lindén, Tord Skogedal (2015), 'The Shark Jaw and the Elevator: Arguing the Case for the Necessity, Harmlessness and Fairness of the Norwegian Pension Reform', *Scandinavian Political Studies*, 38 (4), 386–409.

Esaiasson, Peter and Heidar, Knut (eds) (2000), *Beyond Westminster and Congress. The Nordic Experience* (Columbus: Ohio State University Press).

Esaiasson, Peter and Wlezien, Christopher (2017), 'Advances in the Study of Democratic Responsiveness: An Introduction', *Comparative Political Studies*, 50 (6), 699–710.

Esmark, Anders and Schoop, Sarah R (2017), 'Deserving Social Benefits? Political Framing and Media Framing of "Deservingness" in Two Welfare Reforms in Denmark', *Journal of European Social Policy*, 27 (5), 417–32.

Esping-Andersen, Gøsta, et al. (2002), *Why We Need a New Welfare State* (Oxford: Oxford University Press).

Farrell, David M. and Schmitt-Beck, Rüdiger (2002), *Do Political Campaigns Matter?: Campaign Effects in Elections and Referendums*. Routledge/ECPR studies in European Political Science, 25 (London: Routledge).

Farrell, David M., Kolodny, Robin, and Medvic, Stephen (2001), 'Parties and Campaign Professionals in a Digital Age: Political Consultants in the United States and Their Counterparts Overseas', *The Harvard International Journal of Press/Politics*, 6 (4), 11–30.

Ferrera, Maurizio (2008), 'The European Welfare State: Golden Achievements, Silver Prospects', *West European Politics*, 31 (1–2), 82–107.

Fietkau, Sebastian and Hansen, Kasper M (2018), 'How Perceptions of Immigrants Trigger Feelings of Economic and Cultural Threats in Two Welfare States', *European Union Politics*, 19 (1), 119–39.

Finkel, Steven E. (1995), *Causal Analysis with Panel Data*. Quantitative Applications in the Social Sciences (Los Angeles: SAGE Publications Inc).

Flora, Peter and Heidenheimer, Arnold J. (1981), *The Development of Welfare States in Europe and America* (New Brunswick, NJ: Transaction Books), 417.

Fossati, Flavia (2018), 'Who Wants Demanding Active Labour Market Policies? Public Attitudes towards Policies that Put Pressure on the Unemployed', *Journal of Social Policy*, 47 (1), 77–97.

Fuchs, Dieter and Klingemann, Hans-Dieter (1989), 'The Left–Right Schema', in M. Kent Jennings and Jan W. van Deth (eds), *Continuities in Political Action. A Longitudinal Study of Political Orientations in Three Western Democracies* (Berlin: Walter de Gruyter & Co.), 203–34.

Funkhouser, Ray (1973), 'The Issues of the Sixties: An Exploratory Study in the Dynamics of Public Opinion', *Public Opinion Quarterly*, 31 (1), 62–75.

Geiger, Ben Baumberg (2018), 'Benefit "Myths"? The Accuracy and Inaccuracy of Public Beliefs about the Benefits System', *Social Policy & Administration*, 52 (5), 998–1018.

Giddens, Anthony (1998), *The Third Way: The Renewal of Social Democracy* (Cambridge: Polity).

Giger, Nathalie (2011), *The Risk of Social Policy? The Electoral Consequences of Welfare State Retrenchment and Social Policy Performance in OECD Countries* (London: Routledge).

Giger, Nathalie (2012), 'Is Social Policy Retrenchment Unpopular? How Welfare Reforms Affect Government Popularity', *European Sociological Review*, 28 (5), 691–700.

Giger, Nathalie and Nelson, Moira (2010), 'The Electoral Consequences of Welfare State Retrenchment: Blame Avoidance or Credit Claiming in the Era of Permanent Austerity?', *European Journal of Political Research*, 50 (1), 1–23.

Giger, Nathalie and Nelson, Moira (2013), 'The Welfare State or the Economy? Preferences, Constituencies, and Strategies for Retrenchment', *European Sociological Review*, 29 (5), 1083–94.

Gilens, Martin (1999), *Why Americans Hate Welfare: Race, Media, and the Politics of Antipoverty Policy* (Chicago University of Chicago Press).

Gingrich, Jane and Ansell, Ben (2015), 'The Dynamics of Social Investment: Human Capital, Activation, and Care', in Pablo Beramendi, et al. (eds), *The Politics of Advanced Capitalism* (Cambridge: Cambridge University Press), 282–304.

Gingrich, Jane and Häusermann, Silja (2015), 'The Decline of the Working-Class Vote, the Reconfiguration of the Welfare Support Coalition, and Consequences for the Welfare State', *Journal of European Social Policy*, 25 (1), 50–75.

Green, Jane and Hobolt, Sara B. (2008), 'Owning the Issue Agenda: Party Strategies and Vote Choices in British Elections', *Electoral Studies*, 27 (3), 460–76.

Green-Pedersen, Christoffer (2007), 'The Growing Importance of Issue Competition: The Changing Nature of Party Competition in Western Europe', *Political Studies*, 55 (3), 607–28.

Green-Pedersen, Christoffer (2019), *The Reshaping of West European Party Politics: Agenda-Setting and Party Competition in Comparative Perspective*. Comparative Politics (Oxford: Oxford University Press).

Green-Pedersen, C. and Haverland, Markus (2002), 'Review Essay: The New Politics and Scholarship of the Welfare State', *Journal of European Social Policy*, 12 (1), 13–51.

Green-Pedersen, Christoffer and Jensen, Carsten (2019), 'Electoral Competition and the Welfare State', *West European Politics*, 42 (4), 803–23.

Green-Pedersen, Christoffer and Mortensen, Peter B. (2010), 'Who Sets the Agenda and Who Responds to it in the Danish Parliament? A New Model of Issue Competition and Agenda-setting', *European Journal of Political Research*, 49 (2), 257–81.

Green-Pedersen, Christoffer and Walgrave, Stefaan (eds) (2014), *Agenda Setting, Policies, and Political Systems: A Comparative Approach* (Chicago: The University of Chicago Press).

Green-Pedersen, Christoffer and Wilkerson, John (2008), 'How Agenda-setting Attributes Shape Politics: Basic Dilemmas, Problem Attention and Health Politics in Denmark and the US', in Frank R. Baumgartner, Christoffer Green-Pedersen, and Bryan D. Jones (eds), *Comparative Studies of Policy Agendas* (London: Routledge), 81–94.

Hacker, Jacob S. (2005), 'Policy Drift: The Hidden Politics of US Welfare State Retrenchment', in Wolfgang Streeck (ed.), *Beyond Continuity: Institutional Change in Advanced Political Economies* (Oxford: Oxford University Press), 40–82.

Hall, Peter A. (1993), 'Policy Paradigms, Social Learning, and the State: The Case of Economic Policymaking in Britain', *Comparative Politics*, 25 (3), 275–96.

Häusermann, Silja (2010), *The Politics of Welfare State Reform in Continental Europe: Modernization in Hard Times* (Cambridge: Cambridge University Press).

Häusermann, Silja (2012), 'The Politics of Old and New Social Policies', in Guiliano Bonoli and David Natali (eds), *The Politics of the New Welfare State* (Oxford: Oxford University Press), 111–34.

Häusermann, Silja, Picot, Georg, and Geering, Dominik (2012), 'Rethinking Party Politics and the Welfare State: Recent Advances in the Literature', *British Journal of Political Science*, 43, 221–40.

Häusermann, Silja, Kurer, Thomas, and Traber, Denise (2019), 'The Politics of Trade-Offs: Studying the Dynamics of Welfare State Reform With Conjoint Experiments', *Comparative Political Studies*, 52 (7), 1059–95.

Hay, Colin and Wincott, Daniel (2012), *The Political Economy of European Welfare Capitalism* (New York: Palgrave-Macmillan).

Heclo, Hugh (1974), *Modern Social Politics in Britain and Sweden: From Relief to Income Maintenance.* Yale Studies in Political Science, 25 (New Haven, CT: Yale University Press).

Hemerijck, Anton (2013), *Changing Welfare States* (Oxford: Oxford University Press).

Hemerijck, Anton (2018), 'Social Investment as a Policy Paradigm', *Journal of European Public Policy*, 25 (6), 810–27.

Herweg, Nicole, Huss, Christian, and Zohlnhöfer, Reimut (2015), 'Straightening the Three Streams: Theorizing Extensions of the Multiple Streams Framework', *European Journal of Political Research*, 54 (3), 1–15.

Hjorth, Frederik (2016), 'Who Benefits? Welfare Chauvinism and National Stereotypes', *European Union Politics*, 17 (1), 3–24.

Hood, Christopher (2007), 'What Happens when Transparency Meets Blame-avoidance?', *Public Management Review*, 9 (2), 191–210.

Hood, Christopher (2011), *The Blame Game: Spin, Bureaucracy, and Self-Preservation in Government* (Princeton, NJ: Princeton University Press).

Huber, Evelyne and Stephens, John D. (2001), *Development and Crisis of the Welfare state: Parties and Policies in Gobal Markets* (Chicago: University Chicago Press).

Huber, Evelyne and Stephens, John D. (2015), 'Postindustrial Social Policy', in P. Beramendi, et al. (eds), *The Politics of Advanced Capitalism* (Cambridge: Cambridge University Press), 259–81.

Immergut, Ellen M. (1998), 'The Theoretical Core of the New Institutionalism', *Politics & Society*, 26 (1), 5–34.

Iyengar, Shanto and Kinder, Donald R. (1987), *News that Matters. Television and American Opinion* (Chicago: The University of Chicago Press).

Jacobs, A. (2011), *Governing for the Long Term: Democracy and the Politics of Investment.* (Cambridge Cambridge University Press).

Jakobsson, Niklas and Kumlin, Staffan (2017), 'Election Campaign Agendas, Government Partisanship, and the Welfare State', *European Political Science Review*, 9 (2), 183–208.

Jensen, Carsten and Naumann, Elias (2016), 'Increasing Pressures and Support for Public Healthcare in Europe', *Health Policy*, 120 (6), 698–705.

Jerit, Jennifer and Barabas, Jason (2006), 'Bankrupt Rhetoric: How Misleading Information Affects Knowledge about Social Security', *Public Opinion Quarterly*, 70 (3), 278–303.

Kangas, Olli E., Niemelä, Mikko, and Varjonen, Sampo (2014), 'When and Why Do Ideas Matter? The Influence of Framing on Opinion Formation and Policy Change', *European Political Science Review*, 6 (1), 73–92.

Kemmerling, Achim (2015), 'The End of Work or Work without End? How People's Beliefs about Labour Markets Shape Retirement Politics', *Joiurnal of Public Policy*, Early view, 1–30.

Kingdon, John W. (2011 [1984]), *Agendas, Alternatives, and Public Policies* (updated 2nd edn) (Boston, MA: Longman).

Klingemann, Hans-Dieter, Hofferbert, Richard I., and Budge, Ian (1994), *Parties, Policies, and Democracy* (Boulder, CO: Westview Press).

Knaggård, Åsa (2015), 'The Multiple Streams Framework and the Problem Broker', *European Journal of Political Research*, 54 (3), 450–65.

Knotz, Carlo and Lindvall, Johannes (2015), 'Coalitions and Compensation: The Case of Unemployment Benefit Duration', *Comparative Political Studies*, 48 (5), 586–615.

Korpi, Walter (1983), *The Democratic Class Struggle* (London: Routledge).

Korpi, Walter (2006), 'Power Resources and Employer-Centered Approaches in Explanations of Welfare States and Varieties of Capitalism: Protagonists, Consenters, and Antagonists', *World Politics*, 58 (2), 167–206.

Korpi, Walter and Palme, Joakim (2003), 'New Politics and Class Politics in the Context of Austerity and Globalization: Welfare State Regress in 18 Countries, 1975–95', *American Political Science Review*, 97, 425–46.

Kriesi, Hanspeter, et al. (2008), *West European Politics in the Age of Globalization* (Cambridge: Cambridge University Press).

Kriesi, Hanspeter, et al. (2012), *Political Conflict in Western Europe* (Cambridge: Cambridge University Press).

Krippendorff, Klaus (2004), 'Reliability in Content Analysis', *Human Communication Research*, 30 (3), 411–33.

Krosnick, Jon A. (2002), 'The Challenges of Political Psychology: Lessons to Be Learned from Research on Attitude Perception', in James H. Kuklinski (ed.), *Thinking About Political Psychology* (Cambridge: Cambridge University Press), 115–52.

Kuipers, Sanneke (2006), *The Crisis Imperative: Crisis Rhetoric and Welfare State Reform in Belgium and the Netherlands in the Early 1990s* (Amsterdam: Amsterdam University Press).

Kumlin, Staffan (2004), *The Personal and the Political: How Personal Welfare State Experiences Affect Political Trust and Ideology*. Political Evolution and Institutional Change (1st edn, New York: Palgrave Macmillan US) XII, 260.

Kumlin, Staffan (2006), 'Learning from Politics? The Causal Interplay between Government Performance and Political Ideology', *Journal of Public Policy*, 26 (2), 89–114.

Kumlin, Staffan (2007), 'Overloaded or Undermined? European Welfare States in the Face of Performance Dissatisfaction', in Stefan Svallfors (ed.), *The Political Sociology of the Welfare State: Institutions, Social Cleavages, and Orientations* (Stanford, CA: Stanford University Press), 80–116.

Kumlin, Staffan (2014), 'Informed Performance Evaluation of the Welfare State? Experimental and Real-World Findings', in Staffan Kumlin and Isabelle Stadelmann-Steffen (eds), *How Welfare States Shape the Democratic Public: Policy Feedback, Participation, Voting, and Attitudes* (Cheltenham: Edward Elgar), pp. IX, 337.

Kumlin, Staffan and Esaiasson, Peter (2012), 'Scandal Fatigue? Scandal Elections and Satisfaction with Democracy in Western Europe, 1977–2007', *British Journal of Political Science*, 42 (2), 263–82.

Kumlin, Staffan and Haugsgjerd, Atle (2017), 'The Welfare State and Political Trust: Bringing Performance Back In', in Sonja Zmerli and Tom van der Meer (eds), *Handbook of Political Trust* (Cheltenham: Edward Elgar Publishing), 285–301

Kumlin, Staffan, Kihlström, Daniel, and Oskarson, Maria (2021), 'The Election Campaign Themes Dataset' (2nd edn, University of Gothenburg: Dept. of Political Science).

Lavine, Howard (2002), 'On-Line Versus Memory-Based Process Models of Political Evaluation', in Kristen Renwick Monroe (ed.), *Political Psychology* (Mahwah, NJ: Lawrence Erlbaum Associates), chap. 13.

Lawson, Kay (ed.) (1980), *Political Parties and Linkage: A Comparative Perspective* (3rd edn, New Haven, CT: Yale University Press).

Lazarsfeld, Paul F., Berelson, Bernhard, and Gaudet, Hazel (1944), *The People's Choice. How the Voter Makes up His Mind in a Presidential Campaign* (New York: Columbia University Press).

Lefevere, Jonas, Tresch, Anke, and Walgrave, Stefaan (2015), 'Introduction: Issue Ownership', *West European Politics*, 38 (4), 755–60.

Levi, Margaret (1997), *Consent, Dissent, and Patriotism* (New York: Cambridge University Press).

Levy, Jonah D. (2010), 'Welfare Retrenchment', in Francis G. Castles, et al. (eds), *The Oxford Handbook of the Welfare State* (Oxford: Oxford University Press), 552–69.

Lewis-Beck, Michael S. and Paldam, Martin (2000), 'Economic Voting: An Introduction', *Electoral Studies*, 19, 113–21.

Lewis-Beck, Michael S. and Stegmaier, Mary (2007), 'Economic Models of Voting', in Russel J. Dalton and Hans-Dieter Klingemann (eds), *Oxford Handbook of Political Behavior* (Oxford: Oxford University Press), 518–37.

Lindvall, Johannes (2017), *Reform Capacity* (1st edn; Oxford: Oxford University Press).

Luskin, Robert P., Fishkin, James S., and Jowell, Roger (2002), 'Considered Opinions: Deliberative Polling in Britain', *British Journal of Political Science*, 32, 455–87.

Luttbeg, Norman R. (ed.), (1981), *Public Opinion and Public Policy: Models of Political Linkage* (3rd edn, Ithica, NY: F.E. Peacock Publishers).

McCombs, Maxwell and Shaw, Donald L. (1972), 'The Agenda-setting Function of the Mass Media', *Public Opinion Quarterly*, 36, 176–87.

McGraw, Kathleen M. and Hubbard, Clark (1996), 'Some of the People Some of the Time: Individual Differences in Acceptance of Political Accounts', in Diana C. Mutz, Paul M. Sniderman, and Richard A. Brody (eds), *Political Persuasion and Attitude Change* (Ann Arbor, MI: The University of Michigan Press), 145–70.

MacKuen, Michael B., Erikson, Robert S., and Stimson, James A. (1992), 'Peasants or Bankers? The American Electorate and the US Economy', *American Political Science Review*, 86, 597–611.

Mair, Peter (2006), 'Ruling the Void: The Hollowing of Western Democracy', *New Left Review*, 42, 25–51.

Manin, Bernard (1997), *The Principles of Representative Government* (Cambridge: Cambridge University Press).

Manow, Philip, Palier, Bruno, and Schwander, Hanna (eds) (2018), *Welfare Democracies and Party Politics: Explaining Electoral Dynamics in Times of Changing Welfare Capitalism* (Oxford: Oxford University Press).

Margalit, Yotam (2013), 'Explaining Social Policy Preferences: Evidence from the Great Recession', *American Political Science Review*, 107 (1), 80–103.

Martinsson, Johan (2009), 'Economic Voting and Issue Ownership. An Integrative Approach', *Gothenburg Studies in Politics* 115. https://gupea.ub.gu.se/handle/2077/20037.

Mau, Steffen (2003), *The Moral Economy of Welfare States: Britain and Germany Compared* (London: Routledge).

Meguid, Bonnie M. (2005), 'Competition Between Unequals: The Role of Mainstream Party Strategy in Niche Party Success', *American Political Science Review*, 99 (3), 347–59.

Morel, Nathalie, Palier, Bruno, and Palme, Joakim (eds) (2012), *Towards a Social Investment Welfare State?* (Bristol: Policy Press).

Morgan, Kimberley J. (2012), 'Promoting Social Investment through Work–Family Policies: Which Nations Do it and Why?', in Nathalie Morel, Bruno Palier, and Joakim Palme (eds), *Towards a Social Investment Welfare State?* (Bristol: Policy Press), 153–79.

Morgan, Kimberly J. (2013), 'Path Shifting of the Welfare State: Electoral Competition and the Expansion of Work–Family Policies in Western Europe', *World Politics*, 65 (1), 73–115.

Mortensen, Peter B. (2010), 'Political Attention and Public Policy: A Study of How Agenda Setting Matters Political Attention and Public Policy', *Scandinavian Political Studies*, 33 (4), 356–80.

Mutz, Diana C (1998), *Impersonal Influence. How Perceptions of Mass Collectives Affect Political Attitudes* (Cambridge: Cambridge University Press).

Naumann, Elias (2014), 'Raising the Retirement Age: Retrenchment, Feedback, and Attitudes', in Staffan Kumlin and Isabelle Stadelmann-Steffen (eds), *How Welfare States Shape the Democratic Public: Policy Feedback, Participation, and Attitudes* (Cheltenham: Edward Elgar Publishing), 223–43.

Naumann, Elias (2017), 'Do Increasing Reform Pressures Change Welfare State Attitudes? An Experimental Study on Population Ageing, Pension Reform Preferences, Political Knowledge and Ideology', *Ageing and Society*, 37 (2), 266–94.

Naurin, Elin (2011), *Election Promises, Party Behaviour and Voter Perceptions*. Public Sector Organizations (Basingstoke: Palgrave Macmillan).

Nelson, Moira (2013), 'Theorizing Credit Claiming Opportunities: Exploring the Use of Deservingness Frames in Retrenchment Reforms', Presented at the ECPR General Conference, 4–7 September 2013.

Nikolai, Rita (2012), 'Towards Social Investment? Patterns of Public Policy in the OECD World', in Nathalie Morel, Bruno Palier, and Joakim Palme (eds), *Towards a Social Investment Welfare State?* (Bristol: Policy Press), 91–116.

NOU (2011), 'Velferd og migrasjon. Den norske modellens framtid', Barne-, likestillings- og inkluderingsdepartementet.

NOU (2017), 'Integrasjon og tillit: Langsiktige konsekvenser av høy innvandring'.

Oscarsson, Henrik and Holmberg, Sören (2013), *Nya svenska väljare* (Stockholm: Norstedts Juridik).

Palier, Bruno (ed.), (2010), *A Long Goodbye to Bismarck? The Politics of Welfare Reform in Continental Europe* (Amsterdam: Amsterdam University Press).

Patashnik, Eric M. (2015), 'Paul Pierson's Dismantling the Welfare State: A Twentieth Anniversary Assessment', *PS: Political Science and Politics*, 2015 (April), 267–69.

Peter, Jochen and Lauf, Edmund (2002), 'Reliability in Cross-national Content Analysis', *Journalism & Mass Communication Quarterly*, 79 (4), 815–32.

Peters, B. Guy (1999), *Institutional Theory in Political Science. The 'New Institutionalism'* (London: Pinter).

Petersen, Michael Bang, et al. (2010), 'Deservingness versus Values in Public Opinion on Welfare: The Automaticity of the Deservingness Heuristic', *European Journal of Political Research*, 50, 24–52.

Petersen, Michael Bang, et al. (2012), 'Who Deserves Help? Evolutionary Psychology, Social Emotions, and Public Opinion about Welfare', *Political Psychology*, 33 (3), 395–418.

Petrocik, John (1996), 'Issue Ownership in Presidential Elections with a 1980 Case Study', *American Journal of Political Science*, 40 (3), 825–50.

Pierson, Paul (1994), *Dismantling the Welfare State?* (Cambridge: Cambridge University Press).

Pierson, Paul (1996), 'The New Politics of the Welfare State', *World Politics* 48 (2), 143–79.

Pierson, Paul (ed.), (2001), *The New Politics of the Welfare State* (Oxford: Oxford University Press).

Pitkin, Hanna F. (1967), *The Concept of Representation* (Berkeley: University of California Press).

Pope, Catherine, Ziebland, Sue, and Mays, Nicholas (2000), 'Qualitative Research in Health Care: Analysing Qualitative Data', *British Medical Journal*, 320, 114–16.

Popkin, Samuel L. (1991), *The Reasoning Voter: Communication and Persuasion in Presidential Campaigns* (Chicago: University of Chicago Press).

Powell, G. Bingham (2000), *Elections as Instruments of Democracy* (New Haven, CT: Yale University Press).

Przeworski, Adam, Stokes, Susan C., and Manin, Bernard (eds) (1999), *Democracy, Accountability, and Representation* (New York: Cambridge University Press).

Raffass, Tania (2017), 'Demanding Activation', *Journal of Social Policy*, 46 (2), 349–65.

Rainer, Helmut, et al. (2013a), 'Kindergeld', *ifo Forschungsbericht*, 59.

Rainer, Helmut, et al. (2013b), 'Kinderbetreuung', *ifo Forschungsbericht*, 59.

Robertson, David (1976), *A Theory of Party Competition* (London: Wiley).

Rohrschneider, Robert and Whitefield, Stephen (2012), *The Strain of Representation: How Parties Represent Diverse Voters in Western and Eastern Europe* (Oxford: Oxford University Press).

Römmele, Andrea and von Schneidmesser, Dirk (2016), 'Election Campaigning Enters a Fourth Phase: The Mediatized Campaign', *Zeitschrift für Politikwissenschaft*, 26 (4), 425–42.

Ronchi, Stefano (2018), 'Which Roads (if any) to Social Investment? The Recalibration of EU Welfare States at the Crisis Crossroads (2000–2014)', *Journal of Social Policy*, 47 (3), 459–78.

Roosma, Femke, Gelissen, John, and van Oorschot, Wim (2013), 'The Multidimensionality of Welfare State Attitudes: A European Cross-National Study', *Social Indicators Research*, 113, 235–55.

Ross, Fiona (2000a), '"Beyond Left and Right": The New Partisan Politics of Welfare', *Governance*, 13 (2), 155–83.

Ross, Fiona (2000b), 'Framing Welfare Reform in Affluent Societies: Rendering Restructuring More Palatable?', *Journal of Public Policy*, 20 (3), 169–93.

Rothstein, Bo (1996), 'Political Institutions: An Overview', in Robert E. Goodin and Hans-Dieter Klingemann (eds), *A New Handbook of Political Science* (Oxford: Oxford University Press), 133–66.

Rothstein, Bo (1998), *Just Institutions Matter. The Moral and Political Logic of the Universal Welfare State* (Cambridge: Cambridge University Press).

Rothstein, Bo (2009), 'Svensk välfärdsstatsforskning—en kritisk betraktelse', *Ekonomisk debatt*, 37 (3), 1–21.

Saward, Michael (2008), 'Making Representations: Modes and Strategies of Political Parties', *European Review*, 16 (3), 271–86.

Scharpf, Fritz (1999), *Governing in Europe. Effective and Democratic?* (Oxford: Oxford University Press).

Schmidt, Manfred G. (2010), 'Parties', in Francis G. Castles, et al. (eds), *The Oxford Handbook of the Welfare State* (Oxford: Oxford University Press), 211–26

Schmidt, Vivien A. (2002), 'Does Discourse Matter in the Politics of Welfare State Adjustment?', *Comparative Political Studies*, 35 (2), 168–93.

Schmidt, Vivien A. (2010), 'Taking Ideas and Discourse Seriously: Explaining Change through Discursive Institutionalism as the Fourth "New Institutionalism"', *European Political Science Review*, 2 (1), 1–25.

Schmitt, Hermann and Thomassen, Jacques (1999), *Political Representation and Legitimacy in the European Union* (Oxford: Oxford University Press).

Schumacher, Gijs, Vis, Barbara, and van Kersbergen, Kees (2013), 'Political Parties' Welfare Image, Electoral Punishment and Welfare State Retrenchment', *Comparative European Politics*, 11 (1), 1–21.

Scruggs, Lyle (2008), 'Social Rights, Welfare Generosity, and Inequality', in Pablo Beramendi and Christopher J. Anderson (eds), *Democracy, Inequality, and Representation* (New York: Russell Sage Foundation), 62–90.

Scruggs, Lyle and Allan, James (2006), 'Welfare-state Decommodification in 18 OECD Countries: A Replication and Revision', *Journal of European Social Policy*, 16 (1), 55–72.

Shaffer, Juliet Popper (1995), 'Multiple Hypothesis Testing', *Annual Review of Psychology*, 46 (1), 561–84.

Sigelman, Lee (2004), 'Avoidance or Engagement? Issue Convergence in U.S. Presidential Campaigns, 1960–2000', *American Journal of Political Science*, 48 (4), 650–61.

Slothuus, Rune (2007), 'Framing Deservingness to Win Support for Welfare State Retrenchment', *Scandinavian Political Studies*, 30 (3), 323–44.

Slothuus, Rune and de Vreese, Claes H. (2010), 'Political Parties, Motivated Reasoning, and Issue Framing Effects', *The Journal of Politics*, 72 (3), 630–45.

Sniderman, Paul M., Brody, Richard A., and Tetlock, Philip E. (eds) (1991), *Reasoning and Choice. Explorations in Social Psychology* (Cambridge: Cambridge University Press).

Soroka, Stuart N. (2002), *Agenda-Setting Dynamics in Canada* (Vancouver: UBC Press).

Soroka, Stuart N. and Wlezien, Christopher (2010), *Degrees of Democracy: Politics, Public Opinion, and Policy* (Cambridge: Cambridge University Press).

Soss, Joe and Schram, Sanford (2007), 'A Public Transformed? Welfare Reform as Policy Feedback', *American Political Science Review*, 101 (1), 111–27.

Starke, Peter (2008), *Radical Welfare State Retrenchment* (Basingstoke: Palgrave-Macmillan).

Stephens, John D. (2010), 'The Social Rights of Citizenship', in Francis G. Castles, et al. (eds), *The Oxford Handbook of the Welfare State* (Oxford: Oxford University Press), 511–25.

Stephens, John D. (2015), 'Revisiting Pierson's Work on the Politics of Welfare State Reform in the Era of Retrenchment Twenty Years Later', *PS: Political Science and Politics*, 48 (2), 274–78.

Stiller, Sabina (2010), *Ideational Leadership in German Welfare State Reform: How Politicians and Policy Ideas Transform Resilient Institutions* (Amsterdam: Amsterdam University Press).

Stokes, Donald E. (1963), 'Spatial Models of Party Competition', *American Political Science Review*, 57, 368–77.

Streeck, Wolfgang and Thelen, Kathleen A. (eds) (2005), *Beyond Continuity: Institutional Change in Advanced Political Economies* (Oxford: Oxford University Press).

Strömbäck, Jesper and Aalberg, Toril (2008), 'Election News Coverage in Democratic Corporatist Countries: A Comparative Study of Sweden and Norway', *Scandinavian Political Studies*, 31 (1), 91–106.

Strömbäck, J. and Esser, F. (2014), 'Mediatization of Politics: Towards a Theoretical Framework', in F. Esser and J. Strömbäck, *Mediatization of Politics: Understanding the Transformation of Western Democracies* (Basingstoke: Palgrave Macmillan), 3–28.

Stubager, Rune (2018), 'What is Issue Ownership and How Should We Measure It?', *Political Behavior*, 40 (2), 345–70.

Svallfors, Stefan (2010), 'Public Opinion', in Francis G. Castles, et al. (eds), *The Oxford Handbook of the Welfare State* (Oxford: Oxford University Press), 241–52.

Swank, Duane (2002), *Global Capital, Political Institutions, and Policy Change in Developed Welfare States* (Cambridge: Cambridge University Press).

Taber, Charles S. and Lodge, Milton (2006), 'Motivated Skepticism in the Evaluation of Political Beliefs', *American Journal of Political Science*, 50 (3), 755–69.

Taylor-Gooby, Peter (ed.), (2001), *Welfare States under Pressure* (London: Sage Publications).

Taylor-Gooby, P. (ed.), (2005), *Ideas and Welfare State Reform in Western Europe* (Basingstoke: Palgrave Macmillan).

Thomassen, Jaques (1994), 'Empirical Research into Political Representation: Failing Democracy or Failing Models?', in M. Kent Jennings and Thomas Mann (eds), *Elections at Home and Abroad. Essays in Honor of Warren E. Miller* (Ann Arbor: University of Michigan Press), 237–64.

Tyler, Tom R., et al. (1997), *Social Justice in a Diverse Society* (Boulder, CO: Westview Press).

Vaalavuo, Maria (2013), 'The Redistributive Impact of "Old" and "New" Social Spending', *Journal of Social Policy*, 42 (3), 513–39.

Van Aelst, Peter and Walgrave, Stefaan (2011), 'Minimal or Massive? The Political Agenda-Setting Power of the Mass Media According to Different Methods', *The International Journal of Press/Politics*, 16, 295–313.

van Biezen, Ingrid (2014), 'Introduction: On Parties, Party Systems and Democracy', in Peter Mair (ed.), *On Parties, Party systems and Democracy: Selected Writings of Peter Mair* (Colchester: ECPR Press), 1–24.

van der Brug, Wouter (2004), 'Issue Ownership and Party Choice', *Electoral Studies*, 23 (2), 209–33.

van Kersbergen, Kees (1995), *Social Capitalism: A Study of Christian Democracy and the Welfare State* (London: Routledge).

van Kersbergen, Kees and Vis, Barbara (2014), *Comparative Welfare State Politics: Development, Opportunities, and Reform* (Cambridge: Cambridge University Press), 205.

van Kersbergen, Kees, Vis, Barbara, and Hemerijck, Anton (2014), 'The Great Recession and Welfare State Reform: Is Retrenchment Really the Only Game Left in Town?', *Social Policy & Administration*, 48 (7), 883–904.

van Oorschot, Wim (2000), 'Who Should Get What, and Why? On Deservingness Criteria and the Conditionality of Solidarity among the Public', *Policy & Politics*, 28 (1), 33–48.

van Oorschot, Wim (2006), 'Making the Difference in Social Europe: Deservingness Perceptions among Citizens of European Welfare States ', *Journal of European Social Policy*, 16, 23–42.

van Oorschot, Wim, et al. (eds) (2017a), *The Social Legitimacy of Targeted Welfare: Attitutudes to Welfare Deservingness* (Cheltenham: Edward Elgar Publishing).

van Oorschot, Wim, Roosma, F., and Reeskens, T. (2017b), *The Social Legitimacy of Targeted Welfare: Attitudes to Welfare Deservingness* (Cheltenham: Edward Elgar Publishing).

Vis, Barbara (2011), 'Prospect Theory and Political Decision Making', *Political Studies Review*, 9 (3), 334–43.

Vis, Barbara (2016), 'Taking Stock of the Comparative Literature on the Role of Blame Avoidance Strategies in Social Policy Reform', *Journal of Comparative Policy Analysis*, 18:2 (2), 122–37.

Vis, Barbara and van Kersbergen, Kees (2013), 'Towards an Open Functional Approach to Welfare State State Change: Pressures, Ideas, and Blame Avoidance', *Public Administration*, 91 (4), 840–54.

Wagner, Markus (2012), 'Defining and Measuring Niche Parties', *Party Politics*, 18 (6), 845–64.

Weaver, R. Kent (1986), 'The Politics of Blame Avoidance', *Journal of Public Policy*, 6 (4), 371–98.

Wenzelburger, Georg (2014), 'Blame Avoidance, Electoral Punishment and the Perceptions of Risk', *Journal of European Social Policy*, 24 (1), 80–91.

Wincott, Daniel (2011), 'Ideas, Policy Change, and the Welfare State', in Robert Henry Cox and Daniel Béland (eds), *Ideas and Politics in Social Science Research* (Oxford: Oxford University Press), 143–66.

Zahariadis, Nikolaos (2004), 'Ambiguity and Multiple Streams', in Paul A. Sabatier and Christopher M. Weible (eds), *Theories of the Policy Process* (3rd edn, Boulder, Colorado Westview Press).

Zaller, John R. (1992), *The Nature and Origins of Mass Opinion* (Cambridge: Cambridge University Press).

Zohlnhöfer, Reimut (2015), 'A Coalition Whose Time Had Already Passed ... The Economic and Social Policies of the Second Merkel Government', in Gabriele D'Ottavio and Thomas Saalfeld (eds), *Germany after the 2013 Elections: Breaking the Mould of Post-Unification Politics?* (Farnham: Ashgate), 13–29.

Index

Please note that page references to Figures will be followed by the letter 'f', to Tables by the letter 't', while references to Notes will contain the letter 'n' following the Note number.